THE SOUL
UNEARTHED

THE SOUL UNEARTHED

Celebrating Wildness and
Spiritual Renewal through Nature

Revised Edition

EDITED BY CASS ADAMS

SENTIENT PUBLICATIONS, LLC

Cover design by Stefan Killen
Book design by Bill Spahr

Library of Congress Cataloging-in-Publication Data

The soul unearthed : celebrating wildness and spiritual renewal through nature / edited by Cass Adams.
    p. cm.
Includes bibliographical references.
    ISBN 0-9710786-3-7
1. Nature–Religious aspects. 2. Human ecology–Religious aspects.
I. Adams, Cass, 1961-
    BL65.N35 S68 2002
    304.2–dc21

                                              2001008050

SENTIENT PUBLICATIONS
A Limited Liability Company
1113 Spruce Street
Boulder, CO 80302
www.sentientpublications.com

CONTENTS

CONTENTS

CONTENTS

CONTENTS

$\mathcal{F}$OREWORD

Cass Adams has done us an invaluable service in compiling this anthology. Here, together for the first time, are the voices of wilderness advocates, teachers and guides, supporters of deep ecology, pioneers in the emerging field of ecopsychology, nature writers and poets sharing their love for what is wild within and around us. Their stories reflect decades of experience and insight affirming the role of wilderness in personal transformation.

Through their various works, the authors represented in *The Soul Unearthed* are affecting countless thousands of people. They are reminding us that when we lose contact with the wild, we lose that which springs most spontaneously from our souls. Collectively, they are helping us awaken from the trance of an industrial-consumer society to a world filled with adventure and alive with spirit.

The Soul Unearthed shows how wilderness areas and wild places help us recover realms of our inner lives—realms in which ego and the demands of society have not restricted our experience of innate guidance or our intrinsic compassion. These are spiritual realms, the sacred. This is not "nature mysticism" as some have called it—it is nothing so abstract. The capacity to experience the natural world as sacred is one of the ordinary privileges of being human. It is our birthright. We need only transcend the limits of human-centered thinking. Beyond those limits lies the wild—the far boundaries of home.

The authors in this anthology are mapmakers showing us routes to this far country. Their maps give evidence that this territory is indeed home and its inhabitants are family: mother Earth, brother wolf, sister bear. Among the most touching writings in this book are those describing animal encounters, which allow us to see ourselves mirrored in the eyes and behaviors of the more-than-human world. Who are we really? How shall we live? Such are the questions these seekers bring to the wilderness. And we see that for those who approach in a mindful way, the wilderness offers answers.

I feel especially privileged to write this foreword because so many of the authors in this volume have been my teachers and my colleagues — Steven Foster, Joan Halifax, Dolores LaChapelle, Jed Swift, Elan Shapiro,

Terry Tempest Williams, Elias Amidon, Deena Metzger, David Abram, Antler and others—and they were among the first to show me how to approach the wilderness with respect and openness. Put down your ideas of control and put away your fancy gear, they advised. Go empty-handed and empty-bellied. Slow down, pay attention, wait. Learn to listen and to look. Become friends with the silence and trust the answers you are given. Return again and again. Learn to defend the wilderness that you love.

The intimate contact with wild places that I have come to know does not end when I return to my daily life. Approaching the wilderness as a temple is only a beginning. The best purpose of such journeys is to be able to come back and see all the land about us—agricultural, suburban, urban—as part of the same wild processes that we encountered in the outback, never totally ruined, never completely tamed. As Gary Snyder, our poet laureate of the wild, puts it: "Great brown bear is walking with us, salmon swimming upstream with us, as we stroll a city street." This is the greater work suggested by this collection of writings.

To those who seek personal renewal and reconnection with wild places within and without, this book offers direction. It suggests that we all share in an earthly consciousness, that we have a place in the world, a place we do not have to earn, but a place we are born to because we are part of this planet. It offers community with those seeking intimate contact with wild world, wild self. In the end it does what few books do. It reminds us to put it down, leave it behind and go outside. Don't settle for just reading maps; take the trip!

—ELIZABETH ROBERTS

Wilderness teacher, guide, and coeditor of
Earth Prayers and *Life Prayers*

PREFACE TO THE SECOND EDITION

In watching the first edition of *The Soul Unearthed* unfold, and in reflecting on its contents after publication, an unplanned theme began to make itself apparent. In essence, the book is about that place where the individual sense of separation fades into the vast and open-ended invitation of wilderness. Nature is the more significant character in the story, and the individual plays a pale secondary role. Said another way, if one entered wilderness with a big personal agenda — of adventure, of conquering some formidable challenge, of healing, or even of finding oneness — one returned less sure of their original expectations, more empty of agenda, and much more still inside. In some cases the dissolution was so complete that the mistaken belief in separation from the whole of nature could no longer be held as true. This humbling and blessing was sometimes born out of adversity. Or it occurred through the exposure to wild pristine beauty. Sometimes the bowing came through the simple act of being quiet and being touched by the impersonal loving hands of trees, or through being overwhelmed by the grandeur and sheer immensity of this planet floating through space, or in some encounter with a magnificent and untamed creature. Whatever the means, the personal identity is seen within the context of a larger ongoing cosmological birthing and wholeness, such that the recognition of unity becomes abundantly clear. Gratitude and love replace arrogance and self-importance.

In a true meeting with wilderness there is nothing personal to be gained at all. More true to spirit, such deep exposure results in an erasure of the personal, and is an invitation to a deepening marriage to something larger and more fundamental than the personal. Nature is wild, free, and boundless, and so is the spirit that resides within our hearts. It is this unknowable and uncontainable wildness that we celebrate, and that gracefully lifts us beyond our tiny concerns into a humble and spirit-infused life of simplicity.

In requesting new submissions for the second edition, I invited writings that were written from the heart, that leaned more toward poetry than logic, and that were based in direct experience and actual contact with wilderness, as opposed to being abstract. Interestingly, I chose only poetry. I am grateful for the addition of a handful of fine poems. Some were written by people unfamiliar to me; a few were written by my favorite poets. I believe these new poems have made the second edition of *The Soul Unearthed* a stronger collection. Enjoy.

—Cass Adams

PREFACE TO THE FIRST EDITION

The birth of this anthology occurred on an afternoon in the late fall of 1990, when the leaves were damp on the ground and my soul life was turning inward with the approach of winter. I was sitting on my back porch reflecting about the impact wilderness had made upon my spiritual unfolding. My values, thinking, hobbies, and ecological approach to living, my interest in simplicity, silence, and openness, had all been shaped by nature.

I could say that I had spent time in wilderness to relax, to slow down, to surround myself in great beauty, and to have fun. But on a deeper level, I was aware that some other, hard-to-name healing process and growth had occurred. Being in nature is ointment for personal wounds. Wilderness asks nothing. It is completely detached from the world of human craziness. The openness of wilderness supports us in dropping our attachment to a limited sense of "I." In doing so, we effortlessly expand into and see the vastness that is. Within the peaceful cradle of nature, I had repeatedly found my way back to the larger experience of Self, love, and purpose.

On my porch, as I thought about the significance of my time spent outdoors, I began to imagine how powerful it would be to gather an anthology of writings about the spiritually transformative wilderness experiences of other people. The idea of a collection kept returning in the days and weeks that followed. It was an instinctive soul current, a slumbering river, moving slowly but surely beneath the surface ripples of my mind. This deeper current was insistent; years later, the vision of the book has become a reality. This book belongs to that which is alive and thriving. The earth itself sings through the collective voice of the book's contributors.

The Soul Unearthed: Celebrating Wildness and Spiritual Renewal through Nature offers a view of people in relationship to nature that is based in humility. The anthropocentric notion of humans as caretakers, stewards of the earth, is expanded to an ecocentric — or deep ecology and ecopsychology — perspective in line with the attitude of Chief Seattle's 1852 congressional address — "The earth does not belong to man, man belongs to earth." Humans are viewed within the overall order of nature. We are only one of many beings that have been blessed with life on this planet. And yet, sadly, humans are primarily responsible for the present degradation of the environment. Our arrogance, our failure to see our lives within the larger unfolding of all life, feeds this course of destruction.

In addition to the social, political, and environmental action already occurring on behalf of the earth, a new wilderness aesthetic is emerging to meet the demands of the late twentieth century—a wisdom that embraces the challenges of our current ecological crisis, concurrently, with the age-old reverence that tribal people have held for the earth. A new spirituality of wilderness is necessary, an evolving philosophy and approach to wilderness based in gratitude, humility, respect, and broad vision rooted in real-life experience with real-life connections to nature. The selections in *The Soul Unearthed* are grounded. Through the act of searching for deeper personal connection with the earth, and thereby to themselves, the authors convey a powerful sense of belonging to the larger web of the natural world.

The spirit of the anthology as a whole is one of reverence and celebration of wildness. Wilderness is approached as a place of worship, not as a vacation playground, or as something to be conquered and overcome to sharpen humankind's grandiose spirit of achievement. People are small and wilderness is large. Through the expanse of wilderness, and through grace, we are given the opportunity to stretch ourselves into the greater wealth and depth of being that is abundantly present.

The poems, stories, essays, and interviews included in the book come from the heart of wilderness and reflect how nature transforms us and how we bring this positive change back into the world. As a way of promoting those people whose lives are serving to renew our collective relationship with the natural world, I have selected the work of people who are currently living. *The Soul Unearthed* deliberately offers a diverse range of testimony. Outdoor educators, deep ecologists, environmental activists, storytellers, wilderness guides, rites of passage guides, ceremonialists, gender specialists, therapists, poets, and nature writers are all represented. They are among the finest people in their fields, leading the way to a more ecologically based and spiritual view of life and of wilderness.

My life has been enriched through the anthology. I hope its contents will inspire you and your lives. May this inspiration serve as a catalyst for a wider renewal of our collective spiritual relationship with the earth and may beauty, respect, and true humility be the path upon which we all learn to walk.

—CASS ADAMS

$\mathcal{A}$CKNOWLEDGMENTS

In the acknowledgments for the first edition of *The Soul Unearthed* I thoroughly expressed my gratitude for the help and contributions of many individuals. Due to their extensive editorial assistance, I again thank Lesley Reed and Joan Adams. I am grateful for the love and support I received during the creation of the first edition. Again, thank you all.

For the second edition of the book, I would like to thank Steven Harrison and Connie Shaw for seeing the value of the book and for their enthusiasm to republish this fine collection. Connie, coincidentally, offered to reprint the anthology on my birthday. Given that I was not seeking a publisher, and that the original book had gone out-of-print months before, this was a huge and entirely unexpected gift! Connie's professionalism and sharpness, and her influence on the republication, have been stellar. Furthermore, it has been a pleasure to work with her. I feel very honored to be a part of Sentient Publications at its start.

The tireless service of my partner, Jeannie Zandi, is deeply appreciated. She has been a ready and capable editor of my writing. She accompanied and assisted me during the three-month, car-camping book tour for the first edition in the fall of 1996. In between camp setup, breakdown, and book readings, Jeannie copyedited the completed version and found many unnoticed mistakes. More recently, along with her devoted and exquisite mothering of our young daughter, Sophia, Jeannie supported me financially while I completed the work for the second edition. She also researched, updated, and edited the Periodicals and Journals portion of the Suggested Readings section and the Appendix of Wilderness Resources, and suggested what became the final subtitle of the new edition.

Finally, I would like to express my gratitude to the contributors of the first edition of the book who generously agreed to have their pieces included in the second edition without further monetary reward. Since the publication of the first edition, Sedonia Cahill has passed away. As the book represents those who are still living, and because I was unable to contact anyone from Sedonia's estate, I elected to not include her piece. Her enthusiasm will surely be missed by many. As well, thank you and welcome to the new contributors to this edition.

While many have contributed to both anthologies in many ways, none of the contributions would have existed without the bounty of the earth, which nourishes us daily. And so, I would like to give my utmost thanks to the earth itself for the richness it has showered on me. *The Soul Unearthed* is a small gift that I, on behalf of a larger community of helping hands, offer to the earth and to the beings who live here. This book is a prayer of thanksgiving.

I

Spirit of Place

*P*art of my intention in compiling this anthology is to challenge limiting concepts of what we think wilderness is. For years, my way of seeing wilderness was biased. Nature, in my mind, was rugged snowcapped peaks, remote pristine areas, and the absence of other people. I was a "peak-bagger," having spent a number of years climbing the fourteeners (14,000-foot peaks) of Colorado. I liked the challenge of these hikes. I enjoyed the workout and the grand views. I reveled in the spirit of conquest and in being on the edge of something much bigger than I imagined myself to be.

Such an attitude toward nature is not only common, it is actually encouraged in the vast majority of wilderness education and adventure organizations. While most outfitters and outdoor educators are environmentally sensitive and aware in terms of minimal impact, the whole premise of many outdoor recreation and rehabilitation programs is one of personal growth through having one's limits tested. Nature becomes a worthy opponent, a shaper of character, molding and calling forth the qualities of courage, determination, endurance, willpower, and teamwork. In the world of outdoor magazines there is a plethora of hunting, fishing, rock climbing, and backpacking journals with an endless stream of advertisements offering expensive adventure-based trips. Such publications, and the organizations they support, commonly reflect and reinforce the view of nature as something to be conquered and overcome, separate and apart from man.

Fortunately for me, after my adolescent and college surge of testosterone had settled down a bit, I began to alter my own attitude and approach toward nature. This, in part, was due to the grace of my companions who complained about my insistence to hike into and camp in the most difficult of wilderness terrain. Frequently, I was pushing them—and also myself—beyond healthy and nurturing limits. My obsessive drive caused me to miss much of the beauty and peace that surrounded me.

Slowly and gradually I began to value pacing myself, covering less distance and camping in less dramatic areas. Forests and valleys started to appeal to my tastes as much as did peaks and extreme exposure. These days, when backpacking, I usually set base camp and hang out in the same site for three to five days. I also tend to stay away from the rigmarole, stress, and popularity of the fourteeners. I enjoy quiet, ambling walks on flat trails just outside of town or within city limits.

In the process of approaching the outdoors in a contemplative and low-key manner, my connection has revealed itself to be more rich and intimate than I had ever dreamed possible. The silent and still presence that pervades all of nature has become far more apparent. I have come to realize that my affinity with wilderness is based in consciousness itself—inherent, intact, and overflowing.

What is it that gives spirit to a particular place? I propose that spirit is discovered in our openness and in our receptivity, and that it is not found anywhere in particular. Spirit is in us and it is present everywhere we go. Certain places—mountains, oceans, and sacred sites—may embody an especially strong energy that evokes a feeling of depth and spirituality in us; but it is the quality of our living stillness (and not the actual, external landscape) that ultimately brings us into the recognition of the essence of nature—that which is found both in the woods and in us. Through the simple act of being still inside and resting our minds, we come to know spirit in a very personal and direct manner. And while certain locations may have healing qualities and strong memories attached to them, each time we revisit these sites our relationship is unique, as it is with revisiting an old friend. Nothing repeats itself in quite the same way.

Spirit is not some inert and constricted force. It is not contained in one area and absent from another. It is not even an it. In order to speak intelligently of the spirit of place, I think it is paramount that we look to both the experiencer and to the place, and, more important, to that which carries both the experiencer and the place. If we inquire into the center of this larger field of experience, it becomes impossible and ridiculous to distinguish person from place. Spirit unites these apparent separate realities into a resplendent, expanding, and abundant wholeness.

CATCHING THE SUNRISE

Antler

Antler resides in Milwaukee, spends one month backpacking or canoeing alone each year, and makes a living reading his poems around America. He is the author of *Factory* (City Lights, 1980), *Last Words* (Ballantine, 1986), and *Selected Poems* (Soft Skull Press, 2000) and the winner of the 1985 Walt Whitman Award, the 1987 Witter Bynner Prize, and a 1993 Pushcart Prize. He has been included in numerous anthologies, such as *Earth Prayers, A New Geography of Poets, Erotic by Nature,* and *Practicing Deep Ecology.* His next book is titled *Ever-Expanding Wilderness*. Antler has taught at Esalen, Naropa, and Omega Institutes. "Catching the Sunrise" originally appeared in Antler's book, *Last Words*.

When I see the first light
    touch treetops on the far shore
I launch my canoe without a sound
    and float into perfect calm.
Not till the lake floor disappears
    do I dip my paddle
And begin without a sound
    for the other side.
Not a drip or a ripple
    I go so slow.
When I reach the center of the lake
    the sun is up enough
    the far shore glows.
Soon I'm paddling in sunlight
    mist rises in wraiths.
On seeing the bottom
    as I near the other side
I stop paddling and glide,
    not a breath of wind.
Bird sings. Fish jumps.
Looking back where I came from
    I can see the trees at my camp
    begin to be touched by the sun.

ON THE BLUE GLACIER

Dolores LaChapelle

Dolores LaChapelle's first book, *Earth Festivals,* describes the concept of performing earth rituals throughout the year. Her second book, *Earth Wisdom,* gives the philosophical background for such rituals, as well as being one of the first explanations of deep ecology. Her *Sacred Land, Sacred Sex: Rapture of the Deep — Concerning Deep Ecology and Celebrating Life* is the definitive work on these issues. Dolores LaChapelle is the director of Way of Mountain Learning Center, 9,300 feet high in the San Juan Mountains of Colorado, where she lives and offers workshops. "On the Blue Glacier" originally appeared in her book *Sacred Land, Sacred Sex* (Finn Hill Press, 1988).

In general, modern people begin to recognize that there is such a thing as "sacred land" when traditional peoples, still living on their land, tell us that it is "sacred" to them. But can other types of land be "sacred"? I get many questions like this, so I will explain how I began to get an understanding of "sacred land." It started when I was privileged to encounter such land long ago, before I had ever heard the term. At the time I was part of the Blue Glacier Project.

For sixteen years I spent part of each summer on Mount Olympus in the middle of the Olympic Wilderness in Washington State. I was cook and water carrier and anything else that needed doing for the glacier study project run by the University of Washington. Ed LaChapelle, at the time my husband, ran the project.

The first summer of the project we were camped in tents on the lower moraine of the Blue Glacier. Because our son was only eighteen months old, my life and his were restricted to the moraine itself, which gave me unlimited time between chores to sit in the sun and watch the mountains and plants growing between the rocks. Day after day, for the entire month, I scanned the horizon and everything else within the incredibly beautiful setting of blue ice, white snow, rocks and flowers; however, it was not until the last day that I saw the waters of a pond glistening in the sun. It was clear across the glacier on the lower slopes of a mountain. (I can't give more details because, as everyone knows, to protect any beautiful spot in the natural environment it's best not to say much about the location.) There was no way for me to get there in the remaining few hours before we left; the men were all occupied with the packing of scientific instruments and other gear, so no one would be able to watch my son. But the gleam of water fascinated me. I determined that someday I would find out how a pond could be in that seemingly impossible location.

The following summer was during the International Geophysical Year. A hut was built up on the Snowdome where a plane could land to supply the project. The Snowdome is an immense snowfield lying between the mountains. To the west it drops off in cliffs facing out to the Pacific Ocean. Our hut was on a rock outcropping on the edge of this snowfield. We began to call this rock outcrop Panic Peak, because of the sheer drop-offs on all sides except where the gentle talus slope led down toward the hut.

Almost every afternoon we would all climb to the top of Panic Peak and watch the sun set into the Pacific Ocean, some seven thousand feet below us. During the day, any spare time I had from my chores, I would climb up and search out and identify wildflowers. It was such a wilderness those first few years that I found a flower so rare that it grows only in the Olympics above eight thousand feet. There are very few peaks in the Olympic range that high. But years went by before I could think of trying to get down to my "once seen" little pond.

Then, the year my son was six—four years after I had first seen the pond—I decided he was strong enough to make it down and back. So I put him on a rope and we descended the face of Panic Peak in search of the water. It was a rough climb but small children are very agile. We got off the cliff, finally, and onto a flat place. We walked toward where the glacier would be. Within a few steps we were off the talus rocks and onto moss. A heart-stopping hush came over us. There's no other way to describe it.

As we walked toward the little pond I realized that the star moss had never been disturbed. All around the rim of the pond was a cushion of star moss about ten inches thick. There was no break at all. Nor was there a cut or depression in the moss anywhere. Of course, where we were standing, it was pressed down, but nowhere else was there a mar to the continuous, unbroken surface. Then it came over me with a rush that we were the first humans there; not only that, we were also the first large mammals for a very long time. I don't know the rate that this moss grows but it is very slow. Since that experience I've watched for it in other places in the Olympic rain forest, and over a period of ten years I've not seen it make any noticeable advance. Any large mammal that ever came within sight of this pond would have come to drink. As anyone knows who spends time in the mountains, the drinking places of animals along streams or ponds are very noticeable. But no one had been drinking here.

Now, I had been climbing for fifteen years, having started as a teenager, and I'd seen many awe-inspiring mountain areas and done first ascents in Canada with the thrill of knowing I was the first human in that spot. But this was different. When the hush descended on us I had not yet realized we were the first humans ever there. That's what is interesting. I felt that hush that means "sacred" to me before I knew no one had been there before.

I stood absolutely still and carefully surveyed the entire area. It was paradise. High altitude flowers and a perfect blue jewel of a pond rimmed by star moss. All of it nestled between a vertical cliff of brown rock (which we had just come down) and a lateral moraine. The rest of the world was hidden except at one break where we could look out and up at the blue crevasses showing amid the white ice of the glacier tongue. That was my first recognition of sacred land.

When I began to think again, after the wonder of just breathing it all in, I realized that, truly, we were the first humans ever to see it. Indians did not come into the center of the vast "rain forest" of the Olympic Peninsula. Their legends referred to magic, huge, boundless lake in the center. That was their explanation for the huge rivers pouring out of the interior (actually, glaciers are the source of the water). There was no need for Indians to go into the dark forests. There were plenty of fish and shellfish to eat and a much easier life along the ocean beaches. The first whites never ventured very far from the lower rivers. It was much too fearsome and strange a country. The peninsula was not crossed by white people until modern times, when a Seattle newspaper sponsored the expedition. When mountain climbers began to penetrate the interior, they came only to climb the big peaks — Mount Olympus being the highest in the range. Climbers still follow along the moraine to get high enough to avoid the tangled, crashing ice of the lower glacier and then move on up the steep snow to the Snowdome. From this vast snow basin they have access to all the high peaks. No climber would ever try to cross the jumbled ice of the glacier tongue. Yes, we were the first humans ever to stand on that sacred land!

But how to account for that particular physiological feeling? My six-year-old son was just as hushed and reverent as I was. Yet he had just been untied from the climbing rope. Normally when free from the rope, he would run and jump with sheer exuberance. But not that time; instead he stood in hushed wonder! For years I had no words for the experience. Finally, a couple of years ago, reading David Abram's "Notes from Thami Valley," I found some words. He writes: "I want to ask, finally, if it is possible that our ecstatic or mystical experiences grow precisely out of our receptivity to solicitations not from some other non-material world but from the rest of this world, from that part of our own sphere which our linguistic prejudices keep us from really seeing, hearing, and feeling — from, that is, the entire nonhuman world of life and awareness." With this clue I now think that, possibly, when plants are growing in such a sheltered spot where no large mammals ever come, who might accidentally rip or tear the fabric of their growth, they may put off such a sense of well-being and health, that this somehow registers in our bodies.

What we experienced was not plant devas or elementals or fairies or elves or any of those abstractions. Perhaps the best word is what the primitives call *wakonda*, *orenda* or *mana*, all meaning "the powers" — the connection between my son and me and "the powers" present there. Giving particular names, such as "plant devas," etc., allows us to "objectify" the experience; in other words, to make it into a "substance." But actually, it was a relationship between those "powers" present in that place and us.

Although I had experienced occasional flashes of this feeling during my climbing experiences, before encountering the pond, they came and went so fast—partly because of the danger of climbing—that I could never hold on long enough to think about it. But here in this sacred place I had the chance to ponder what was happening. To attempt the impossible by putting words onto my experience, I feel that if one is able to stop the merely human reactions in such a place long enough, then one is able to join in the "play" of the ongoing natural relationships of all the living beings of that place and, of course, this is the sacred.

THE WAY OF THE MOUNTAIN

Joan Halifax

Joan Halifax is a cultural ecologist and Buddhist teacher who has long been at the forefront of cultural and spiritual exploration. She is the author of *Shaman: The Wounded Healer* and *The Fruitful Darkness: Reconnecting with the Body of the Earth*, the coauthor, with Stanislav Grof, of *The Human Encounter with Death*, and the editor of the anthology *Shamanic Voices*. She lives in Santa Fe, New Mexico, and is the founder and president of Upaya, a Buddhist studies center of environmental inquiry. "The Way of the Mountain" is an excerpt from her book *The Fruitful Darkness: Reconnecting with the Body of the Earth* (HarperCollins, 1993).

Everybody has a geography that can be used for change. That is why we travel to far-off places. Whether we know it or not, we need to renew ourselves in territories that are fresh and wild. We need to come home through the body of alien lands. For some, these journeys of change are taken intentionally and mindfully. They are pilgrimages, occasions when Earth heals us directly.

Mountains have long been a geography for pilgrimage places where peoples have been humbled and strengthened. They are symbols of the Sacred Center. Many have traveled to them in order to find the concentrated energy of Earth and to realize the strength of unimpeded space. Viewing a mountain at a distance or walking around its body, we can see its shape, know its profile, survey its surroundings. The closer you come to the mountain, the more it disappears. The mountain begins to lose its shape as you near it. Its body begins to spread out over the landscape, losing itself to itself. On climbing the mountain, the mountain continues to vanish. It vanishes in the detail of each step. Its crown is buried in space. Its body is buried in the breath.

On reaching the mountain's summit, we can ask, What has been attained? The top of the mountain? Big view? But the mountain has already disappeared. Going down the mountain, we can ask, What has been attained? Going down the mountain? The closer we are to the mountain, the more the mountain disappears. The closer we are to the mountain, the more the mountain is realized.

Mountain's realization comes through the details of the breath. Mountain appears in each step. Mountain then lives inside our bones, inside our heartdrum. It stands like a huge mother in the atmosphere of our minds. Mountain draws ancestors together in the form of clouds. Heaven, Earth and Human meet in the raining of the past. Heaven, Earth and Human meet in the winds of the future. Mountain Mother is a birth gate that joins the above and below. She is a prayer house. She is a mountain. Mountain is a mountain.

Mountains are extolled not only for their qualities but also for their effect on those who relate to them. Taking refuge in them, pilgrimaging to them, and walking around or ascending them has long been a way for the shaman and the Buddhist to purify and realize the mind of the mountain. The surface of inner and outer landscape, of the above and below, meet in the mountain body. The sense of place is confirmed in the mountain body. The spirit of place is confirmed when the mountain disappears into the landscape of the mind. Thus one reveres mountains.

Some of us are drawn to mountains the way the moon draws the tide. Both the great forests and the mountains live in my bones. They have taught me, humbled me, purified me, and changed me: Mount Fuji, Mount Shasta, Mount Kailas, the Schreckhorn, Kanchenjunga. Mountains are abodes for ancestor and deity. They are places where energy is discovered, made, acquired and spent. Mountains are symbols, as well, of enduring truth and of the human quest for spirit. I was told long ago to spend time with mountains.

In Praise

John Daniel

John Daniel has had a varied career as a college student, jogger, railroad inspector, rock climbing instructor, hod carrier, cook, and poet-in-the-schools. Daniel has taught creative writing and composition at Stanford University and as a writer-in-residence at colleges around the country. He is poetry editor of *Wilderness Magazine* and the author of two books of poems: *Common Ground* (Confluence Press, 1988) and *All Things Touched by Wind* (Salmon Run Press, 1994). *The Trail Home*, his collection of essays on nature, imagination, and the American West, was published by Pantheon Books in 1992. He is a winner of the 1993 Oregon Book Award for Creative Nonfiction and the 1995 John Burroughs Award for an Outstanding Natural History Essay. "In Praise" was first published in *Zone 3* (1992). It also appears in *All Things Touched by Wind*.

High in the pines the rising night wind lifts me awake
to stars and silhouettes of shifting trees,
their boughs alive with a passing spirit
whose deep sounding stirs in me
an older, vaster spirit
streaming from the source of time —
spirit that breathed these trees into being,
the ground that holds them as they sway,
and I who lie here listening,
told in a tongue I almost know
of where I came from and what I am,
how the power that imagined me moves through me
and beyond, far past my own imaginings
of what it is, and beautiful the flowing of its song.

The Water Way

Brenda Peterson

Brenda Peterson has lived in Seattle for twenty years, half of the time on Puget Sound, her daily muse and mentor. *Living by Water* (Alaska Northwest

Books, 1990) and *Singing to the Sound* (New Sage Press, 2001) reflect this
passion for the Pacific Northwest coast. She is the author of thirteen
books, including the recent memoir *Build Me an Ark: A Life with Animals*
(W.W. Norton) and with coauthor Linda Hogan, the new National
Geographic book, *Sightings: The Gray Whales' Mysterious Journey.*

If landscape is character, then northwesterners are most like water. We
are shaped by the voluptuous shores and salt tides of Puget Sound, the
deep currents of the Columbia, Salmon, and Snake Rivers; finally, we are
held back from falling off the proverbial edge of the world by a Pacific
coastline whose nurturing rain forests and rocky peninsulas face the sea
like guardians. Being surrounded by water, we cannot impose our own
rhythms on nature as easily as a bulldozer does on a southern California
canyon. We find ourselves subtly in sync with the rise and fall of tides, the
ebb and flow of the natural world.

This distinction that we northwesterners are more changed by our
environment than it is by us is crucial to understanding our character.
Once a convention of New Yorkers visited Seattle. On the harbor cruise
to Blake Island, birthplace of Chief Sealth (Seattle), for a salmon feast
hosted by Native Americans to re-create the first salmon bake and pot-
latch ceremonies that defined tribal life here for thousands of years, the
tourists commented that everything seemed in slow motion.

"We've had to shift gears," said one New Yorker, somewhat anxiously.
"Everything's so laid back. Maybe it's all those negative ions in the atmosphere."

Another visitor said, "How do you stand traffic jams on those floating
bridges? Can't they just pave a part of Lake Washington?"

Finally, a rather pensive, bespectacled literary agent remarked, "Now I
know why Seattle is single-handedly keeping New York's book business
alive. You have to go inside in all this gray and wet. I feel like I'm dreaming."

"Must be why Seattle has espresso carts on every corner and some of
the world's best coffee," someone laughed. "It's to keep yourselves awake!"

Northwesterners are a dreamy lot. We're in a fine tradition of dream-
ers. According to the Wasco Indians along the Columbia River, the tribe
knew long before the white people came to settle at Alki Point, in 1851,
that a change was coming. As told in Ella E. Clark's classic *Indian Legends
of the Pacific Northwest*, one of the Wasco elders dreamed that "white people
with hair on their faces will come from the rising sun." The strangers were
prophesied to bring with them "iron birds that could fly," and "something—
if you just point at anything moving, that thing will fall down and die."

They also brought new tools such as axes, hatchets, and stoves. Along with this new technology, the white people brought a philosophy of individual ownership of the land.

The Native Americans knew that the land could never be owned, just as it was impossible to section off the vast winding lengths of the emerald-clear body of Puget Sound, so like a watery dragon embracing the land. Even now, after over a century of non-Indian dominance, Puget Sound property rights ebb and flow according to the tides, not the set boundaries of so-called landowners. If even our ownership of northwest land is called into daily question by changing tides, how much more deeply are we affected by water?

Northwesterners not only reckon with water shaping our physical boundaries, we have learned to live most of the year as if underwater. Rain is a northwest native. Our famous rainfall is perhaps all that shelters us from the massive population and industrial exploitations of nearby California. The rain is so omnipresent, especially between late October and June, that most northwesterners disdain umbrellas, the true sign of any tourist.

Widely acclaimed Port Angeles poet Tess Gallagher tells it this way: "It is a faithful rain. You feel it has some allegiance to the trees and the people…. It brings an ongoing thoughtfulness to their faces, a meditativeness that causes them to fall silent for long periods, to stand at their windows looking out at nothing in particular. The people walk in the rain as within some spirit they wish not to offend with resistance."

One must be rather fluid to live underwater; one must learn to flow with a pulse greater than one's own. A tolerance for misting gray days means an acceptance that life itself is not black and white, but in between. If the horizons outside one's window are not sharply defined but ease into a sky intimately merged with sea and soft landscape, then perhaps shadows, both personal and collective, are not so terrifying. After all, most of the year northwesterners can't even see their own literal shadows cast on the ground. We live inside the rain shadow. We tolerate edges and differences in people and places perhaps because our landscape blends and blurs as it embraces.

There is a strong Asian influence here in the Pacific Northwest. Seattle's expansive harbor is a gateway to the Orient, and the strong, graceful pull of that more feminine culture is felt here. In fact, the classic *Tao Te Ching*, by the ancient Chinese master Lao-tzu, could well be a description of the Puget Sound landscape and character—we are flexible and fluid.

If water is our northwest character and rainy reverie our temperament, it follows that those of us who stay long in the Pacific Northwest must develop an inner life to sustain us through the flow of so many changing gray days. This means that ambition is not only an outward thrust toward manipulating our environment; ambition may also be an inner journey, not to change but to understand the often unexplored territory within, what Rilke calls "the dark light." Are we a more mystical region and people? Let's just say the climate is there and so is the water way.

KENAI FJORDS

Chris Hoffman

Chris Hoffman is an ecopsychologist, poet, and counselor. He is the author of the acclaimed ecopsychology book *The Hoop and the Tree: A Compass for Finding a Deeper Relationship with All Life* (Council Oak Books, 2000). His poetry has been published in various chapbooks and magazines. He lives in Boulder, Colorado, with his wife and son. "Kenai Fjords" originally appeared in *Sea Kayaker* magazine and was also published in the *Men's Council Journal*.

This little kayak gives me an ocean for legs.
I stand where the pelagic sea birds float
and slide beside sleeping otters
rocking in their big bay cradle.
My kayak's prow skims through the water
parting a vee as delicate as a raindrop's ripple,
gracefully tracing fine and vanishing calligraphy,
sensitive and eager as a lover's first intimate touch.
I will go with my kayak to the place of glaciers,
to where the ice age crouches by the ocean,
probing with thick fingers of ice,
stilling its chill breath
and hoping for a long, cold winter.

I glide past the incessant gnawing of ocean at cliffs,
past the slack and bloom of wavelets plashing
on beaches cobbled with black stones.
Braided streams like long lace
from the white linen tablecloth of icefields and snowfields
plunge reckless and tangled in their abundance

down steep verdant slopes—
numberless unnamed waterfalls pounding and roaring.
Flurries of wary puffins whack the water
in their take-off runs.

Orange beaks make bright wedges
in a misty grey-green grey-blue grey-grey world.
Here are the shores where the bear's tongue tastes
blueberry and sweet red cloudberry by multitudes—
taut sacks bursting in wild explosions of flavor.
Here is where the bear's paw
pulls miraculous salmon from the thronging streams.
A bald eagle flies to its nest, sculpting the air with its wings;
Mew gulls and kittiwakes swoop and pluck at the water;
An arctic tern hovers over the beach, wheeling and crying;
In the distance, rugged mountains in three shades of grey
kneel into the sea.

O to go buoyant on the liquid muscle of the sea
and to be so small in this immensity, but present and alive!
In my speck of kayak
I balance on the gilding swell and dancing chop
and watch the crystal beads that fallen raindrops make
before the ocean sucks them in.
I reach with my paddle and push my boat forward
and breathe with the rhythm of sliding along.
The ocean supports me and welcomes my paddle
and I move like a swimmer immersed in a song.
I move like a swimmer, I move like a swimmer,
and I move like a swimmer immersed in a song.
To be here this way is something delicious and forbidden—
like being in a warm safe night, outdoors and naked.

In this little kayak I glide towards the glacier;
and I hear the tomb of ancient winters slowly speaking—
muttered booms cushioned by the silence of deepening cold.
Seals slide into the water and simply watch—
scores of grey-headed periscopes with soft eyes.
I pass islands of ice that sometimes pop and crackle as they melt.
The water is milky blue-grey and barely salty;

and through the kayak it drinks the heat from my body.
The wall of ice grows and grows taller and taller,
wider and wider as I drift closer.
It is white and dirty black
and the piercingly impossible edge of blue —
a barrier of grotesquely beautiful shapes hundreds of feet high
and hundreds hundreds wide.
A still and terrifying calmness descends on my soul
in the expanse of this unseen presence.
A young sandhill crane, poised in single-pointed weight,
turns and graciously walks away.
This world in its rawness is ever sacred.

Ten Years Later

David Whyte

David Whyte makes his home in the Pacific Northwest, where rain and
changeable skies remind him of his other, more distant homes: Yorkshire,
Wales, and Ireland. He travels throughout North America, Europe, and
Asia, reading and lecturing, bringing his own and others' poetry to large
audiences. He is one of the few poets to bring his insights to bear on
organizational life, working with companies at home and abroad.

He's the author of the following books of poetry from Many Rivers
Press: *The House of Belonging* (1996), *Fire in the Earth* (1992), and *Where Many
Rivers Meet* (1990). "Ten Years Later" first appeared in *The House of Belonging*.

When the mind is clear
and the surface of the now still,
now swaying water

slaps against
the rolling kayak,

I find myself near darkness
paddling again to Yellow Island.

Every spring wildflowers
cover the grey rocks.

Every year the sea breeze
ruffles the cold and lovely pearls
hidden in the center of the flowers

as if remembering them
by touch alone.

A calm and lonely, trembling beauty
that frightened me in youth.

Now their loneliness
feels familiar, one small thing
I've learned these years,

how to be alone,
and at the edge of aloneness
how to be found by the world.

Innocence is what we allow
to be gifted back to us
once we've given ourselves away.

There is one world only,
the one to which we gave ourselves
utterly, and to which one day

we are blessed to return.

THE LAND:
A Sense of Home

Bill Weiler

Bill Weiler coedited the collection *The Earth Speaks*. He has also written *Humor in the Balance: Nature Laughs Last* (a collection of environmental cartoons) and *The Night Mare* (fiction). Bill is the Pacific Northwest representative for the Institute for Earth Education, the planet's largest environmental education organization, and works for the Washington Department of Fish and Wildlife as the Regional Volunteer Coordinator. "The Land: A Sense of Home" is excerpted and edited from the introduction to his book, *Close to the Wind: A Northwest Naturalist Is Dreaming*. The article was first published in the seasonal international journal, *Talking Leaves*, by the Institute for Earth Education.

> *Whatever evaluation we finally make of a stretch of land, no matter how profound or accurate, we will find it inadequate. The land retains an identity of its own, still deeper and more subtle than we can know. Our obligation toward it then becomes simple: to approach with an uncalculating mind, with an attitude of regard. To try and sense the range and variety of its expression — its weather and colors and animals. To intend from the beginning to preserve some of the mystery within it as a kind of wisdom to be experienced, not questioned. And to be alert for its openings, for that moment when something sacred reveals itself within the mundane and you know the land knows you are there.*
> —BARRY LOPEZ, Arctic Dreams

Since the first human couple, home has always been more than a structure to sleep in. It was the land that supported the family, the land that supported buffalo, cows or corn. For pockets of Americans, there is still a tenacious love affair with the wild landscape and an understanding that the true wealth of a piece of land is considered not by what it's worth economically, but what its worth is spiritually.

My own undeniable urge to live in a natural setting grew in proportion to my deepening love for the outdoors. By high school, when I resided in Los Angeles, a formulating dream preoccupied my thoughts. Over the years, and despite the setbacks of some five dozen prospective homelands and numerous land partners, the dream, though slippery and changed from its original intent, lived on. My initial plan of a place far from any crowd dissolved. I could be secluded but not isolated. Six years of treadwearing narrowed my ragged topography maps to two locales: southern Oregon, world headquarters for the survivalist movement, the state's banana belt; or north-central Oregon/south-central Washington, distinguished by its proximity to a natural showcase, the Columbia River Gorge, and a welcomed sunny climate. When my latest land-hunting partners, Marc and Brook, took the gamble and moved to an outpost apartment on the eastern edge of the Columbia River Gorge, our decision was locked. I liked the combination: a gentle land, drier than the "umbrellaed" west-of-the-mountain climes, small, comfortable communities, mountains of mythical proportions, nearby waterways, cheap land, no McDonald's in sight or in the crystal ball, down-to-earth people and vistas that laid beauty before the eye and encompassed the heart.

The search sharply narrowed. One area that Marc had praised, I could not even get close to due to the owner's ominous warning signs. Another hilltop seemed too remote for my liking. Marc and Brook swallowed hard at my reaction almost to the point of wondering if I was still interested in the land pursuit, but kept on searching and came through. They acted swiftly on a local ad: the owner of forty inexpensive acres desired to take flight to the less civilized shores of wild Alaska.

This Columbus-like discovery of Marc's soon sent a thunderbolt of energy catapulting through us, reviving our optimism. I had been involved in this undertaking for eight years now, pursuing an elusive dream, which, like the ebb and flow of ocean waves, seemed repeatedly close to reality, then far out to sea. Marc watched me intently as he introduced this latest serene acreage, five miles from the two-block town of Lyle, Washington. We had shared the windy silence before and had been disappointed more times than we cared to remember, yet this place felt different. People react to heart-moving experiences in their own ways. Some, like game-show winners, jump up and down, hugging anyone in sight; others cry for joy, while still others (and I typically fall into this group) take it all in silently, the mind analyzing, while its counterpart, the heart, sings in the background. Inwardly, I was leaping, though I failed to show my joy outwardly. Marc left depressed over what he perceived as my tepid reaction.

What made this earth prize appealing was that not only did it favorably compare to our land list of requirements, but it offered something intangible, a song directed at me, a planetary echo most audible to those who spend their lives with their ears close to the earth. Barry Lopez, in *Arctic Dreams*, bears witness to similar experiences: "A man in Anaktuvuk Pass, in response to a question about what he did when he visited a new place, said to me, I listen. That's all. I listen, he meant, to what the land is saying. I walk around it and strain my senses in appreciation of it for a long time before I ever speak a word. Entered in such a respectful manner, he believed, the land would open up to him."

Once in a lifetime, if we're lucky, we non-native, city-evolved humans with dulled senses are able to listen purely to what the land is saying. In our stillness, in our open receptivity, we link hearts with the source of our being. The music seeps in, and, like a live orchestra, comes emanating from all directions. And between the notes, a silent drumroll beats and the soul understands: The rapture. Here I belong!

Although many other nature places we explored spoke to me, they were more whispers than song. Some areas, like the clear-cut spot, had lost their voices completely. To test the skeptical notion that my first visit might have been an aberration, I returned on several occasions, and every time, no matter where I stood on the property, the ethereal voices followed me.

It wasn't long before Marc knew of my ecstatic leanings. This time, nothing would prevent us from signing the purchase papers. This was the place. It was time to give away the land-buyer manuals to the next person poring over the real estate ads. Once you've reached home, you still need to plod through the official formalities but they become low priority. You zoom through the wrappings to get to the present hidden underneath. When the young girl in the movie *Miracle on 34th Street*, lost in a fog of doubt, looks up to find the clear vision of her dreams, the house she has longed for, she screams for joy in recognition of her "new" home. She becomes a believer in dreams and of wishing. I became a believer that first day overlooking the Klickitat River Valley and my future.

The Spirit of the Forest

Michael J. Roads

Michael Roads is the author of *Talking with Nature, Journey into Nature, Simple Is Powerful, Journey into Oneness*, and *Into a Timeless Realm*. He has also written an organic gardening book published in Australia, *The Natural Magic of Mulch*. He emigrated from England to Australia in 1964. After a decade of farming in Tasmania, he became a founding member of a holistic community and then an organic farming consultant. He is now a full-time metaphysical writer and gives talks and retreats around the world.

I scramble up the steep rocky incline toward the alpine plateau. It is a unique place, towering above a multitude of small valleys in the New England National Park in New South Wales, Australia. On reaching the top, I behold forest as far as the eye can see.

Collectively forest, yet on the ridges grow the sparse, sclerophyll forests, while deeper on the plunging slopes grow rain-forest trees, each environment clearly defined. From above, it appears rather as a patchwork quilt of varied hues of green, spreading in undulating waves over the hills, slopes and valleys beneath me.

On this small, bleak, windswept plateau grow many natural bonsai. Ancient sprawling trees cling with tenacious roots, roots that have penetrated deep into the rocky cracks and fissures of time. Brown and blackened moss clutches at the bases of the dwarfed trunks, defying the adverse environment. Before me, no more than knee high, a tiny tree, gnarled and twisted by age, shames my bonsai art by its natural perfection. Its tiny leathery leaves draw moisture from the night's atmosphere, its roots searching the deep rock. Perhaps a hundred, maybe five hundred years have passed while this dwarf tree has struggled to survive.

How different from the forest giants, so close beneath the parapet, yet, environmentally, so far away. The trees below have had little struggle in their efforts to grow, reaching tall from the decaying biomass of a natural forest. Is it not likely then, that the dwarfed trees that have battled a relentless environment for each new leaf, each inch of growth, contain far greater energy than their giant cousins in the sheltered forest?

I eat my lunch while green and black butterflies flit in swift, erratic swoops from flower to flower in the profusion of heath on the cliff edge. I have a feeling of wholeness of infinite connections with the Nature that contains me. I do not feel myself to be an intruder in this wild place, rather, I feel that my surroundings are no more than an outer reflection of the inner spaces of my greater Being. I disengage myself from separation, becoming One with this wild Nature.

When I descend from the plateau, I take a remote track, plunging down the slopes into milder rain forest, noisy with gurgling, newborn creeks. A dramatic change takes place. Leaving behind the cool climate silvertop gum, manna gum and mountain gum with their rocky terrain and sparse undergrowth, I enter the moist, shaded, twilight environment of the huge southern beech. Wow! What a tree. Host to an incredible variety of vivid mosses, lacy-fronded ferns, sickly yellow lichens and strange primitive liverworts, each tree in this cool, humid microclimate is testament to the extravagant art of Nature.

As I follow the track, I gaze up at many varieties of orchids, often hidden behind a bridal veil of hanging moss. I breathe softly, walking slowly, awed by the rich immensity of life. Over fifty species of evergreen trees grow here, while liana vines loop from tree to tree like thick, primeval serpents. As I pass, I pay homage to the magnificent red cedars, the grand monarchs as they stand among their subjects, the booyong, hoop pine, yellow carabeen, corkwood and a whole host of others.

I duck beneath the wicked barbs of the wait-awhile vine, then squat to smell the rich, pungent biomass of the forest floor. I continue quietly on my way, looking, feeling, being with. I have no particular focus, few thoughts. I am open to the forest and very aware of the subtle undercurrents of energy that are an intangible part of the physical forms all around me. The Spirit of the forest is as evident in its tangible absence as the huge trees with their imposing presence.

I gaze at a strangler fig, a tree that has clutched and squeezed the life from an unfortunate forest giant. Developing from a frail slender root, which began its tenuous journey to earth from a seed high in a host tree, the fig's massive network of thick powerful roots and limbs has replaced, over several decades, the unwitting host. These trees are an impressive sight. I pause for a while, gazing at the decaying shell of the host tree, long dead, leaving a stairway through the strangler formed by the barrel of its collapsing, rotten trunk.

The trees appear as though they were once engaged in a violent conflict, a life-and-death struggle of imperceptible sound and movement. I am mesmerized by my speculation. Gradually, in my silence a different Silence overwhelms me, and in my consciousness, I hear the Spirit of the forest.

The strangler fig and its host tree may appear to the human eye as though locked in conflict, but this is the deduction of a reasoning mind and the conditioning of separation. Humans can see the manifestation of a physical order, interpreting it according to their consciousness. Yet within this forest many levels of order are manifest.

The strangler fig and its dead host are a graphic demonstration of death within life, life within death, for in a higher expression, nothing is born and nothing dies. Life IS. You can relate to the trees as victor and vanquished, or, with insight and perception, you can see to the heart of a shared synthesis, where a mutual expression of one life moves through forms that know nothing of separation.

Humanity's belief in the illusion of separation is the cause of your preoccupation with competition and defeat. This belief causes you to interpret the relationship between these trees as a fight for survival, instead of seeing a synthesis of diversity within a framework of unity.

I look at the trees with a new appraisal. I am again reminded that unless I am focused in the moment, then I am in automatic, stuck with its program of the past. Stepping around a very large, unattended cobweb, I continue along the track, moving deeper into the rain forest.

Close by, the towering plateau rears above the forest, but I can see nothing of it. Even light has difficulty reaching the forest floor, such is the density of vegetation. Soon I come to where a mammoth tree has crashed to earth, probably felled by a wild storm. Its trunk is massive, the girth higher than my head, its limbs crushed and twisted by its colossal weight.

I stare in awe at the bulk and enormity of the tree, wondering what could cause such a giant to topple, but as I clamber around the base, I find the reason. It is rotten, the trunk full of soggy pulp. Only the thick bark had been holding the tree erect, while vainly pumping sap through the huge system. All around the tree sunlight cascades into the forest gloom, and among the tangled vegetation a race is in progress, a race to reach ever higher to the sunlight. Vines and shrubs, small flowers and sapling trees, all reach out to absorb the energy of light.

I smile. This time I do not see competition and conflict. I now realize these are human concepts, for I have learned that Nature is a participation of life, and that the birth and death of physical forms are but the movement of consciousness. I linger for a while, enjoying a few rarely seen understory plants as they briefly bask in the sun, then I move on. Before long I am in very deep shade. I watch the soft tree fern unfolding vibrant new fronds, each wrapped in clinging threads of gold. I am witnessing the birth of hidden beauty.

I follow the forest track as it meanders among the trees, when I spy one of my favorite creatures, a lizard. It basks in a tiny shaft of sun on a moss-covered rock. There is an extensive variety of reptiles here, ranging from the large monitors to dragons and geckos, not forgetting numerous varieties of snakes. Frogs abound, but one that is worthy of mention is the recently discovered sphagnum frog. This little amphibian lives in burrows tunneled deep into sphagnum moss. The tadpoles develop in comparatively large eggs in there until ready to emerge as tiny replicas of the adult frogs.

I swat at a few mosquitoes, checking my ankles for leeches. I accept that paradise has its parasites. As I follow the track, an enormous richness and variety of insects are evident, filling every available ecological niche with the perfect species. I stop to examine a huge, ungainly stick insect that moved just enough to catch my eye. It is a beauty. Flitting over the park's cold creeks are some of the smallest dragonflies in the world, while hovering like primeval helicopters in the damp rain forest are the largest. I look for one of these as I walk along, for I love the large dragonflies, but I see none. I am rewarded, however, by the sight of a grotesque praying mantis, the ferocious predator of all insects. I also see some butterflies. Over fifty species hover and flit about the park, feeding from the flowers of the heath and scrub or the nectar of fragrant blossoms high in the forest trees.

As I near the end of the track, soon to emerge near my car, I reflect on the immense diversity of the forest. Life teems in seething abundance, living and dying in countless myriad forms. If there is anywhere that I can encompass life as the movement of consciousness, as continuity, it is here, for only in Nature am I free of emotional attachments. In moments like this, I feel and perceive that all is a vast and complex order. I am aware that nothing happens by accident in this forest; order is the very pulse of Nature. And if this is so, is it not so for all life?

As I walk in the deep silence, it takes little imagination to realize that a forest is not just a lot of trees. A living forest demonstrates oneness, for even while embodying physical separation it is empowered by its subtle spiritual connection. I am catching the occasional glimpse of just a fraction of the vast array of forest life, life forms which depend on and interrelate with each other in a wondrous holistic balance. For brief moments I perceive the interface between this dense physical reality in which we are so entrenched and the metaphysical realities that so easily elude us.

While I study my physical surroundings in all their rich diversity, I am held by the images of my eyes, but when I pause, my eyes no longer seeing out, then, it seems, the fabric of the forest is no longer quite the same. For timeless moments the reality of other ways of being gently intrude. I find it easy to connect with the nature of the forest, yet in this mystic energy I feel an even greater connection. Here, hidden and shielded in a dense forest, it seems that the distant stars are also connected, for as I pause before a pepper vine, my hand on the smooth bark, I feel only moving energy. Not the energy of a physical nature, but that of metaphysical movement, a movement unrelated to time or distance, unhindered by form. My hand rests on the vine, yet into my awareness come images of a thread of connection between all life forms throughout the whole universe — a thread of endlessness, of continuity. The words I hear seem to come from somewhere very distant, yet no more than a breath away.

Where humanity sows no discord, you may reap a higher vision. A pure Nature evokes that which reaches into the space of the mystic Self. Here you will find a gift — the gift of in-sight.

As I drive away, I thank the Spirit of the forest for my experience, and I remind myself that wholeness is my ongoing truth, not momentary, in an enchanted forest.

Solitude Late at Night in the Woods

Robert Bly

Robert Bly is the author, editor, and translator of numerous collections of poetry. Among his recent books are *The Night Abraham Called to the Stars* (HarperCollins, 2001), *American Poetry: Wilderness and Domesticity, The Winged Life* (about Henry David Thoreau), *Iron John: A Book about Men,* and his collected prose poems, *What Have I Ever Lost by Dying?* He lives near Minneapolis, Minnesota. "Solitude Late at Night in the Woods" was originally published in *Silence in the Snowy Fields* (Wesleyan University Press, 1962).

I

The body is like a November birch facing the full moon
And reaching into the cold heavens.
In these trees there is no ambition, no sodden body, no leaves,
Nothing but bare trunks climbing like cold fire!

II

My last walk in the trees has come. At dawn
I must return to the trapped fields,
To the obedient earth.
The trees shall be reaching all the winter.

III

It is a joy to walk in the bare woods.
The moonlight is not broken by the heavy leaves.
The leaves are down, and touching the soaked earth,
Giving off the odor that partridges love.

II

Quests and
Rituals of Renewal

*A*ny true quest, any true ritual, if you are lucky, will bring you into contact with silence and with Self. The beauty of turning to wilderness as teacher and healer is that wilderness is entirely impartial to our human affairs and struggles. It just is: disinterested, unattached and, yet, totally in relationship to itself and to us. Nature presents us with a stillness and a silence that is not the absence of movement or the absence of noise, but active stillness and active silence.

The opportunity offered in the sanctuary of nature is one of turning inward toward the source, of seeing beyond surface appearances. This plunge is a plunge into the peace and joy of being. Nothing else is needed. Removing ourselves from the busyness of our lives and meeting the depths of presence and beingness found in the outdoors is a gift we can give ourselves at any time.

There are traditions of wilderness rites of passage throughout human history that serve to bring us into the arms of the pulsing and dynamic mystery of life. The Aboriginal walkabout and the initiations of shamans throughout many indigenous cultures are examples. From the continent of North America, within various Native American tribes, there is a long history of solo quests in wilderness, often involving much ritual preparation, community support, and fasting. The ritual concludes in an all-night vigil of prayer, in which the quester asks to be given a vision. The famous story of Black Elk's vision of the sacred hoop, in which he saw all of the world's peoples as belonging within one circle of humanity, is probably the most well known version of this rite.

Many of the contributions in this section speak to individual experiences of this simple archetypal form. Most of these accounts are written by non-Indian people who draw upon pan-cultural sources and borrow from Native American ceremonies. It is not—in any way, shape, or form—my intention to be disrespectful toward these traditions. In fact, I have deep admiration and gratitude for the depth and strength of the many earth-centered ceremonies of prayer that have been passed down over the ages and that influence us collectively. I have included these essays in the book because they convey the potential transforming effects of time spent in wilderness.

We all come from histories that have had wilderness rites of passage as part of our culture. We all are made up of matter. Our bodies are sustained by the food of the earth. All peoples are intimately interwoven within the richness of the earth and with one another. We can no longer afford to live isolated from the beauty of one another's culture.

It is my perspective that any practice or ceremony that brings us into true relationship with nature and Self—if it is done with heart, respect, care, and love—is worth supporting. The integrity and quality of the offerings of each writer and guide will need to be tested on an individual basis.

A SACRED PASSAGE

Adapted from an interview with John P. Milton

Lauren L. Dasmann

John P. Milton is the founder of the Sacred Passage wilderness programs. He was an early pioneer of the deep ecology movement and has conducted numerous expeditions and field projects in wilderness areas throughout the world. John has served as chairperson and director of several public foundations, as professor of environmental studies, and as a consultant in environmental protection and renewal. He has authored numerous books and articles on ecology, environmental conservation, and inner development. Sounds True recently published his six audiocassette tape complete course on spiritual practice in nature, entitled *Sky Above, Earth Below.*

Lauren Dasmann participated in a Sacred Passage program with John Milton in 1989 and felt moved to get the word out, and so interviewed John about his work. She was raised by an ecologist and grew up in tents in the wilderness. She is currently living in Bisbee, Arizona, with her husband and child. "A Sacred Passage" first appeared in *Chrysalis* magazine.

> *The great sacred spiritual paths of the world traverse a varied landscape of culture and tradition but nearly all have passed through and been strengthened by time alone in the wilderness.*
> —JOHN P. MILTON

There has been growing interest in recent years in the revival of a traditional rite of passage, the vision quest. In this interview, John P. Milton, founder of the Sacred Passage wilderness programs, explains the value of the vision quest: how it can serve us in modern society and how important it has become as a tool for reconnecting with the earth and with the spirit, healing the imbalances of our personal lives and of the planet as a whole.

LAUREN L. DASMANN: Can you tell us a little about the historical role of the vision quest?

JOHN P. MILTON: It's a very basic rite of passage which helps awaken the heart to the profound unity of all life. It's been used throughout the world, for thousands of years, as the most direct and powerful way to contact guidance, inspiration, renewal and the sacred view.

Traditional peoples, for whom the quest was the rule, lived in a way very closely integrated with the earth and with the spirit, and they remained so closely integrated partly as a result of the vision quest. Most often, this was the ritual that defined passage from childhood to adulthood. On quest, people received deep and powerful insight into their true nature, contacted the purpose of their lives, received their true name and made the transition into a new phase of life with a deep understanding and respect for the interconnectedness of all life.

LLD: And how does the quest experience you offer today compare with the traditional vision quest?

JPM: Traditionally, questers went without food, shelter, clothing, sleep, and, in some cases, even water. Today we haven't been raised with the same preparation or with the same trust and familiarity with nature. So now we take a few more supports: water, a sleeping bag, a little food, clothing, and a small tent. Also, where traditionally questers were confined to a very small spot, we've extended the site to a circle of 108 yards. We tend to be very distracted, given the state of modern culture, and staying within this "sacred circle" helps us to settle down. While on solo, we become thoroughly integrated with our site, one with it. It becomes the foundation of our Sacred Passage.

We've also extended the time spent on solo from the traditional two to four days to a minimum of seven days out alone. As people develop a commitment to the process, we extend that to two weeks and then to a full lunar cycle.

LLD: For most people even two days alone in the wilderness could seem difficult. Why have you chosen to extend that?

JPM: We've found that seven days seems to be the ideal time period for modern people to begin with. Also, it seems to resonate with what people realize, at some level, is the necessary time to accomplish major internal breakthrough.

We are so totally out of balance with the earth and with the true opening of the spirit that a shorter quest just doesn't give us enough time.

Modern people tend to go through three phases during solo. First is several days of purification and elimination. There's then a spontaneous opening to spaciousness and bliss and an opening of the heart. And that is followed by a deep period of integration. A shorter quest usually doesn't allow us to go beyond even the initial purification phase.

Traditionally, the shorter quest was the culmination of long training and focused ceremony. We still recommend a year's preparation but, in fact, people often don't even decide to go on a quest until very shortly beforehand. And on top of this minimal preparation, our culture hasn't given us the background to really deal with the quest experience. The training we provide before and after quest helps a great deal, but the extended time on solo is also necessary. Also, we've worked to tailor Sacred Passage to meet the realities of modern culture. The quest requires only one full week off work. It's great when people can give themselves a longer period, but almost anyone can take a week off if they really want to.

LLD: What do you think brings people to a point where they want to?

JPM: There's a push and a pull involved. The push comes from realizing how crazy our lives have gotten. We live in a state of high stress and distraction and we seek to fill our needs through material means. We are pressured and distressed in many ways and at some point we awaken to feel that something's really wrong with this. The push may also come from realizing that we are facing an environmental crisis which threatens the earth and all life. And we are brought to the pull side when we want to find a way to help change ourselves, others and the planet as a whole. The pull comes from a desire for change, from a desire to simplify our lives, and from recognition for the need and real possibility for reconnection with the earth and with pure Universal Spirit. It's important to emphasize that great peace and a natural state of happiness come very spontaneously through a Sacred Passage. It is the bliss and the profound opening of the radiant heart that is central to the quest. If people know that, it can help in overcoming the obstacles to allowing themselves this experience.

LLD: Does Sacred Passage require a particular spiritual orientation?

JPM: No. Our training does point to the basic essence found within all traditions that lead to enlightenment, but it is nondenominational and integrates with any orientation. This is a very earth-based tradition, which serves to bring us into harmony and balance with earth, but it also goes far beyond that to provide a tremendous reconnecting with the spirit that moves through the whole universe. That's important, because as we've lost our connection to earth we've also lost that greater connection, the connection to pure spirit.

LLD: Can you tell us a little more about the training you offer?

JPM: Much of our training is aimed at opening to the fundamental universal nature in ourselves and in other people. Reconnecting with nature is not confined to the wilderness; it includes other people and all forms of life. We use a variety of meditation practices and Tai Chi movements, which help us to deepen our experience of union and pure being. We emphasize three principles: decontraction (total relaxation and opening), non-distraction (from pure being), and the opening of the radiant heart (of unconditional love).

LLD: What's the value of having this training? Some people would prefer to go out on their own and not get involved with a group or a guide.

JPM: If people are able to do it on their own, that's great. That's how I started myself over thirty years ago. But it's important to realize that this is a very powerful process for which our culture hasn't prepared us, so we do emphasize a need for guidance. It's easy to get caught in astral or other illusory experiences. And totemic experiences, where animals appear as guides, can also be exciting. These experiences do arise and must be understood and honored. But if you don't have a way to interpret them that takes you beyond them to their source, you can begin to hold them as your goal. That would be tragic as there's so much more that's possible. We need also to realize that a tremendous amount of deep emotional material is released through Sacred Passage. In some cases this could lead to amplified neurosis or psychotic breaks. Without a good guide who understands the process, a quest could be damaging for some people. And the same is true with our mental processes. When they first encounter the spaciousness of the quest experience, people often find that their minds run away with them.

Good guidance is also very important after return from the quest. We spend several days on the re-entry process and provide a program for continuing integration and cultivation of the heart wisdom received while on Passage. We also remain available to people for ongoing help with integrating this profound experience into modern life. Again, traditionally the vision quest was a part of long training and spiritual guidance. People didn't just go out there "cold" so to speak.

LLD: What are the main obstacles that block people from allowing themselves the experience of a Sacred Passage?

JPM: Resistance usually stems from a very basic fear of change. For some there's a fear that the quest might precipitate a kind of "dark night of the soul." But, in fact, the quest brings people a true taste of their own inherent bliss and a chance to follow it very deeply and directly, to bring it back into their lives, and to learn to "give it away" to other people.

Sometimes people are so unfamiliar with nature that they're quite afraid to be out there alone. The quest, of course, is even safer than a normal camping trip. And, although you don't see anyone during your solo, you leave daily signs to show that you're all right. There's someone checking on that who can help if there's any difficulty.

And then there are those people who have spent a lot of their lifetime close to nature, and who feel they've already experienced the depths of what's possible. Their belief system is that they've already done it when, in fact, they've barely scratched the surface. Unfortunately, these are often some of the most resistant people, because they've set a limit, a barrier, for themselves. Along the same lines, some people think this is like a glorified camping trip, and, of course, it's not. It's completely different.

The pull to go through a Sacred Passage, to overcome the resistances, is often generated through direct contact with the radiance of people returning from solo time. We welcome visitors during our initial training and re-entry. This gives people a chance to see the incredible, blissful, living energy and empowerment shining out of the quester's eyes. People returning from a solo often look as though a thousand suns are lit up inside: that speaks so much more clearly than words, just one look at a face like that.

LLD: You also have an extensive background as a professional ecologist, and our environment is critically threatened. Why have you chosen to focus your work on the vision quest?

JPM: It's a natural thing for earth-oriented leaders to emerge through the Sacred Passage process. There are always those who are pioneers and who help to guide other individuals and the culture as a whole. Almost without exception, when people go through this experience, they afterwards evolve into leadership roles. It's become obvious that this is going to produce very powerful leaders in what we call deep ecology or sacred ecology, and this is going to have a profound effect on our culture. People emerge from Sacred Passage with a tremendous amount of inner insight, wisdom and energy, almost as if they receive an initiation directly from Mother Earth herself. And that empowers them to go on and do things that are often unbelievable in their effects. As more people and institutions begin to recognize the value of this, I foresee the quest becoming an incredibly powerful vehicle for positive and healing change in our culture.

WILDERNESS KINSHIP

Anne Stine

Anne Stine, M.A., MFT, is an experienced ecopsychologist and wilderness rites of passage guide with extensive experience in symbolic processes and wilderness therapies. She teaches Applied Wilderness Ecopsychology at Sonoma State University. Anne is founder and director of Wilderness Rites, which is dedicated to offering initiatory earth-based healing rites and practices as well as trainings for guides that assist people in reclaiming their true place within the wisdom and cycles of nature. Her programs have been offered in the wilderness areas of California, Idaho, and Oregon, and at various universities. "Wilderness Kinship" came out of the transformative impact of her first quest for vision in a remote desert valley. It is her hope that this essay will inspire others to mark their own life transitions in a meaningful way through a return to a place of belonging in the natural world.

I did not know that my life was in such need of renewal and transformation when I entered the wilderness and, for the first time, the sacred circle of my life's purpose. I had been thinking about and preparing for a vision quest for nearly ten years. I understood this ancient human journey of renewal to be a rite of passage, which facilitates transitions from one stage of human life to another and is necessary for the continuation of the species and culture. With this in mind, I drove my old GMC truck over the Sierra Mountains and down into the Great Basin. I am a native Californian and had driven across the barrenness of this unique desert land numerous times but, typically, had never bothered to stop because "nothing was out there."

I had the naive eagerness of a child and the adventurous spirit of an adolescent as I drove toward the unknown. I was also restless and empty, and my dreams were telling me that something basic and instinctual was deeply hurt and needing attention. In some fundamental way, I was alienated from my life force. I had not yet ventured into the deep spaciousness of my own psyche with its vast silences and apparently unyielding mysteries. There was so much I didn't understand about how I felt, for my basic nature had slipped away from its home in the instinctive world.

I was reading Sylvia Perera's *Descent to the Goddess* at the time and I resonated with her description of modern women as "unmothered daughters of the patriarchy." Lacking "an adequate sense of our own ground and connection to our own embodied strength and needs," there has developed a "fault in the basic levels of our personality, a deep split." The dark Goddess, Ereshkigal, embodies the rejected female powers. She was carried off into the *kur* (a word for desert, wilderness, a desolate alien place). This event coincided with the human departure from living consciously within nature, the feminine, and the body. I was compelled by the idea of wilderness holding lost, forgotten and rejected parts of personal and collective life. My own urge to return reflected a drive to heal some basic split that holds us humans captive in a deeply shared pain.

My heart pounded as I neared Big Pine, a small desert town on the edge of the Great Basin and home of the School of Lost Borders, which is managed and staffed by two people who grew right out of the desert floor, Steven Foster and Meredith Little. I called the school for final directions, partially hoping that no one would answer and I could abort my plans. I was soon to learn that this fear that shook my guts and immersed me in dizzying rushes of energy was the "quest" arising from deep within my ancestral memory. At the same time, it made me want to run.

I am impressed by an instinctual response to an ancient calling from within as I set foot in the desert for the first time. At base camp, we are offered a clean slate upon which to write our lives. Nothing marks the spot and there are no traces that anyone has ever been here before.

Our first task is to find the power place where we will fast in solitude for four days and nights. My fellow questers deliberately put their day packs on and set off in various directions. They seem to know what they are doing and I wonder what prompts them to go where they go. The old vision quest saying comes to mind: "Vision questers find their power place in the same way they find their place in life." As within, so without and it goes both ways. Similarly, one's power place mirrors one's own unique psychic world and its requirements for such things as growth, healing, regeneration, and celebration. Does it call for a view, for openness and expansion, for enclosure and protection, for trees or boulders? It is powerful because one considers it so and sanctions it through meaningful ritual, deriving from a relationship to the earth place itself.

I usually find my place in any new situation by initially exploring all options. There is no way to do that here. Vast and endless space stretches out all around me. How do I choose where to start? I panic inside. Doubts and fears paralyze me. My guide asks me where I am going to begin. I have no answer.

I wait and scan the horizon. I listen. Then, within the paralysis, a faint inner prompting slowly emerges and urges me south. It is the urging of a long buried instinct, in the body, in something that is of the earth, inside me. I have made a beginning. I have connected with something the mind cannot grasp, nor even be helpful with other than to note the experience.

Within five minutes base camp has disappeared. Another severance and I am alone in the desert with no sound except the sand moving under my feet and the soft wind blowing. Otherwise, it is still, empty. Although I don't know what is out there, something draws me on and I "know" where I am going. I walk on looking for snakes, scorpions, tarantulas, crystals and arrowheads. I can see nothing but sand, rock, creosote bushes and a vast, still sky overhead. I am watchful, apprehensive. Will I know my spot when I find it?

Then I see a circle of large boulders in an open space at the base of a rocky peak. This is it, I think. I love stone circles, what luck. My heart lightens and I am already mentally settling in when I see it is occupied by another quester. I think about how quickly I attach, as my heart sinks and I feel confused and lost again.

I instinctively retrace my steps and am drawn up the side of a canyon, along a wash bed. The smooth sandy floor of the bed is dotted with boulders and creosote bushes, creating a series of semienclosed spaces. I follow the wash up to its source where the sides of the canyon meet in a vortex of boulders. The sandy openness stops at the base of a huge boulder with a flat top. I climb on top and the valley opens out below me, endless and breathtaking. This is it, I breathe out slowly and quietly. I'll settle somewhere down in the wash with the canyon to my back and the valley stretched out below me.

The following morning, as the rising sun spills over the Last Chance Range, I begin my journey of solitude into the vast, silent, and stark land-

scape, inner and outer. I am impressed by a dream, clear and vivid, awaiting my wakefulness. In it there are rattlesnakes of all sizes and shapes.
The dream focuses my fears, heralds changes and, above all, keeps me
vigilant in my solitude. So begins my threshold phase of four days and
nights alone in this alien, yet strangely familiar place.

Expectations of grandiose visions soon give way to living my life on
the land in an intimate and simple way. Survival is basic and I find myself
learning to read the signs of my body's needs for water, shade, rest, movement, stimulation and warmth. The chatter of the daily mind, with its ten-
dencies to moralize and divide me from my natural, instinctive life in the
body, is slowly dragged off its throne. At first, the shift is imperceptible as
I fuss over my power place and avoid the existential solitude of my condition. But the wind, sun, quiet, rock, lizard, quartz, creosote bush, sand,
darkling beetle, dryness of my environment gently and relentlessly grind
down this crusty armor.

Timelessness and spaciousness slowly replace this mental activity
with images, sensations, strange words and sounds that faintly represent a subtler life lying beneath the surface. What began as "nothing out
there" continues to reveal itself as "something in here." The arid landscape yields hidden life forms, insects, a startling flower, and then a gentle
voice moving within. I have to be still, emptied out, receptive, consent-
ing, vigilant.

At first tentatively, then more deliberately, my life begins to unfold
within and around me as a story, gently laid out in image/word. The darkling beetle on its march somewhere is both a solitary survivor and a mes-
senger of pacing and of long-range tactical strategies. The wind is both a
coolant for the hot, dry air and a courier for simple poetic phrases, a subtle
voice for the one I can't yet hear from deep inside. As I walk the desert
pavement, hour after hour, my mind melting, with only the sound of the
sand and boot connecting, chants arise:

Spirit breathe, in and out
take it in, give it out
Spirit shows us in Its way
how to live our lives each day.

The rhythm of the chants connects me with myself, at my own pace —
sound, word, movement, synchronizing together without thought.

By the third morning, I am weak, nauseated, disoriented, lethargic,
the ingredients of solitude, fasting and the wilderness setting bringing me

to a threshold. There's great emptiness, longing, my heart is pounding. My system feels poisoned as it grapples with the deeper levels of toxic waste that often appear around the third day of a fast. I write down another dream about snakes—this time it's cobras—and stare at it as if it will tell me what it means. But I feel sick and stupid and nothing comes.

Like a sick animal I move slowly from the rising sun and its warmth to seek refuge in the shade. I am all body now, my mind is remote and lumbering, thoughts come and go, I move without knowing where I am going nor the outcome. It's a hot, dry, merciless day and I am deep within myself.

Suddenly one of my guides approaches me. She comes from the world I have left behind and I am startled by the sudden contact. We crouch down in the sand and, as she talks to me, I watch my world alter completely. A large earthquake has hit the San Francisco area. She gives me all the details of the damage, gently and thoroughly. While it is unlikely that my home and loved ones have been hurt, strong feelings burst forth from the dark withdrawn world I have been in. The life I have built is precious, and without the personal life and community, the sacred has no anchor, no manifestation, no meaning.

I return to my power place for the day, to sit and take in the news and feel its full impact. I think about priorities and values and watch the mind rush in to split experience into sacred and profane. I struggle with guilt and selfishness and try to find the "right" decision—should I stay in the desert or return to my suburban home? I try to force myself to choose one over the other, but I can't. What's in my heart is more than either/or. The separation I feel is my own difficulty in moving back and forth between worlds, unable to live in the interpenetration of the two. No one will tell me what to do; I have to know my own heart and follow it. I begin to feel more receptive to the great forces that guide our lives, including earthquakes and fasts.

I leave my home in the desert that evening to make a phone call to my community. As I confront the chaos, fear and demands of my life, which has been completely shaken up by this massive communication from the earth, I feel shocked. Waves from the earthquake reverberate in the stillness, sending tremors throughout my psyche, and indeed around the world. While I deal with the news, and my decision to complete the quest, I am unaware that as the earthquake is making permanent changes in the body of the earth, so is it heralding radical shifts in my own life.

I return in my truck to my power place in the middle of the night, in the middle of the desert, with nothing to mark the final turnout to my destination. Some internal homing device guides me and I rejoice at being back in the desert. This ability to find my way back home confidently in the dark reveals a gift that I will rely on as I navigate my way through the life that awaits me—to find my way into and out of the darkness in order to respond to the needs of my community and to survive radical changes.

As I walk from the truck to my desert home, my footsteps rhythmically touch the earth. I sing wildly and with abandon. I feel naked, stripped down; somehow I am relieved of my burdens. Being up close to myself has a quality of ecstasy about it. Now I am looking for crystals. I have been given some guidelines for this search. It requires a certain kind of "seeing"—one's eyes must adjust to glancing at color, texture and contour. The body sees, not the eyes. The skin, hair, lips, ears and heart see, quietly, softly, no straining, content in the process itself, nothing to find.

Suddenly, my eyes are caught by an odd shape, half buried in the sand, imperceptible except under this close scrutiny. I brush off the dirt and my heart leaps as I hold a delicate arrowhead in my hand. It is finely crafted out of pure white stone and I turn it over repeatedly, examining the tip, the edges, the place it would attach to the wooden shaft. An ancestor has fashioned this tool with much love and skill and I give thanks for the gift and for the forces that preserved it for so long.

In this vast expanse, this offering signals a joining of some part of myself with the earth. The arrowhead is old and whole, a tool for survival, and it has endured a long time under harsh and varied conditions. The discovery of this buried treasure in the earth also reflects a treasure hidden within my own nature. The arrowhead calls attention to the source within human nature, a core that remains intact and emerges unscathed no matter what our conditions. What needs to be preserved will be preserved and it has to do with the mystery of why we are all here. The vision fast has ladened me with gifts, teachings, tools, questions and many indications of my place in human mythology.

The years that followed this initial re-entry into the wilderness were difficult and challenging. By finally submitting to an encounter with the natural world, immersing my own nature in its original environment, I could plumb the depths of my own life, hear the voice of my own essential way. The gifts that came from that liminal world of wilderness, the realization of human nature existing as a part of nature, not apart from nature, the intimate reacquaintance with lost parts of myself, all had to be tested in the harsh light of daily life. I had learned from Steven Foster that for a seed to germinate it must be planted in the dark of the earth. To incorporate oneself into the community, to contribute to the continuation of the culture through renewal and regeneration, one can only take what is truly needed, what is no longer important falls away, the wheat must be threshed from the chaff.

I return regularly to the wilderness as a vision quester, as a wilderness guide for others seeking their unique story and circle of life's purpose. I notice repeatedly how this intimate encounter with the earth community reawakens people to their nature and to the reality of the survival of all life forms together. Again and again, the personal human story is the story of the earth, the body of each reflected in the other.

THE MORNING OF THE LAST DAY

Steven Foster

Steven Foster (Ph.D. Humanities) retired from college teaching (San Francisco State University) in 1971 to devote his time to the reintroduction of ancient passage rites into the mainstream of modern culture. In 1976, he married Meredith Little, and together they founded and co-directed Rites of Passage, Inc., and have guided thousands of individuals through the initiatory steps of wilderness passage rites. Since the establishment of the School of Lost Borders in 1981, they have trained hundreds of persons from many fields and nationalities. The fruits of their research, teaching, explorations of natural solitude, and apprenticeship to a variety of medicine teachers are set forth in several books: *The Book of the Vision Quest: Personal Transformation in the Wilderness* (1980, '87, '88), *The Trail Ahead: A Course Book for Graduating Seniors* (1983), *The Sacred Mountain: A Vision Fast Handbook for Adults* (1984), *The Roaring of the Sacred River: The Wilderness Quest for Vision and Self-Healing* (1988), and *Betwixt and Between: Patterns of Masculine and Feminine Initiation* (1987), edited with Louise Mahdi. "The Morning of the Last Day" is from the revised edition of *The Roaring of the Sacred River: The Wilderness Quest for Vision and Self-Healing* (Prentice-Hall, 1988; Lost Borders Press, 1996).

> *It is better to prevent misery than to release from misery:*
> *It is better to prevent error than to forgive the criminal.*
> *Labor well the Minute Particulars, attend to the little ones,*
> *And those who are in misery cannot remain so long*
> *If we do but our duty: labor well the teeming earth.*
> —WILLIAM BLAKE, "JERUSALEM"

I watched the old man coming up the ridge, an ant with a bum leg. Awake, I was disinclined to get up to greet him. I was exhausted, unable to sleep, my eyes riveted open like portholes on a deep-diving vessel, mouth wracked with unnerving desires for water, nose trying to run but unable to spare more than the briefest dew, body a mass of specific aches and pains — back, legs, ass, elbows, stomach, throat, head. I was satisfied just to sit and watch the old man do the work.

Mentally, I felt shaken and uncertain. At first light I'd checked all around the creosote bush for signs of the sidewinder. At the time it seemed reasonable to assume there existed a corporeal representative of the being I'd talked to the night before. I found nothing but the piece of dried root. It lay approximately where I'd left it. There were, however, scuffle marks in the dirt, signs of an encounter with something or other. And my thoughts were burdened with words left there by the snake, words having to do with the human world.

Without visible proof, how could I accept my experience of the night before as real? What could I tell this old man coming up the hill? The "encounter" had hardly been of the classic American Indian variety, at least of the sort I'd read about in books. The Aztecs and Mayas had rattlesnake goddesses, but I couldn't conceive of their behaving as my rattlesnake had. An anthropologist would shoot such an experience full of holes. It bore few of the classic signs of the vision quest or shamanic journey. Besides, it was the experience of a white man.

Now the old man was in plain view, black pants, blue jacket, and cowboy hat clear in the pre-dawn light. The day promised to be cloudless and hot. The storm that had passed through the day before (it seemed an eternity ago) had vacuumed every molecule of hydrocarbon from the air. From an armchair desert lover's perspective, it was a magical morning. The rising sun was dusting Sudden Peak in the Inconsolable Range with golden pollen. The fourth and final day had arrived. By my calculations, it was a Thursday morning. Easter Sunday was three days away. If I stayed up here, I'd emerge from my grave on Good Friday.

It was a hard climb for the old man. I could see why he'd been reluctant to take me on. Five days in succession he had to get up before dawn and make his way up that slope. Why should he want to do this, not only with me, but with all the others who came to him?

Panting hoarsely, John reached the circle, grinned, and looked hard into my face. "How's it goin', sonny boy?" A little sweat from under his hat ran down his gray temples. He took the hat off, wiped his forehead with a jacketed sleeve. "A little bird says you ain't doin' so bad."

"Hullo, John." It was painful to speak out loud. All night I'd talked to that sidewinder without moving my lips, which by now were cracked and hard, my tongue a block of balsa. "I'm O.K. But it's getting hard. Pretty hard." God, how I wanted to spit!

John spit for me. Then he let himself down on his cane, like he always did, and wheezed, "Nobody said it was easy." He fumbled inside his jacket for the ubiquitous pouch of tobacco and rolling papers. "It ain't easy for me, and I done it ten-twenty times. It's never easy. You just gotta keep on prayin'."

He offered me a smoke. I considered its effect on my desiccated lungs, shook my head no.

He accepted my refusal with a nod. He knew what I was going through, and was probably glad he wasn't me. "Yeah. I've been praying."

"What you been prayin' about?"

"Yesterday I prayed to Grandmother to save my ass."

His face broke into a thousand wrinkles as he laughed, and his dark eyes glazed over with a certain knowing that could only come from experience. He slapped his knee. "Now that's prayin'!" He assumed the expression of a little gnome that hides in the cupboard. "And you know what? I was prayin' too. I was scared that lightning was gonna hit your little toy car and blow my house to bits!"

I had to laugh, the effort painful and rewarding. Yeah, it had been pretty damn funny, me groveling like a worm in the dust, praying hysterically to my Grandmother. "Not my car. Just your house," I replied.

John guffawed then got serious. His dark eyes buttoned themselves to mine. "Otherwise you wouldn't be breathin'. I saw them thunder arrows hit up here. I thought mebbe they got you."

A bowl of shadows, the Inconsolable Valley was filling up with light, the glow climbing toward them on the eastern slope of the Noname Range. Soon, sun fire would touch us. I faced an important decision. I couldn't put it off any longer. This would be my last chance to go down with the old man.

"John, I think I'm ready to quit," I mumbled.

"You what?"

"I think I'm ready to go down. Three days and nights is enough."

"You sure about that?" Behind his wrinkles there was the faintest suggestion of a grin. Did he know something I didn't?

"No. I'm not sure about anything anymore. I just don't think I can make it."

He thought for a minute. "You got some time to answer me some questions, Professor?"

"What?"

"Who's your people?"

"Who's what?"

"Who's your people. You know, the people you serve. The people who come to you for healin'. The people you care about."

The old man had a good one there. I'd been wrestling with that one most of the night. In the aftermath of the visitation by the rattlesnake, my thoughts had turned toward the human world, which suddenly seemed an insurmountable mountain. Given the fact that I had no profession, no mate, no prospects, how would I make it through?

Had the hippy professor come to a thoroughly unprofessional end, playing in the dirt of a distant desert with a twisted creosote root? Could I ever go back to the culture that had spawned me? I might never again succeed there. What game would I play?

"All that time you were really looking for me," the sidewinder had said, stitching the silence with needlepoints of inaudibility. "Now that you know the inseparability of you and me, you can say good-bye to your mother. You'll be living with your Grandmother."

"And where does my Grandmother live?"

"Everywhere you go. She's in everything, including human beings. In the land, in the culture, in technology, in the mass psyche of your people."

In silence thick with the burden of cold air, I contemplated the reality of the culture and land I lived in. It was spring, 1972, and America was a dark place. I'd had but the slightest taste of its evil, intolerance, and injustice. Still, I'd been beaten and imprisoned for championing the rights of minority people. I'd been judged by hypocritical colleagues on the relative morality of my nonprofessional life. I'd been labeled a sinner and the spawn of the Devil. Even now I was being ejected from the system as a malcontent and rabble-rouser, a stench in the nostrils of "decency."

I'd be returning to a land ruled by little boys who played with apocalyptic nuclear toys. There would be violence, fraud, propaganda, greed, rape, and murder in the streets, homes, workplaces, and churches. Diseases without cures, addictions without diagnoses, conflicts without resolutions, twistedness without growth, would be floating in the very air I breathed. Real dragons would be out there somewhere, and so would the Baptists with suppressed libidos, rednecks, conservatives, liberals, corporate pigs, establishment pimps, television whores, sexist boys, angry feminists, polluters, exploiters, rapers of the earth, people without jobs, without homes, without food in their bellies, without shoes on their feet, without hope or love.

"It's a foul world I return to," I thought.

"The cynic always turns away from the stink of his own clothes," said the sidewinder. "Your body, your blood, your senses, your heart, your mind, and every expression of your corporeal will belongs to Grandmother, wears her colors, exudes her smell. If it's a foul world, you're befouled by it. You're of it."

The song I'd been singing that same evening came back to me. This time I had a new verse to add to it:

I'm fasting on the mountain
And I sure wish it would rain.
Remembering all the people
Drowning in their pain.

How could I be optimistic if so-and-so had decided to run for U.S. senator? How could I take heart if three out of five Americans believed that American soldiers should not be brought to trial for the My Lai massacre? Could I like being human and loathe being human in the same breath?

"The question is the extent to which you love your fellow humans. Are you or are you not willing to serve them?"

"I have mixed feelings about my fellow humans. You see, I simply can't figure out what to do to improve the mess. As a college teacher, I could tell myself I was contributing, in my own infinitesimal way, to the betterment of humankind. But what will I do now? I'm a hybrid and a radical and a loner and a fool and no one in their right mind would hire me. I'm not sure I'd want to work for them anyway." Something caught my eye. A flitting shadow in the moonlight—four tiny white feet, a file-tail. It hit me. The stick of gum I'd stashed away for the last night. I looked for the stone on which I had set it. The gum was gone! Damn! For a moment, I felt a pang, like a knife shoved deep into the lung.

"Persistence and trust," said my ally. "Persistence like the rock rat, trust that sooner or later you'll turn up a piece of chewing gum."

"You mean, persistence in looking," I sneered.

"Persistence in looking on the level where the gum is. If you're willing to humble yourself to the size of a rock rat, to snake-eye level, then the prize you seek will loom and glitter."

"You mean, get down in the gutter."

"Maybe. In gutters you find what has been lost, rejected, or overlooked. That's praying: groveling in the dirt like you did yesterday. No one to applaud your piety. That's finding your true place on the earth. If you can't grovel and know your Mother, you can't even begin to know your contribution to the welfare of your people."

I thought about the thunderstorm, about how I'd made it through the dark passage by chanting, "Please, help me, Grandmother!" over and over again, until the chanting had possessed my body with a rhythm, an elemental pulse that raged to live.

"You mean, praying is like looking for a way through fear?"

"Through fear of dying. You confronted what being human is all about. You faced death. Civilized humans hate doing that. All too often they dish it out, but they can't take it. They'll do just about anything to ignore or forget that they, too, will die. This fear makes them ignorant of the ways of their true Mother. Do they secretly hope they'll escape her in the end? She'll take back what she gave — her own body."

I hadn't slept in a long time. With every passing hour, thirst was nudging me closer to death. I was cold, tired, and infinitely sore. But my eyes were wide open. My mind was crystal, clarified by moonlight. "The secret of praying is yielding to the reality of death? But I don't want to die!" I protested. "I want to live. More than anything else, I want to live!"

The sidewinder had caressed me with stark words. "How do you think it will be on the last day of your life?"

The shadow line would hit us in ten minutes. I still hadn't decided if I was going back down with the old man. His question was, "Who are your people?"

"I serve Grandmother," I said.

"Yeah, but who are your people?" The old man was rolling another smoke like he had all the time in the world. He spat on the ground (wasting water!) and licked his paper, gazing at me with innocent bird eyes. "You don't come up here just for yourself. You got folks you feel responsible for."

Aside from my parents and a few others, there were none. Students — but that responsibility would soon be gone. Those who were praying for me — but that would soon be over. There were plenty of people with whose causes I sympathized, whom I admired or respected. But they were hardly "my people."

The old man took a drag and blew smoke into the cold air, the steam vanishing across the shadow line only a few yards away. The old guy had pulled a fast one. He was right. Who did I serve? How did I serve them?

"You got a point, John." My tongue was thick with thirst and feeling.

"You gonna stay?"

I wanted to cry. "Yeah."

"Good," he said softly.

His look said, "Life is just a lark."

SONG OF THE EARTH

Brooke Medicine-Eagle

Brooke Medicine-Eagle is an American native earthkeeper, teacher, ceremonial leader, sacred ecologist, songwriter, Feng Shui practitioner, and catalyst for wholeness, whose dedication is to bring forward the ancient truths concerning how to live a fully human life in sustaining harmony with All Our Relations. Her wilderness spiritual camps have brought many people to a deep appreciation of the beauty of spirit, alive in Mother Earth. She is the author of a spiritual autobiography, *Buffalo Woman Comes Singing;* and her new book on the transformational practices of earth magic and ascending into our greater humanity, *The Last Ghost Dance.*

> *Oh, Mother, send me your voice*
> *Teach me what I'm to say*
> *Show me how I'm to live*
> *To walk a medicine way.*
> *Way oh hey, hey oh way,*
> *Way nay hey hey oh!*

This song was given by Spirit, singing through our sweet Mother Earth to one of my students as she sat upon the mountain calling for a vision. Before this group of vision seekers had left for their individual places on the sacred mountain, I reminded them that their visions could come not only as something seen, but through every sense, every means of perception. I told them specifically that many of our native people in times past received a song—a song meant for their personal empowerment alone, or a song to be given to all the people for their enjoyment and growth.

So Molly listened with her heart and she heard this song. It came to her near the Scapegoat and Bob Marshall Wilderness areas in Montana, where I gather people together for "spiritual awakening" camps. It is an exquisitely beautiful place, secluded and radiant. Yet this song of the earth can sing itself to you wherever you quiet yourself on the land. And it is important that this song be heard by more and more people.

We know, through ancient as well as modern science, that vibration and sound are the basis of all things earthly and physical. If something has no vibration, it simply does not manifest upon this plane of experience. In every creation myth I have studied, there is always reference to the time before things were manifest—a time of chaotic, abundant energy held in a magical bowl or womb. Then Creator spoke a word, or more likely sang a song, and the world became manifest. This symphony of creation began to spread across the waters and land, and life on earth began.

> Oh, may I walk a beauty path
> With every step I take.
> And may I sing a beauty song
> With every word I make.

In present-day understandings of how to manifest and create what is wanted in one's life, there is always emphasis on the emotional, expressive, and vibratory phase of the practice—on where one sends the image to become manifest. Native people often make their prayers aloud, with the understanding that we must bring our inner experience and express them through sound. They remember the old stories that tell of the nine-pointed star under which the golden dream of peace, abundance, harmony, and full expression will be made real. This star seems to correspond to the Aquarian Age, and is symbolized as the throat chakra. Both Eastern and American Indians acknowledge this center as the place of manifesting and making real, following exactly the prescription given us in the creation myths. It is sound, vibration, song that is key to creating the world we all want.

And what more beautiful song to sing than the song of Mother Earth's and Father Spirit's harmony as we experience them in the pristine wilderness? What more exquisite song could we sing than one of natural harmony, balance, sweetness, of clean air, sparkling streams, bird song, deer and elk grazing, and of us at peace? We go into the wilderness to find such peace and beauty, and the songs we take away with us can help awaken others to this same possibility. We can become Mother Earth's ambassadors, inspired and thus able to inspire others.

It is clear to all of us who are paying attention that the magic, mystery and crucial understandings brought to us through the wildness are fast passing away. We must not only take ourselves into the quiet and sweetness, but also return to the paved roads of humankind, making real our inspiration for re-greening the garden, respecting all things in the circle of life, and listening to the Great Voices around us for counsel. We must sing the song of our hearts, the melody given us by Spirit, in our home, our workplace, our community—sounding aloud for all to hear the notes of harmony, cooperation, respect, and balance. The creative vibration we put out will come as well from our dance of life, our rhythm, the lightness of our step, the way we live our lives, and who we are in the world. Then we can call out to each and every thing in the circle of life, as Molly shared through song:

Oh, eagle, send me your voice …
Thunder beings, send me your voice …
Oh, pine tree, send me your voice …
Singing waters, send me your voice

Teach me what I'm to say
Show me how I'm to live
To walk a medicine way.
Way oh hey, hey oh way,
Way nay hey hey oh!! Ho!

VIKING HIKING

Christopher Manes

Christopher Manes is an attorney and author of *Green Rage: Radical Environmentalism and the Unmaking of Civilization* (Little, Brown, 1990), which was nominated for a *Los Angeles Times* book award, and *Other Creations: Rediscovering the Spirituality of Animals* (Doubleday, 1997). His articles on environmental themes have appeared in such publications as *Los Angeles Magazine, Northern Lights, Environmental Ethics,* and *English Language Notes,* as well as anthologies such as *Eco-Criticism: Essays in Literary Ecology* (University of Georgia Press, 1995), *Place of the Wild* (Island Press, 1994), *Listening to the Land* (Sierra Club Books, 1995), and *Postmodernism and Environmental Ethics* (SUNY Press, 1995). His documentary, *Earth First!— The Politics of Radical Environmentalism,* was screened at the 1ˢᵗ Annual Environmental Film Festival in Colorado Springs, Colorado, with excerpts appearing on "60 Minutes," MTV, and numerous news programs.

Magnus and his girlfriend drive me east on the Ring Road out of Reykjavik, Iceland's capital, past the town of Hveragerd, with its row upon row of hothouse banana trees looking incongruously luxuriant against a horizon of pale glaciers. It's midsummer, the time of year when Arctic terns occupy every coastal heath to nest on their tiny turquoise-colored eggs. They're winsome little black and white birds with the disposition of a Hitchcock movie, strafing and defecating on anyone foolish enough to wander onto their nesting grounds. I speak from experience. At the moment, they seem appropriate symbols of the unforgiving temperament of Iceland's interior wastelands, the destination of this trip.

We travel up the Thjorsa Valley east of Mount Hekla, whose last major eruption in 1783 killed a quarter of the country's population in one casual puff of lava and poisonous gas. Road's end is north of Thorisvatn, Iceland's second largest lake, where the boggy heaths give way to black sands and razor-sharp lava beds. This is the edge of what the Icelanders call the *eyðu*, "the empty place," no-man's-land: fifty thousand square miles of uninhabited lava fields, glacier rivers, and volcanic ash so inhospitable NASA practiced the moon-landing there in the sixties.

Wishing me well, Magnus grins and sighs, *"kanur"* — Icelandic slang for "American." Icelanders don't do much trekking and leave the eyðu to irresponsible foreigners like myself. Every year a few Germans or Americans die of exposure, drown in flash floods, or plunge through the unstable soil near volcanic sites. Magnus drives back to the Ring Road for a more conventional coastal trip of hotels and hot tubs until we meet up in Akureyri in a week or so. With luck.

The eyðu is wilderness absolute, no signs of humanity, no reason for humans to put their signs there. But I prefer to think of it more as an exercise in sacred geography. In his poetry and art, William Blake envisioned England as a physical landscape overlaid with the spiritual map of biblical Israel. The same synchronism of nature and myth can be found in the eyðu, except here the cosmology is Old Norse or Viking instead of Christian in character. Since the days of the sagas a thousand years ago, the interior wastelands represented the final refuge for the exiles and outlaws of Icelandic society, many of whom, in literature at least, were victims of a community increasingly dominated by greed, intrigue, and brute force. For the *saga* writers, the outlaw-hero could encounter in the eyðu the other world of spirits, trolls, and *"seiðerers"* — the Norse equivalent of shamans — whose knowledge could be brought back to enlighten a society in need of moral clarity. Some of these fugitives, such as Egils Skallagrimson, were said to be shape-shifters, with the ability to take on animal form. Egils' grandfather was called, appropriately enough, Kvoldulf: "Evening Wolf." Symbolically and literally, this wilderness of ice was a place of transformations.

It's late afternoon, and I cast a long, Gumbyesque shadow. But sunset presents no problem: at midsummer, at this latitude, there are twenty-three hours of sunlight to walk by.

I trudge along the gravelly terrain, the blue wall of Vatnajokull, the largest glacier in Europe, to my right. To my left lies Hofsjokull, Europe's third largest glacier, in whose hidden ice-caves Grettir the Strong, one of Iceland's greatest warriors, was said to have cohabitated with three beautiful troll-daughters for several sex-filled years. Grettir had many other, less pleasant, encounters with the spirit realm, most notably when he fought with Glam, an evil revenant terrorizing a farmstead. Grettir slew Glam, but the specter placed a curse on Grettir, forever dooming him to banishment and ill luck in his dealings with society. The story embodies the paradox of Icelandic history, which counts exiles and fugitives among the nation's foremost heroes. The narrative seems to suggest that our encounters with the wilderness beyond the city gates must inevitably estrange us from the protocols of civilization. But in recompense, they fortify our independence and awareness.

In a few hours I'm alone in the heart of the Sprengisandur, "the broken sands," the name for the easternmost desert of the eyðu. There are no obvious signs of life, not even vegetation, only a rippled black desert of what is technically called "palagonite tuff," a porous rock covered by shifting volcanic ash and glacier mud. Scoured continuously by unhindered winds, the rock surfaces take on the weird, random shapes of bears, gargoyles, dead Elvises. Why would anyone want to come here?

The eyðu has that absolute solitude common to all deserts, a silence so profound that it is as tangible as the stones and as insistent as the bad weather. Isaac Bashevis Singer writes in one of his short stories about the silences within silences where God ultimately dwells. This is just the disturbing silence human culture everywhere banishes from its domesticated life. But here in the eyðu, it remains. By the time I'm halfway to the Tungnafell glacier, I am out of range of everything human, except for an occasional contrail from some unseen commercial jet, quickly whisked away by the constant winds, as if intentionally to keep this wild place free from the tokens of modern life. I may be the only human, not to mention mammal, not to mention vertebrate, within a fifty-mile radius—with the exception, perhaps, of a stray ice climber up on Vatnajokull. There are very few places left on the globe that offer such profound solitude.

Nonetheless, I still carry civilization with me like a head cold, wondering if I left the coffeepot on back in California, or whether an *ex parte* motion I filed will be granted (I am, alas, an attorney). "Won't someone please stop me from thinking all the time?" pleads Morrissey in one of his songs. Yes, the eyðu will.

I begin to pay attention to where I am. On larger stones, colonies of green and gray lichen do the real work of ecology by breaking down inorganic material into soil. Perhaps after a million years of this lichen labor, Iceland will have coniferous rain forests again, as it once did eons ago. Yellow algae cling precariously to the shifting banks of rivulets that occasionally cut the landscape. Here and there a bunch of lyme-grass, sea-pink or fescue appears, growing out of the *loess*, the glacier mud accumulated in a crevice or depression that retains water like a flowerpot. Very rarely, I stumble over small oases of cotton grass, heather and moss, most of which cover an area no larger than a kitchen table.

I make camp near a small nameless lake just south of the Tungnafell glacier. The black waters have death wish written all over them. If there is anyplace on the map that should still contain the words, "Here be dragons," this is it.

Late that night in my tent I'm awakened by a strange, unearthly cackle. I'm southwest of a mountain called Trolladyngja, "Troll Heap," and my imagination runs wild. It takes me a while to realize the noise is coming from a raven. I go outside and see him flying low against the horizon, where a diffuse sun sits like a blob of red oil. The bird is preternaturally large and black, and his uncanny vocalizations sound like the scales of a deranged xylophone. He swoops down and lands a stone's throw from my tent.

Perhaps he's looking for water, or a storm blew him off the regular flyways, or the red color of my tent attracted his attention. I sit on a large rock, throwing him pieces of cheese, watching him gobble them up as he watches me. We are alone out here in the desert.

I call him Hugin, after one of the pair of mythic ravens sent out each day to observe the world by Odin, the chief god of the Norse. Hugin and Mugin, they were called—"Thought" and "Memory."

For all except professional warriors, ravens were bad omens, emissaries of the warlike divinity they served, a threat to order and civil society as embodied in the havoc of battle their black wings presaged. With the red reflection of the midnight sun in his eyes, Hugin could be the rook of the Apocalypse.

Hugin's ambiguous presence makes me uneasy. The same and yet not the same bird you see on a telephone wire or soccer field in Reykjavik. Like the bully who waits outside the classroom for the smart-ass kid, he has caught me as a wasteland solitaire, drained of civilization's assurances, a minimal man. We meet as equals, as one animal to another in neutral space. I can see myself through his untamed eyes, and suddenly understand the shape-shifters who have preceded me out here. I might smash him with a rock. Or just as likely, two days from now, after I turn an ankle and get lost in a gale, he might be standing on my chest, pecking out my eyes for food. We are united in these equivocal possibilities, a bird and a man aglow in never-ending daybreak, as if nothing else in the world existed.

Then, just as unexpectedly as he came, Hugin takes several hops to reach flight speed and flies away.

A week later, I greet Magnus at the Hotel Edda, leg-weary, slightly more knowledgeable about Iceland's geography, and infinitely more aware of the ravens that perch so darkly on Akureyi's brightly colored rooftops.

On Climbing the Sierra Matterhorn Again after Thirty-One Years

Gary Snyder

Growing up in Washington State, Gary Snyder worked on his parents' farm and seasonally in the woods. In 1955, he moved to Japan for a ten-year residence abroad. During that time he studied and practiced Zen Buddhism. In 1969, he returned to North America and built a house in the Sierra Nevada foothills with his family. He continues to travel widely, reading, lecturing, and working with various groups of environmentalists and indigenous peoples. He is the author of fourteen volumes of poetry and prose, including the Pulitzer Prize–winning *Turtle Island* (New Directions, 1974). "On Climbing the Sierra Matterhorn Again after Thirty-One Years" is reprinted from *No Nature* (Pantheon Books, 1992).

Range after range of mountains
Year after year after year
I am still in love.

4 X 40086, On the summit

BEYOND THE QUEST: BRINGING IT BACK

Fred Swinney/Graywolf

Fred Swinney/Graywolf, B.Sc., MA., psychotherapist, philosopher, author, shaman, and guide is helping shape consciousness science through his pioneering work in dreams and natural healing processes. Founding member of the Association for Chaos Theory in Psychology and contributing editor of the journal *Dream Network*, he lectures and teaches internationally. Graywolf leads "self-healing" journeys at Asklepia Retreat in Wilderville, Oregon, and is writing a series of books and articles about his work. "Beyond the Quest: Bringing It Back" originally appeared in *Dream Network*.

I was once told by a doctor that I would probably be dead within three years. That warning forced me to consider that my preoccupation with success, science and technology had become a threat to my life. My training as an engineer had led me to be objective and removed from all human processes except logic and intellect so that I might manipulate the world about me. This training and these pursuits occupied most of my life and had led to my considerable success as an engineer executive.

But to succeed, I had given up my natural humanness and had forged myself into a detached, objective machine, which had impacted on my ability to live. Since I was out of touch with my body, it had badly deteriorated; hypertension, a weakening heart, a developing ulcer and hypoglycemia were among the more imminent threats.

I was scared, so scared that I dropped out and got interested in health and healing. I trained as a psychotherapist, and worked out most of the emotional issues that had kept me trapped in my type A personality. I got so busy having fun, I forgot I was supposed to die. But in rare moments of deep self-honesty and appraisal, I admitted that while my health and my life were improving, they still left much to be desired. There was a discomfort tugging at me, a vague sense of unease. I felt an incompleteness with the psychologies and the healing methods I was learning. I used a wide and eclectic variety of theories in my practice and was considered a good therapist, but something was missing. I was not really addressing the full human condition in either my clients or myself.

I was also considering the deeper issue of my personal survival. Not my desire to survive—I had already affirmed that by changing my high-stress lifeless style—but the question of whether or not I believed I could survive in the chaotic world of the 1970s. I was more than half convinced of the imminent demise of civilization through economic breakdown, nuclear war or ecological disaster. But there was also, deep within me, a core of insecurity, a frightened self who was not sure of my ability to survive if left to my own wits and efforts.

To confront this fear, I decided to put myself into an alien environment, one where I would have only myself, my wits, and, I hoped, a dormant survival instinct to get me through. In late July 1976 I found myself alone in my canoe, about three days from the last sign of civilization, on my way to James Bay in the wilderness of northern Ontario. I had with me basic survival tools, but no food; I had decided to rely mainly on my wits to provide for me. Three days and that far from the nearest civilization, I was not in very good shape.

It was dark. I was camped on a peninsula on a small lake. I had never felt so utterly alone in my entire existence, and I was terrified. A simple sprained ankle and I might very well have died alone in the wilderness.

A loon pierced the night with water demon and spirit voices and the pale flickering light from my fire pushed at the edges of the haunted forest, barely keeping the dark at bay. I huddled in this precarious island of safety, so terrified that for the previous two days I had been unable to keep the half-raw fish and berries I foraged in my stomach. Cold writhing snakes slithered and pushed at the pit of my abdomen and from time to time sank their fangs into its walls, sending tremors of pain through my groin. My neck and shoulders were petrified into numb rocks. Tears forced their way past my tightly clenched eyes to tangle in my beard. Although I had been an atheist for the past twenty years, I sobbed, "Oh God, please, please help me."

"Breathe deeply and slowly," the psychotherapist in me said. I closed my eyes. "Focus on the breath and relax." Eventually I relaxed into fear, and sleep claimed me. I dreamed I was pursued through the clinging woods by predators; they were gaining on me and I could only run in slow motion. Just as I felt the damp heat of their breath, and their sharp fangs closing on the back of my calves, I woke.

I opened my eyes and focused on the smoldering red coals of my fire. Beyond, in the shadow of the forest was a deeper shadow and two yellow-green eyes that trapped mine and pierced through into my soul. Simultaneously, I stared into the eyes of a wolf and back into the eyes of the human. Fear melted into surrender and I flowed in the circle of birth into life, into death, into unknowable yet comforting chaos, into birth. The snakes in my abdomen transformed into a warm almost wet pool of deep red power and energy. It was like letting go of an orgasm and it took me to a sense of boundless self, of all one . . . the trees and forest beings, the creatures of the woods, even the humans far to the south. My abdomen filled with a swirling kaleidoscope of memories, knowledge and wisdom, an infinite storehouse to be drawn on when needed.

The eyes of the wolf brought me to this consciousness and held me there. There was a magnetic attraction; we communicated without words or sounds, open and vulnerable to each other. We seemed to exist in an endless moment beyond time and space. Eventually I noticed that the wolf shadow and eyes were gone but wolfness lingered in my mind. I was wolf! And then it was dawn and I knew I would survive.

It was the essence of wolf that empowered and carried me through that time; I lived in a timeless state, foraging, intuitively finding roots, berries and other plants to supplement the fish I caught. I returned to civilization about four weeks later by the calendar, but an eternity later in subjective time. And that was when things really began to get difficult.

Back in my rational, ordered, civilized world, the wolf experience took on scary overtones. We are often drawn into the psychotherapy professions out of a need to help ourselves, and moreover we are often drawn to specialize in the area of our own pathology. I had specialized to a large degree in schizophrenia and my mind now seemed split in two, wolf and man. *Schizophrenia* is derived from two Greek words: *schizein* (to split) and *phren* (mind). Were my problems deeper than I had originally thought? Had a latent schizophrenia surfaced in me? The wolf experience had all the signs of hallucination, and I had certainly suffered from what my rational psychotherapist self termed "thought disorders, and reality and sensory distortions." The term "lycanthropy" describes a delusion in which a person believes himself or herself to be a wolf. At the very least I could assume that diagnosis. I knew that within the native Amerindian culture experiences such as mine were common and acceptable, but that didn't diminish my fears.

"Has my insecurity yielded to an underlying and deeper insanity?" asked the pedantic psychotherapist part of me. Fearing the answer, I attempted to blot the experience from my mind. On rare occasions, with a few trusted and intimate friends, I discussed it in intellectual terms, or as an unusual experience, but I avoided as much as I could the reality of the wolf within. Whenever I relaxed, images of wolf eyes filled my mind. "Clearly a compulsion," diagnosed my inner critic. Graywolf had helped me to survive in the woods, but of what possible benefit or use could he be in my civilized, rational life? Why did he keep bothering me?

The answer came slowly as wolf consciousness began snaking into my therapy sessions, often giving me visions and insights that defied all explanations of my rational therapist's mind. I would return to the timeless moments of wellness in the wilderness and this state of consciousness would lead to strange intuitive images which, when shared with my clients, often seemed to trigger quantum therapeutic leaps. Graywolf's intrusions and timing were impeccable and eventually I was forced to admit that this wolf therapist in me far outshone the rest of my abilities.

I began to explore wolf, reading books and doing deep inner searching. I found solace, support and confirmation for the deepest and often secret levels of my being. Aspects of shadow self that I had previously thrust away in shame became valued and transformed as wolf. A natural unprogrammed self began to emerge, and self-esteem and empowerment gently began to replace insecurity and self-judgment. My quest to the wilderness was being answered, my inner shadows transformed by Graywolf.

Finally, in 1980 at a Humanistic Psychology conference, I found the courage to share my wilderness wolf experience. I took the name Graywolf before a large group of the very peers who I had once feared would judge me insane. I found both acceptance and encouragement, if not a little envy from many of them. Later, at an outdoor Paul Winter concert, the siren howls of "Wolf Eyes" resounded off the surrounding mountains and seemed to at last welcome Graywolf into the world. The vision lived on and grew.

This recognition (or was it acquiescence to an inevitable process?) accelerated the changes in my life. For the first time, I formed a deep and meaningful relationship with a woman, one that still endures (the wolf mates for life). I left my practice and, with my family, took to the road to follow the wolf's instinct. Through the years since, we have made many decisions and taken turns that to outsiders seem strange. But when guided by vision and intuition, that's often the case.

My brief encounter in the wilderness with Graywolf was a pivotal point in my life. It has been a never-ending source of empowerment and inspiration that helps me on the often rocky path. I now live a life based on inner freedom, creativity and ongoing evolution, not fear and constriction. The split has healed and wolf and man exist in harmony. I am at last at ease.

PRAYING IN DEATH VALLEY:
A Letter to My Father

Elias Amidon

Elias Amidon is a writer, wilderness guide, and teacher in the Sufi tra-
dition. With Elizabeth Roberts, he runs the Qalandar School in Boulder,
Colorado, which offers solo wilderness quests and spiritual retreats in
Colorado, Utah, New Mexico, and abroad. Elias is president of the
Institute for Deep Ecology and coeditor of the books *Earth Prayers, Life
Prayers, Prayers for a Thousand Years,* and *Honoring the Earth.*

March 5, 1994

Dear Pop,

I write this from Death Valley in one of the most remote places I've ever
been, on the fourth day of a solo fast. I feel quite weak, but peaceful. It is
so quiet here. Time is nearly still—as still as my breathing. I have very
few things with me—a sleeping bag, a tarp, some clothes. There are no
distractions.

I think of the luxuriant green of your surroundings, the wind through
a million leaves. I hope the hibiscus we planted survive after the cows got
at them. I love the image of you chasing them off with a slingshot!

Here the valley and mountains are bare—just scattered creosote bushes
on an undulating expanse of rock and sand. As my friend Meredith says,
you sit on Grandmother's bones out here.

My little camp rests between two smooth hills that rise up on either
side of me like breasts—I'm in the bosom of the earth. As I look up from
this page, I see for miles across Death Valley to the Last Chance Mountains. This area is full of portentous names ...

Why do I do this? Certainly not because it's fun (it isn't), though tomorrow, when I hike out of here, will be wonderful and joyous. The thought
of a piece of good bread, or a strawberry! No, I do this for some reason
that remains half-hidden from me, that keeps surprising me. I do it to
burn up the dross that collects in my soul. I do it to burn up my forgetfulness and sloppy ways of living. I do it to remember simple gratitude.
The ordeal of going without food or companionship or things to do is a
surprisingly hard teacher—and an honest one.

I've been praying a lot out here. "Praying!?" I hear you say. I can imagine the idea of prayer may strike your Unitarian soul as superstitious or sentimental. And it's true, superstition and sentimentality are demons in the spiritual heart—I do my best to keep vigilant. Out here in this Big Quiet I rise in the first light before dawn and climb to the top of one of these hills where I can see for miles and miles. I do the same at sunset. And there I sing my prayers for a long time as the sun slowly rises or sets. I pray for the well-being of everybody and everything that I can think of. I pray that your days will be many and filled with love, that your heart will be open and your mind free and your body strong. Simple things. I pray that all those who suffer will find peace and be comforted, that all those with vicious intent will be blessed with mercy, that all the hands about to commit violence toward another will be stayed. I pray for all my loved ones and family and friends. I pray that my life will be an offering to grace the beauty of the world.

And to whom do I pray? Who listens? No one. The God I pray to is unknown to me. I know that any conception I have of God is not God. Of course I address this unknown God with many names: *Oh Gracious One! Oh Spirit of All! Oh Earth beneath my feet! Oh Loving Sun! Oh Moon and Mountain and Water of Life! Oh sweet Spirit of the Air! Oh you billion stars! Oh All Those who have come before me! Oh Generous Heart that beats through the world in ways known and unknown! Oh Great Mystery! and many more ...*

These names of the Nameless open up the ground I stand on and the air I breathe and the light we all share, and suddenly Everything is Listening! Rock, lizard, crow, cloud—everything listens! I feel as if I partake in the Great Kindness of the universe—my prayers melt me into that.

Do you remember what Einstein asked, what he called the most fundamental question: "Is the universe benign?" I agree that the question is fundamental, but the answer is easy. To me the universe is so obviously "good"—though ruthless and indifferent at the same time. I believe that what we have emerged from, and what we will return to, is the indescribable essence of Blessing. This is not to say that I can turn away from or trivialize the world's suffering—whoever does that trivializes themselves—but even in the face of suffering, even in the midst of my own, a kind of Unfathomable Tenderness holds us, an Unbounded Grace—although these words—*Tenderness* and *Grace*—are only distant approximations of what is.

How did such an old humanist/atheist like you spawn such a wide-eyed pantheist like me? Actually, I suspect beneath the exteriors you're a wide-eyed pantheist yourself. Maybe come Judgment Day we all will be.

I came upon the remains of a wild burro down in the wash the other day. Mostly bones—she had been picked pretty clean. Her skull was grinning, as all skulls do. What's the joke I wonder? Somebody once told me that at the very moment of our death we wake up laughing. That old burro did.

Just before I started this letter I was sitting here gazing out at the Quiet and you came to my mind. I thought of your eighty-two years and that very likely, though not for sure, you will die before me, and suddenly I was filled with a great pang of missing you. I haven't written anything since I've been out here—it's too distracting—but that pang made me get out my pen and paper. The idea of a world without you in it makes me lonely, though who knows, you might be dead even as I write this, or I might be as you read this. We live mostly in an illusion of our own projection. And maybe that is the magic of prayer and its power: It calls us to dive deep into what matters most to us, to find it, acknowledge it, and bring it up into the air. That's why singing my prayers aloud in my singsong chanting way up on this hill with no one listening fills me with such love and gratefulness. An illusion of my own projection, which becomes truth. Like existence itself bursting out of emptiness, we mimic that incomprehensible act in our own little ways.

But what do you think? Is there a purpose or a meaning to all of this, or is it senseless? I wonder if the answer might be neither, or someplace between meaning and meaninglessness. It's like that beautiful painting you did years ago of a hand lifted up and open to the cosmos—all we have is the gesture. Meaning falls away, and meaninglessness falls away, in the beauty and thoroughness of each momentary gesture. And that's how I believe in prayer—it's a gesture, an offering flung up into the wind and blown away, an act of creation with no grasping for the results. *So be it!* I sing, *"So be it! Oh bless them and heal them and love them and make the way open before them in beauty! So be it!"* And then? Only the Quiet remains, taking the prayers within it like invisible seeds, and I am left not quite who I was, no different from anything else, though so very me.

My subjectivity loses its edges out here. I remember reading somewhere that Jacob Boehme said, "Whatever the self describes, describes the self." And so this projection, this gesture of prayer, describes us. It is a chance to unfold ourselves through what matters most to us—like great music and art and dance and poetry. But then, all of our gestures carry the potential of prayer within them—a handshake, a kiss, making a meal, making love, wishing each other good morning, good night, have a nice day, be well! Prayers to the heart we share, and the Silence that holds us so tenderly. And yet, for all this high-minded talk of prayer, it's really not so special—in fact, it's quite ordinary. It's simply what we give. Prayer is what we give. We give thanks, we give love, we give support, we give respect, we give solace, we give compassion. Prayer is our gift back.

Well, maybe that's not always true—there are the prayers I sing for myself and those are gifts to myself …. *"Oh Dear Heart, bless me with strength and responsiveness, free me from self-pity, teach me graciousness when I am self-centered, make of my life an offering…."* But look, there it is again, the gifting. We seek to rise above our heaviness and self-preoccupation. Why? To give and live more authentically, to love each other beyond conditions.

That's why I come out here, and why I guide others to come, because in some mysterious way it completes the circle, allowing me to touch without distraction all that I care for and value, and to offer my life to that.

Of course it's also uncomfortable, and boring, and lonely—the wind blows incessantly or it rains for days or you can't keep your mind off food—but in the end you know it is the ordeal itself that transforms you. Strange, isn't it? Tomorrow, when I'm finally back in the world of towns and traffic, I'm going to find a strawberry and eat it slowly—and may I never again forget the blessing of that taste!

Well, I hope all this talk of prayer hasn't put you off. The demon of sentimentality lives off words—so often when we try to express the Ineffable it turns into pap. That's why I love singing my prayers all alone out here—the words matter so much less than the spirit they carry. Writing them down like this is much more treacherous. Perhaps a higher way would be to learn how to pray without words. Can we do that?

In the end I think prayer simply calls from us our deepest sincerity about what we love. When it does that, it escapes superstition and sentimentality and heals our isolation.

In this spirit I pray your days will be gentle and fulfilling and your nights full of peace.

… but now the wind is up, blowing sand in my face, telling me Enough Words! So may the Silence bless you.

Love,
Elias

III

Men, Women, and Wildness

*B*eing in the out-of-doors has a way of bringing us into our instinctual selves, the part of us that responds naturally to life in an intuitive way. After a long walk in the woods, or even more so, after an extended camping trip in a wilderness environment relatively free of the day-to-day demands and craziness of our usual lives, we tend to settle into an interior space that is relaxed, open, and responsive. Our minds calm down and our capacity for insight becomes sharper. We inhabit our bodies more fully. The senses of sight, hearing, touch, and taste are heightened. We experience a stronger connection to our essential maleness and femaleness, to our sexuality, to our wildness, and to the body of wilderness. We feel ourselves to be animals amongst other animals living in response to the natural currents that move inside and outside of us.

This experience, as I have witnessed leading wilderness retreats with men and backpacking with male friends, is amplified when we spend long periods of time in the outdoors surrounded by the company of our own gender. The commonality of having been born in a male body and the awareness of the absurd and oppressive conditioning that comes with this fate forms an inherent and understood bond between us. Men understand what it is like to be men in a way that women can never really know, and vice versa. Being in the woods, without women present, men feel less inhibited about certain things. A kind of playfulness, roughness, and an honesty of being find release and expression in the company of our own gender. I have no doubt that women experience the same sense of camaraderie and freedom when alone with other women in the sanctuary of the woods.

As much as I believe we need to celebrate and relish our differences, we also need to embrace the mystery of the mixing of the sexes, and of our naturally given sexuality. The contributions in this section begin with pieces that are more gender specific and then move toward writings that reflect the beauty, joy, and magnetism of the meeting of man and woman within the context of wildness. And while wilderness brings forth and highlights the differences between the genders, it also serves to make clearer our common humanness.

However—with all of this said—I believe, that in the deepest ground of our beingness, we are joined in a way that cuts completely across the boundaries of our sexuality. The inherent wakefulness that we all share has nothing to do with our bodies or our gender; this presence is far deeper—without limits or constraints—already established in an unbreakable intimacy with the body of trees, rivers, oceans and with the unfathomable body of the cosmos. If we are fortunate, we drift freely past our conditioning and past the nearsighted view of identifying ourselves as being only our bodies, our sexuality, our thoughts and our experiences in the phenomenal world. Our longing returns us to the realization that we are the quiet, radiant, and empty presence that pervades all of life. Then, wherever we turn, we see ourselves in all things and in all circumstances. We reach the center of our aliveness and live our lives freshly from this pulse.

FINDING OUR PLACE ON EARTH AGAIN

An Interview with John Stokes

Forrest Craver

John Stokes runs the Tracking Project, a nonprofit community education group in Corrales, New Mexico. In his travels, he helps to spread awareness about Native people and the natural world. His teachings include tracking, traditional survival skills, story, music, dance, and the martial arts. In past years, he has presented tracking skills at men's conferences around the country with Robert Bly, Michael Meade, James Hillman, and Robert Moore.

Forrest Craver has worked for twenty-five years as an organizer, volunteer, and participant in peace, environmental, and human rights movements with organizations such as Amnesty International, National Organization for Women, AIDS Action Council, Native American Rights Fund, World Wildlife Fund, Defenders of Wildlife, the Wilderness Society, Center for Marine Conservation, Sierra Club, the New Warrior Network, and *Wingspan: Journal of the Male Spirit*. His life mission is to create sacred harmony between all beings through initiating, training, and empowering men to missions of service to the world. He lives with his wife, Susan, in Arlington, Virginia. The Cravers are the parents of two grown sons. "Finding Our Place on Earth Again" first appeared in *Wingspan: Journal of the Male Spirit*, Summer 1990.

FORREST CRAVER for *Wingspan:* What do men have to learn from nature?

JOHN STOKES: What men have to learn from nature is that the natural world is the backdrop to the whole human experience. When we go into nature, we encounter the world we have lived in from the beginning. We hook up with our ancestors and the bodies of all who have gone before us. With this comes humility—something that makes it possible for us to be here. Taking a place in the grand line-up of life moves us away from our egocentric behavior, away from our anthropocentric behavior. When men go out to nature, they see the balance of life and death, hot and cold; they can go beyond the duality in nature. They discern a force that holds it all together. This third force is what leads us away from duality.

We need to learn more about predator-prey relationships in order to learn the love each being has for all the others, to understand the symbiosis of nature and the place of carnivores. All the books in the world cannot add up to the Holy Book of Nature! When you read this Book, you can feel it and move with the great circle of life. When you see the gentleness/ferocity of animals, when you see a volcano, when you watch certain trees bend in the wind and others stand firm, you realize there is a range of emotion and response and that there are many, many different ways to be. We urgently need to rediscover that great diversity. Nature helps us to see that we do not have to be one certain, fixed way.

Wingspan: How does the male history of hunting, violence and warfare shape our current relationship to nature?

STOKES: We are finding that our knowledge of prehistory has been guided by historians and anthropologists in a distorted way. Hunting is not a violent activity per se. It has become so because of the types of weapons used and the loss of respect for the animals. Neither hunting nor warfare was nearly as violent as what we do today. The old ways of killing only when there was a need for food, using all of the animal, asking forgiveness of the animal's spirit and not concentrating on the biggest, strongest animals brought people more in contact with the world they lived in, for they were close to the source of their own survival. Hunting in this way was usually authorized by the animals themselves and these rules were often given to the people through dreams or through the medicine people. It is an attitude that men who enjoy hunting could come back to today.

I have worked with many different native peoples in North America, Australia and the Pacific Basin. I have heard about their traditions and how things have changed. Earlier in history, it seems, warfare was governed by checks and balances. For example, you might have a tribe divided into a red and white clan. Only the red clans could make war, the white having to remain peaceful. Among the Tohono O'odham (formerly called Papago), when two sides fought, a man who had killed another would blacken his face and move to the edge of the battle. When two such men stood aside, the fighting would stop. Among the Haudenosaunee or Iroquois, there were peace chiefs and war chiefs. We should not assume it is in the "hard wiring" of men to be violent—no more so than for men to be peaceful and understanding. Today, we rely on warfare as our first line of defense. In earlier times, among some people, clear thinking was the first line of defense. It seems to be our job to learn to use the peaceful way once again—to learn how to manage our human resources so people don't fall through the cracks. Remember, it is not only men who suffer in war— it is the children and the women who suffer also from violence. We have to learn that one death is enough. Statistics of thousands and millions killed no longer have any meaning to us.

Wingspan: Where did we lose our relationship to nature?

STOKES: The moment we said something was inanimate, or even before, when we stopped wandering as seminomadic groups. As majestic as the Greek world was, it split the animate from the inanimate world. That was a tragic loss. Native people teach that all things are alive, that everything has a spirit. From the misunderstanding that certain things don't have spirit came the further misunderstanding that certain peoples didn't have souls, that they were somehow less than human. The fine Seneca scholar John Mohawk has studied this break from nature and how it manifested in the attack on native peoples. He found around 1770 a group of German scholars who coined the term "Caucasian" and who began to intentionally over-emphasize and distort the role these "white" people had in history. Giving them a much larger and grander place in civilization, they air-brushed out any positive contribution by dark-skinned people, such as the Huns, the Turks, the Egyptians, the Native Americans. Carried on, this projection ultimately led to the Nazi madness. Once we stepped out-side the circle of life, all manner of craziness became justifiable.

Wingspan: What experiences in nature speak to men and get them back into a right relationship?

STOKES: After taking about seventy-five thousand people out into the woods, I have found that the simplest experiences have the deepest impact. Like going out and learning how to listen. As Robert Bly noted regarding the poetry of Rainer Maria Rilke, "Listening creates a pathway to the other worlds." Many cues in nature are not visual, they are auditory. All men should go out and stalk. Take off your shoes and move silently through the landscape. Move to bless and caress the earth. This is probably a good time to mention the word "love." Men must be humble and listen. Walk. Feel. When your heart opens, you hear things your ears cannot hear.

Just going out, sitting and breathing and becoming conscious of your own breath is important. The Great Peacemaker of the Iroquois confederacy brought a three-fold message for peace and one of his tenets is health. Health of body and mind. But health also means peace, because when minds are sane and bodies are healthy, men desire peace. For men in this country, we must be healthy in our bodies to think healthy thoughts. And there are always group activities for the ecosystem—picking up bottles, cleaning refuse from streams, planting trees. The male vocation is to care for this world. Men feel good when they do it. It's time for men to come out on the land and bring this land back!

Wingspan: What can men in urban centers do for the environment?

STOKES: Basically, we all need to become aware—aware of what we need as human beings to live. Whether we live in an urban center or out in the bush, the needs remain the same—shelter, water, fire (heat and cooking source) and food, at the physical level, that is. There is a movement in North America which is hooked up to a global movement and it has been called "bioregionalism." You become aware that you live in a natural system, that your water comes from a certain place and your plants and animals are in a unique balance. The soil here is different from the soil in Seattle or Denver. What one person does within the bioregion directly affects the others who live there. We discover that an environmental strategy that might be good for one area is no good for your bioregion.

What men in urban areas should do is take a deep interest in where they live. Find out the names of the native peoples who once lived there. What happened to them? How many of them are around today and where do they live? How many edible plants can you find on your way to work? What plants in your area are hardy enough to poke up through the cement? What plants are common? What is your annual rainfall? Where is your nearest reservoir? And so on. … People have been working for some time to "green the cities"—plant millions of trees, create parks and rooftop gardens, safe parks and more of them, bring animals back into the city. Some men are working to get the foxes and falcons back to the cities. Nature is all around us, and the animals have taken to living in our attics because that's the only place we've left as habitat. I was pleased to see a hawk circling over the hotel in Seattle, four jackrabbits all in a line one hot day in the shadow of a light pole in Albuquerque, a coyote on the runway at the Denver airport. I sometimes see more animals on my way from one city to the next than others might see on the Nature Channel. They're all around us, but they have become very elusive. Some are nocturnal now that used to move by day. But what I'm getting at is that nature stays close to us—it is the people who drew away. We call some of these animals vermin and try to eradicate them. Men in the cities—as crazy [as the cities] may be at times—must begin to remember that nature is there, too.

Wingspan: Where did this throwing out of nature and animal life start in this country?

STOKES: The history of European colonization of the Americas is basically a "kid in the candy store" scenario. After a while, as the idea of Manifest Destiny took hold, all kinds of policies were enacted to clear the land and pave the way for development. Native peoples and animals were brutally pushed aside. The forests were cut. Today, we have the Animal Control Division of the U.S. Department of Agriculture—since the late 1800s they have been responsible for the control of "vermin" such as wolves, mountain lions, bears and other species. In 1988 alone, the agency shot, trapped or poisoned 76,000 coyotes, 30,000 beavers, 200 mountain lions, 300 black bears, and 4.6 million birds, mostly grackles, starlings and blackbirds around airports and urban centers. They have a budget of thirty million dollars and this year they received an increase. ... They call these animals vermin. And a plant you don't like in your garden is a "weed." Our civilization has created a lot of vermin and weeds.

Wingspan: What are the best learning tools on nature?

STOKES: Well, there's no substitute for being out there. It's not in books. I want to refer men to the great manuscript of nature itself. In "The Gospel of Peace of Jesus Christ," Jesus tells the people they should "do the law," and they respond that they do the law, even as it is written in the Holy Scriptures. And he answers back:

> *Seek not the law in your scriptures, for the law is life, whereas the scripture is dead. I tell you truly, Moses received not his laws from God in*

writing, but through the living word. The law is living word of living God to living prophets for living men. In everything that is life is the law written. You find it in the grass, in the tree, in the river, in the mountain, in the birds of heaven, in the fishes of the sea; but seek it chiefly in yourselves. For I tell you truly, all living things are nearer to God than the scripture, which is without life. God so made life and all living things that they might by the everliving word teach the laws of the true God to man. God wrote not the laws in the pages of books, but in your heart and in your spirit.

Jesus sounds very much like a Native American. It is the reason why native peoples sound similar all over the world. We must learn to read the Book of Nature everywhere. I use the stars. The law of nature is written in the stars. If you go back in literature and in the Bible, you find people being informed by the stars. The Hopi people followed stars in their migrations....

Any good poetry or mythology will help, too. It's important that poets are leading the movement of men because it is beauty that leads men out into the wilds. I say again that so much of our imagery about the natural world has been shaped by a mistaken past—we must learn to see again. Poets help us to see again. Freshly.

Wingspan: In your experience, does the mother earth metaphor hold together across native cultures?

STOKES: No, not really. It seems that in these times it is an easy way for people to begin to see "relations" in nature, but most of the old understandings I've come across have been that there is not just a "mother earth" and a "father sky"—there are male and female components to the earth, male and female sites. Some use a term that means something like "parent earth." It's true the earth nurtures us and feeds us. We are children, children of the earth. Usually the names for things in nature that I have come across have reflected not only this nurturing, but a whole extended family of relationships between the people and the world they live in—uncle, aunt, grandpa, grandma....

Wingspan: What is your urgent plea to men?

STOKES: I can be real succinct. Wake up!! Men have traditionally been the guardians of the earth. The true vocation of men was to guard the earth, love it, care for it. We are only caretakers stopping over here for a while. We are supposed to pass it on in an even more beautiful state than we received it in. People should go back and read the accounts of North America in the eyes of the first European explorers. It was a paradise here. This entire continent was kept in a state of radiant beauty. It's time for men to wake up and take this historical role again. We need to define the new warriors. Men are called to be warriors for the earth. You love this earth so much you would defend it to the death and become a warrior for the earth. There is nothing more important than this world that gives us everything, our entire life. If men will awaken to that call, everything else follows. When a man walks in nature, his humanity is turned on and he becomes complete. That's why I sometimes describe aboriginal men as simultaneously tough and gentle. The natural world can bring this integration to full flower within men.

Wingspan: What personally led you out into nature and being with native peoples?

STOKES: My own suffering and grieving. My personal grief over a loss was so great it was to nature and the animals I went. They fixed me up when no man could have really helped me. The natural world brought me back to the world of the humans. For over six years, I spent most nights in front of a fire and I watched and I listened. This was my preparation for the work I'm doing now. From my long time of sitting and listening, I learned who were my allies and friends in nature. Men need to know and have allies in nature. Every man must go out and find his informants. Only with their help can he become fully who he is supposed to be.

Wingspan: How did this evolve for you?

STOKES: My family lived in Cleveland, Ohio. My father would encourage me to go out into nature and watch the birds. I would go out, watch animals, build forts, stay out until it was dark. I also remember seeing a photo of an Apache warrior when I was young. He had a knife, almost no clothing and he was walking out into the desert. I knew somehow that this man had everything he needed to survive. It left a deep impression on me of what a man could be.

Our notions about native people are so shallow and distorted. When I first went out into the bush with the aboriginal Australians, it was a humbling experience. In the desert, they asked me what I would find to eat. Where would I find water? I said I didn't know. They said for a teacher, I didn't know much about life. They were right! They let me know in a positive way that they could help me learn how to live in nature. A bushman or tracker has to know botany, astronomy, linguistics, the food chain and lots more to survive. You can get a Ph.D. in a few years, but it could take all your life to become a good bushman.

Wingspan: How can we tune in and be in nature?

STOKES: We have a lot more available to us than we think. I wonder how many people greet the sun each morning. How many give thanks for the sun that makes life on earth possible? Who thanks the water or the rain when it comes? These things are simple, but we have to go back to the beginning. Go outside and really see what is there. Our roots are in nature. Who thanks the Wind? We don't need rules to go back to nature. A friend who was trained in Guatemala tells a story of First Man, how he comes here and doesn't even know that he doesn't know. And the Sun's stipulation has been that this new creation can stick around if it can survive by listening. So he listens and things begin to speak to him and he learns why he is here. The earth is telling us how to be right now if we would only listen. …

There has been too much suffering at our hands, in the human and nonhuman worlds. We have a lot of work to do to heal this earth and the time is now for all of us to get busy. In the end, the human being is very beautiful. We have a place here. We need to find our place once again.

$\mathcal{H}$EALING THE $\mathcal{W}$OUNDED $\mathcal{F}$EMININE THROUGH THE $\mathcal{N}$ATURAL $\mathcal{W}$ORLD

Anngwyn St. Just

Anngwyn St. Just, Ph.D., has served as somatic advisor in the Drug and Alcohol Studies program, University of California (Berkeley) School of Public Health. She has traveled widely in Europe and Russia, teaching innovative ways of healing generational trauma with a special focus on issues around "Men, Women, and War." Anngwyn lives and works in the red rock canyons of Lyons, Colorado. "Healing the Wounded Feminine through the Natural World" evolved from Anngwyn's deep commitment to finding innovative methods for trauma education and recovery as well as from her own experience of the unbroken web of nature as a path to "immediacy" and the direct experience of wholeness.

Over the past several years I have been involved in exploring ways that wilderness experience can be used to heal the traumatic aftermath of over-whelming life events. During the summer of 1990 I worked in the High Sierras in a wilderness program for people suffering from post-traumatic stress. All of the women there had sustained some form of childhood or adult physical abuse, sexual abuse or torture. As these women shared the ways they found to use the natural world in their own healing, I began to see that at the core of women's identity is a distinct and vital self that is often wounded simply by the process of growing up female in cultures that have not valued women's connectedness with themselves and the earth.

Later I joined with several other women in exploring traditions that still use the natural world in healing the wounded feminine. We asked Brazilian shamana, Maria Lucia Saur Holloman, a gentle, light-hearted woman of leonine grace and great spiritual depth who embodies genera-tions of shamanic wisdom, to serve as teacher, "technician of the sacred," and guide during an experiential quest for women in nature. Together, we invited women from the healing and helping professions to join us in ex-ploring how we might find our own ways of healing and renewal.

Realizing that healing for women would require both time and an ap-propriate setting, I searched for a retreat site that would be strongly evoca-tive of the feminine. Interested women suggested a place near Salt Point Marine Preserve, on the north central coast of California. This surreal stretch of rocks and cliffs, known as "the moon," was rich in elements of the archetypally feminine with erotic hollows and ocean caverns hidden among sensuously undulant sandstone formations from the upheavals of the Eocene era. With its juxtaposition of land and water, wilderness and safety, the area was also rich in "edges" where familiar things come to an end and something else begins. Edges define limitations in order to deliver us from them. While being close to the marvelous power of the edge height-ens perception, nearness to an area of safety is also important for women who are survivors of rape and other forms of violation.

We established our particular edge at Gerstle Cove, where the vast-ness of the air and the enormous indistinct power of the ocean come to-gether along a stretch of sea-sculpted shoreline. We felt this interface — of sea and shore, unconscious and conscious, nature and civilization — would be conducive to exploring our processes of healing and transformation. We began with a walk along the edge of Shell Beach, passing first through thick groves of cypress and eucalyptus, then onto a meadow filled with tall grasses and abundant wildflowers. We saw iris, variegated lupine, orange poppies and wild mustard; bush rabbits, white-tailed deer and ground-nesting quail. Gentle breezes smelling of anise and a faint fishy rankness grew stronger as we approached the shoreline. Gulls circled high above the waves while a single file of brown pelicans skimmed the surface of the water. We spent a long, leisurely afternoon exploring the intertidal region of sea-sculpted rocks and sand bounded by the ocean and a drift of seaweed and shells that marked the high-tide line.

Curiosity had drawn Maria and the other women farther along the shoreline and, just beyond a sheltered cove, they had made a discovery. They waved and signaled us upward; we followed a steep path that emerged on the top of a rocky cliff where, within a few steps, we found ourselves at the edge of an enormous sea cavern. Looking down into the cave, we saw emerald green mosses and delicate ferns on the shady side of the interior and a freshwater spring that trickled gently down the rock face into the salt-water currents below. We were fascinated with the variegated patterns of light and shadow that played across the moist rocky surfaces, refracting down into the dark, churning waters of unknown depth.

The women felt this cave was "enormously feminine." "The Dark Feminine," someone said. "Mother Earth" and "uterine" were terms that arose as the group contemplated the site. We were mesmerized by the murmur of rhythmic splashes with echoes and roaring that reverberated at irregular intervals, as the surging tide hurled wave after wave against the cavernous walls. There was something deeply primal, and primeval, about this place.

Caves represent inner esoteric knowledge, hidden knowledge; they are places of initiation, burial, ceremonial rebirth and mystery. Caves are secret (sacred) places, their entrances hidden by labyrinths or accessible only by dangerous pathways. As such, they are often the sites of initiations or rites of passage. The cave is also the feminine principle, the womb of Mother Earth in her sheltering aspect.

Maria stretched herself out on a rock ledge facing downward, her head oriented toward the rim of the cave. Several of us did likewise. Lying on my belly, near the top of the cave, my soft mammalian body could feel the surf vibrating upward through the rock. Settling into those vibrations and the rhythmic sounds below felt strangely familiar and deeply soothing. Womblike. Connected. Grounded.

"Rocks," Maria said, "are very ancient beings. They have been on earth for so long that they have much to teach us. So, what I am doing is just lying here, slowing down and being receptive … just being with them. Rock messages don't come in thought form. They come into my body as softening up. Opening up. Not having to push myself so hard. Because they are rocks and they have been here for so long they don't have to do much. They don't have to move much. They are prints, encoded records, of what's been going on here on earth for eons. They have felt it and everything is recorded in them."

Lying at the cave opening, I was grounded more completely than I could have been standing. The women near me were lying face down, squatting quietly, or sitting on the ground with legs apart. They had not done this on other retreats when men were with us.

Later we talked about physicality and the way that women know by contact. At the beginning of life, it seems that we know mother, and later father, through contact, a kind of direct knowing. We realized, however, that there was something about the way that the women were making direct contact with the earth that was specific to an all-female setting. I continued to notice this throughout the retreat: women sitting on the ground, women sitting on rocks, women straddling rocks and ledges. At times I saw them rock forward to bring the alignment up the spine, or arch their backs to bring more of the perineum into contact with the ground. Consciously or unconsciously, we experimented with a pleasurable connection with the earth.

Women who have been sexually traumatized often seem to "lose ground." From my experience with such women, both as a bodyworker and psychotherapist, I knew that the aftermath of this kind of trauma was often the withdrawal of awareness from the lower half of the body, particularly from the pelvic area. Survivors of sexual abuse and pelvic trauma "lose their legs." Most of their awareness becomes centered above the diaphragm. The work of the dome-shaped diaphragm then is to "keep a lid" on the unwanted feelings and sensations arising from the lower body. As a result, many abuse survivors suffer a variety of symptoms that involve the organs just beneath the diaphragm. I began to realize the importance of restoring awareness to the lower half of the body in a gentle noninvasive way that would be empowering.

Being out with women in the natural world, I began to see that some kinds of healing are best done in same-sex settings. In the sea cave, I realized that women know a lot about healing other women and that it is important to explore the richness of their innate knowledge together with the resources of a natural setting.

Nature offers a mirror of wholeness in the often shattering aftermath of overwhelming life events. The ocean with its powerful rhythms of ebb and flow was part of an expansive environment that merged with the atmosphere and with the land to form a single dynamic system. A felt sense of origins emerged along the edge of the sea. The sounds of gentle rhythmic splashes and the roarings of the surging tides evoked deep memories of evolutionary and gestational continuities.

This kind of experience in the natural world may have very specific value for individual women in search of healing. More important, however, it may be a step toward developing new models for healing women. In many parts of the world the time, money, facilities, and trained staff for individual psychotherapy are lacking, white there are vast numbers of women struggling with physical, social, cultural and political survival. Any hope of interrupting ongoing cycles of generational trauma in areas of devastation must include treatment for traumatized women. Because professionally trained people are in short supply, it seems urgent that innovative ways be found to train not only mental health workers but paraprofessional workers and volunteers as well. In this respect, the natural world offers a potent resource.

It is increasingly clear that the issue of the wounded feminine is, or should be, a global concern, but we are still far from universal recognition of the crucial relationship between respect for the feminine and the fate of the earth. While the natural environment remains largely available as a resource for personal healing, we must also recognize that its continued degradation seriously compromises both personal and planetary healing.

OCTOBER, YELLOWSTONE PARK

Maxine Kumin

Maxine Kumin is the author of ten books of poems. *Up Country* won the Pulitzer Prize for poetry in 1973, and her collection, *Looking for Luck*, was nominated for the National Book Critics Circle Award in 1993. Her latest book of poems is *The Long Marriage* (Norton, 2001). She has taught at a number of colleges and universities, including Brandeis, Columbia, and Princeton. She and her husband live on a farm in New Hampshire where they raise horses. "October, Yellowstone Park" originally appeared in *Plowshares* magazine (Fall '92). It also appears in *Connecting the Dots*, (Norton, 1996).

How happy the animals seem just now,
all reading the sweetgrass text, heads down
in the great yellow-green sea of the high plains —
antelope, bison, the bull elk and his cows

moving commingled in little clumps, the bull
elk bugling from time to time his rusty screech
but not yet in rut, the females not yet in heat,
peacefully inattentive — the late fall

asters still blooming, the glacial creeks running clear.
What awaits them this winter — which calves will starve
to death or driven by hunger stray from the park
to be shot on the cattle range — they are unaware.

It is said that dumb beasts cannot anticipate
though for terror of fire or wolves some deep
historical memory clangs out of sleep
pricking them to take flight. As flight pricked the poet

dead seventeen years today, who for seventeen
years before that was a better sister
than any I, who had none, could have conjured.
Dead by her own hand, who so doggedly whined

at Daddy Death's elbow that the old Squatter
at last relented and took her in. Of sane mind
and body aged but whole I stand by the sign
that says we are halfway between the equator

and the North Pole. Sad but celebratory
I stand in full sun on the 45th parallel
bemused by what's to come, by what befell,
by how our friendship flared into history.

Fair warning, Annie, there will be no more
elegies, no more direct-address songs
conferring the tang of loss, its bitter flavor
as palpable as alum on the tongue.

THE SOUL UNEARTHED

Climbing up switchbacks all this afternoon,
sending loose shale clattering below,
grimly, gradually ascending to a view
of snowcaps and geysers, the balloon

of Old Faithful spewing, I hear your voice
beside me (you, who hated so to sweat!)
cheerfully cursing at eight thousand feet
the killers of the dream, the small-time advice-

laden editors and hangers-on. I've come
this whole hard way alone to an upthrust slate
above a brace of eagles launched in flight
only to teeter, my equilibrium

undone by memory, I want to fling
your cigarette- and whiskey-hoarse chuckle
that hangs on inside me down the back wall
over Biscuit Basin. I want the painting

below to take me in. My world that threatened
to stop the day you stopped, faltered
and then resumed, unutterably altered.
Where wildfires crisped its hide and blackened

whole vistas, new life inched in. My map
blooms with low growth, sturdier than before.
Thus I abstain. I will not sing, except
of the elk and his harem who lie down in grandeur

on the church lawn at Mammoth Hot Springs,
his hatrack wreathed in mist. This year's offspring
graze in the town's backyards, to the dismay
of tenants who burst out to broom them away.

May the car doors of tourists slam, may cameras go wild
staying the scene, may the occasional
antelope slip into the herd, shy as a child.
May people be ravished by this processional.

May reverence for what lopes off to the hills
at dusk be imprinted on their brain pans
forever, as on mine. As you are, Anne.
All of you hammered golden against the anvil.

PIPIT LAKE

Thomas Lowe Fleischner

(for Ed Grumbine)

Thomas Lowe Fleischner is a naturalist, conservation biologist, and poet whose three great teachers are the mountains of the Pacific Northwest, the desert canyons of the Southwest, and his young children, River and Kestrel. Cofounder of the North Cascades Institute, he now teaches in the Environmental Studies Program at Prescott College in the Central Highlands of Arizona. He is the author of *Singing Stone: A Natural History of the Escalante Canyons* (University of Utah Press, 1999).

Into these meadows
autumn's slanted light
has gathered all the colors of the year,
and we eat them through our pores
as we leap like deer down the slopes

At moonrise our camp sits
where firs and meadows mingle,
and sound of moving water surrounds us

This ring of mountains is complete
and in its fullness we lie silent and at peace

Being human ain't so bad!
Even the luckiest of deer cannot share green tea
with cherished friend
at moonrise
in this place of beauty

A WALK WITH THE KING

Gabriel Heilig

Gabriel Heilig is a poet, editor, and speechwriter to federal and corporate executives. He and his wife recently developed a multimedia CD for the U.S. Chamber of Commerce that will help 70,000 young people trained each year by Job Corps to be hired by businesses across the United States. A former Vietnam-era conscientious objector, he is the founder of Action Resumes, the only resume service with an office in the Pentagon. "A Walk with the King" first appeared in *Wingspan: Journal of the Male Spirit*, Spring 1990, and later in the book, *Wingspan: Inside the Men's Movement* (St. Martin's Press, 1992).

Fincastle, Virginia, October 1989. Southeastern Regional Men's Conference. Silent hour. Time to encounter the void.

I walk up an old trail by myself. In five minutes I'm gone from the group of over a hundred men. I'm looking for a treehouse I was told about: some temporary north-star to orient the rowboat of my life.

As the trail leads me on, I feel my uncomfortableness with the forest's silence, my anxiety at having no map, no agenda. Yet I'm also beginning to feel at ease with the silence and hush of the woods. It smells good. The privacy is refreshing. For a suburban kid like myself, who grew up without much in the way of city street smarts or country wisdom, trails into the woods hold a sense of foreignness and fear. I keep expecting something to happen, something I won't be able to handle.

Soon I find myself calling out. At first, the usual self-announcements. Banal stuff. My hellos to the trees. But as I do it a few more times, I begin to feel more comfortable with the sound of my own voice in the woods.

I begin shouting. I'm alone in that there are no other people, yet the woods are alive. I feel an ancient part of myself begin to reawaken. The hunter, reentering his forest kingdom. I start getting into it. I shout more.

Before long I'm bellowing. "I'M THE KING OF THIS FOREST." Wow! Where did that come from?

No one's telling me to shut up, so I shout it out again. "I'M THE KING OF THIS FOREST."

I listen to the echo of my own voice thundering unrestrained through the woods. Its tone has enough authority that I believe these words myself. I don't know where this king's been hiding, but he sounds real. My body feels fantastic as his presence rumbles through me.

I try it again—I'm into it now. No doubt about it: Kings definitely have more fun. I spot a sign: "Treehouse this way." I head off the trail, bellowing out every few yards. This king... I like him.

Snap of twigs as I leave the trail, following a sign pointing toward the treehouse. After about ten minutes of winding around, guessing at where the trail leads, I get to a clearing with two large treehouses. I climb a ladder and find mattresses and a roomy space. A few minutes there and I know I'm in the woods for something else. So I clamber down the ladder and begin walking back the way I've come.

Tonight there'll be a poetry reading and I want to memorize a poem I'd written about my own "bucket work," my effort to get down into the dark psychic swamp where the Wild Man lives, his power chained, like mine has often felt.

I get back on the trail, slowing down now that there's no treehouse to find, no goal to reach. I start giving my poem to the woods, full throttle on the volume. What the hell—I'm king here.

"Muffled bubbles from below ..."

As I begin, the tone of my voice downshifts to something I've never heard before in myself—a low growl, carrying the force of my words in a way I didn't hear even when I was writing them. I sound like a cement mixer or an old bull serenading the birds overhead. It dawns on me that I feel like a Shakespearean actor pounding out his soliloquy. And I feel old, at least twenty years older, like an actor playing Lear or some other aging king roaring his majesty across the forest stage.

I keep on giving the tone, loving it even more.

"... like angry raindrops falling upward ..."

I'm boiling with it. Probably I'm possessed by an archetype or some Jungian complex, but I could care less. I stand there for fifteen minutes or so, booming out my lines, bringing my poem off the pages of memory and back into my body.

A question forms: Why don't I talk like this all the time? Not a bad question. But I'm not in the woods for self-analysis. I'm here for self-expansion. That much I can feel. An unexpected door down into an old castle room has suddenly blown open, and there's a king down there.

Is he my king? I don't know if he's mine or not, but he feels good to me. Yet I have to ask: Where has he been all my life? Or, where have I been? Whatever the answer, he's here now.

I roar on, back down the trail toward the gathering of men, and Robert and Michael, James and John, our teachers. As I come over the rise of the last hill before joining the road, I have another moment, another opening.

I'm not a large-bodied man, yet standing on that ridge, about to descend toward the lodge, suddenly I feel like Paul Bunyan. There's a flowing extension across my shoulders and a spacious warm feeling around
my body. I feel like Ulysses home from the wine-dark seas or a hunter
back from the hunt.

I feel GOOD.

I stride into the hall where dinner's already being served. Suddenly, I
feel an animal wildness filling me. Suddenly, this gathering of men and the
work of the past few days seem tame and forced, like we're trying too
hard, trying to get underneath our trying. Yet for this brief moment, I've
gotten beneath it. I feel filled with something primal: animal, ancient and
unmistakably male.

I make my way to the food tables. I don't want any silverware. I just
want the food—and I don't want to be nice about it, either. I grab a plate,
pile some food on it and sit down. The man next to me tries not to look too
startled as I bury my face straight down into the chow.

I munch away happily, like a famished horse. Who cares what I look
like? I've been waiting forty-six years to feel like this, unthinking of what
others think of me.

All right, you Jungians and therapists. Probably I'm inflated, right?
Probably my archetypes are having a royal feast on my ego-state. But I'll
tell you what—I don't give a sweet shit. These archetypes know how to
have one helluva good time.

I spot Ed, one of my brothers from Washington, D.C. He smiles at me
with a "go for it" wink. You got it, Ed. I'm gone.

Munching onward, I even get dessert down. It's good to know how
the animals do it. Not bad, either. Lots of contact here.

Eventually, the mood evaporates. The room closes back in, and I shrink
back to my normal identity. The question is: Which one is actually mine?

My feelings feel like they're stuck in a crowded elevator No room to
move their elbows or swing out. My ego-casing is back, securely around
me again.

And then I see it. Out there on the trail I met some presence who lives
far from the suburbs where I was raised and taught to live. The work in
the lodge with the men and our teachers was preparation, coaxing the ego
to let go a bit, so I could move toward the dark voice that waits beneath
my trained politeness.

I feel the same roaring tone a few nights later, when Michael gives a
toast to our final night's feast. He raises his glass toward us; we raise ours
toward him. His Irish blessing, "Slancha," slices through the room like a

thick spear of sound. Suddenly I feel like I'm in a medieval tavern with a band of soldiers, about to ride off to war. The toast rattling across the room is utterly male, without fear of death, and binding.

This is no longer a lodge in Virginia or a men's conference. These are men. Period.

Thinking back on my walk with the king, I know that for a moment's brilliant grace I released myself, initiating myself somehow on my own male ground. Some buried part of me rose up and claimed me. The tone in my voice touched it. My words carried it out of me, bucket by bucket, feeling by feeling. And the woods held me in it, a spacious container.

Whatever did it, whoever was down there waiting for me—God bless you, you furious old soliloquizing bull-king sergeant-major. You can sign me up.

*W*ILDERNESS IN THE *B*LOOD

Lorraine Anderson

Lorraine Anderson is a freelance writer and editor with a special interest in women's experience and the natural world. She edited *Sisters of the Earth: Women's Prose and Poetry about Nature* (Vintage, 1991), and co-edited *Literature and the Environment* (Longman, 1998) and *At Home on This Earth: Two Centuries of American Women's Nature Writing* (University Press of New England, 2002). A native Californian, she was educated at the University of Utah, Naropa University, and in the West's wild places. She lives in Davis, California.

Our blood is a remnant of the great salty ocean in us. It flows with the tides, subject to the moon's pull.

My blood comes unexpectedly while I'm on my vision quest in the Sierra Nevada; I am not prepared. The September air is soft against my skin as I squat naked, soft as I watch the dark stream trickle from between my thighs, soft as my blood splatters and runs on the lichen-covered slab of granite that serves as my altar. The day is bright with the thin rays of autumn sun. But I see the rains coming soon, washing all trace of my blood into the earth; I see the snow lying on the land; I see the snowmelt and the tiny plants springing from the pungent earth, nourished by my blood. I see the circle close.

Our bodies are the earth of us. They follow the laws of everything else in nature: birth, growth, decline, death, decay. Blood courses through the rivers in our bodies, irrigating our lands.

In my sacred circle of stones, on my granite slab, quiet and inward in the mountains, I see how our culture teaches us to ignore all evidence of our connection to the wild. We are taught to catch our blood with neat white pads, bleached with deadly dioxin; we are taught to flush our blood down white enamel toilets. We are not taught how to complete the circuit, from earth to blood, blood to earth. This knowledge is kept from us, this knowledge of how securely we are woven into the web. This is the knowledge that is forbidden in our culture and so we live lives of mistaken identity.

A wild rhythm pulses in our blood. A wild river pulses in our blood.

I know a woman who gathers her blood on cloth pads, soaks them in a bucket of water, uses the enriched water to nourish her garden. What an appropriate gesture to honor the truth of our lives. Back from my vision quest, I often let expediency rule my life, instead of beauty, or appropriateness, or truth, or wilderness. But I know now, and I don't have to go to the mountains to remember, because my blood in the wilderness woke me to the wilderness in my blood.

BONDED BY SPIRIT ON BROKEN HAND

Jed Swift

Jed Swift, M.A., is an adjunct faculty member at Prescott College, The Naropa Institute, and Antioch University where he teaches ecopsychology, deep ecology, rites of passage, and transpersonal psychology in the wilderness. Jed is also a codirector of Earth Rites, Inc., a nonprofit educational organization that offers wilderness rites of passage and renewal courses for adults and teens. Over the past eleven years, he has successfully guided hundreds of people on spirited journeys into the inner/outer landscapes of Colorado, Arizona, and Utah. "Bonded by Spirit on Broken Hand" originally appeared in the 1990 Outdoor Leadership Seminar Trainings brochure.

We were in sight of the summit when it became clear that something in the weather pattern was shifting more rapidly than we had anticipated. You could feel the danger and darkness lurking on the far side of Broken Hand, the 13,800-foot peak in Colorado's Sangre de Cristo Range, which our Breaking Through group had climbed every year since 1979. Even at the halfway point we seemed to be in good shape as all twenty-six of our participants and staff, an equally mixed group of men and women, appeared strong and the weather still showed traces of sun amidst the heavy cumulus clouds to the west.

With all of his years in the wilderness, Rick Medrick (the founder and director of Outdoor Leadership Training Seminars) was the first to sense that something was wrong. He called for a rest stop on a slender ledge in order to consult with Dolores LaChapelle, another wilderness expert. As the large group snacked, gathered the odd remnants of mountain goat hair lying about, and took in the spectacular view of the pristine Crestone alpine valley below, Rick and Dolores quickly recognized that each of their nature "radar systems" was on high alert. In the next moment Rick was addressing the whole group with the news that we were to begin a cautious yet hasty retreat back to our base camp in the valley below. I personally was relieved—the light snow and swirling winds that began to surround us while we rested seemed like enough of a sign to me.

The entire group thus began to move in that special way that develops when people have bonded with each other over several days in the wilderness—hands reaching out to hands, words of comfort and support echoing through the mists and gusts, and eyes sharply focused on both the next step ahead and the progress of those nearby. Within moments of our first retreating steps, the ominous darkness from the far side of Broken Hand suddenly moved overhead and brought with it rapidly plummeting temperatures, driving blizzard-like conditions, and treacherous footing.

I had spent many years in the outdoors myself and had heard stories of the fury that nature could unleash, but had never seen the likes of this. Nor was I prepared for the human drama that unfolded as our weary tribe reached its major obstacle for a safe return—a steep and slippery ledge that would require everyone roping up. As staff, I waited in the last position on top and did my part to assist each person in using the rope to lower themselves the necessary twenty to thirty feet. This seemed to be taking hours and as the last participant grabbed the rope, I felt the sleet slide down my neck and back from the places where it had worked its way under my rain gear.

As the shivering began to spread through my body, I cursed the thought of hypothermia and the troubles it could bring, but I also realized that if I was feeling this then surely many of the less experienced members of our group must be in similar danger. I stared into what had now become an impenetrable sheet of snow and wind and wondered what to do. The Great Spirit that moves in all things answered my prayers as just then the first muffled chorus of the group below reached my ears. It seemed incongruous—a lovely symphony of human voices chanting and singing, while all around nature seemed determined to drown out all but her own raging song. Word quickly made its way to me from other staff that I could now begin my descent. I did so swiftly and safely so as to see what miracles waited around the rock outcrop below.

The sight will remain with me for the rest of my life, especially when I am feeling cynical or pessimistic about our ability as humans to work for common purpose and survival. There, fifty feet ahead of me through the veil of fog and gray, was the entire group of twenty participants huddled together in a huge embrace. They had spontaneously formed this protective energy field, pulled their weakest and coldest members inside, and begun to chant, sing and allow their strength of spirit to meet the harsh conditions head on. Chills of a different nature swept over me. I was witnessing and was part of a human community that had decided its group survival was as important as the welfare of any one member. What an inspiring model of what seems to be missing on a cultural and planetary level where our struggles are so often self-centered and isolated.

Song and laughter guided us down the remainder of the icy slopes and back into base camp in another hour or two. There were several members who were in need of immediate attention to prevent hypothermia, but, miraculously, no one suffered any lasting or damaging effects from the ordeal. In fact, in our group sharing circle around the campfire that evening, there was a unanimous feeling of having shared in one of the deepest and most powerful community experiences of a lifetime. For me, it was a further wake-up call to both the awesome power and mystery of nature and the indomitable strength, beauty, and goodness of the human spirit. Nature has always been my greatest teacher and this lesson only served to deepen my understanding of how connected, mutually interdependent, and capable of service beyond the small self we truly are.

North McKittrick Canyon

Janet Lowe

Janet Lowe is a poet and essayist living in the red rock country of Moab, Utah. Her poetry has appeared in a variety of literary journals across the country, including *Puerto del Sol*, *Earth's Daughters*, and *New Letters*, and has been collected in several anthologies, including *Passionate Hearts* and the Moab Poets and Writers' first book, *Glyphs*. Her most recent book is *Into the Mystery*, a guide to the rock art of the Moab area published by Canyonlands Natural History Association. She is at work on a collection of personal essays as well as a local history and cookbook for the Moab area.

I have never been this deep
into the wilderness before.
I have not moved through the membrane
that separates the woods from wilderness,
not parted the invisible lips that shield
the well-worn trail
from the path of the mule deer.
In the canyon, with you, I crossed over,
passed into a world with no time,
through a gravitational boundary
that left us floating
in the lungs of the canyon
like the sunfish we found suspended
in the spring pool.
Draped like snakes over the boulders,
our shirts peeled,
the limestone hard on our backs,
the desert sun on our chests,
we touched the water gently
as if our fingers could shatter the surface.
You lifted a piece of burnt-red madrone bark
from the stream, pressed it
first against one cheek, then the other,
molded it to your arm, then mine,
to my cheek, to my breast,
returned it to the water
with the faint intaglio of

your fingertips, my nipple.
This is all we left of ourselves.
We could have stayed, stained the rock
with our love, erected
a monument to our union
but that would give us too much importance
in a place where lizards are
more essential than man.
A wind wrinkled the pool;
it was the canyon, exhaling,
pushing us outward.
Three miles out,
we pierced the membrane again,
felt it seal behind us.
I have never been this deep
into the wilderness before;
I will remember its soft breath
on my back.

PROWLING THE RIDGE

Judith Minty

Judith Minty's first book, *Lake Songs and Other Fears* (University of Pittsburgh Press, 1974), received the United States Award of the International Poetry Forum. She is the author of four chapbooks and five full-length poetry collections, most recently *Walking with the Bear* (Michigan State University Press, 2000). She has taught at several colleges and universities in the United States, but considers the North Woods of Michigan her permanent home. "Prowling the Ridge" first appeared in her book *In the Presence of Mothers* (University of Pittsburgh Press, 1981).

You, husband, lying next to
me in our bed, growl
like a wild dog or wolf
as you travel the woods
of your dream.
I feel your legs running

from or after some
thing. Now you turn
and curl from the moon.
Away from me, you
prowl along ridges, hunt
with the pack. You rest
your paws on wild fur, bare
teeth to raw meat.

If I reach out and touch
the curve of your haunch,
brush my hand over your skin,
I can tame you
back to this room, to this wife
still outside
your blanket of sleep.

But it's your dream
I burn for, the other
place and time.
Wolf, leave tracks now. Ouick.
Let me follow your scent.

MADULCE CABIN:
A Fantasy

Paul Willis

Paul Willis grew up in Oregon and has spent many years rambling in the
Cascades and Sierra Nevada. He has taught writing and literature at
Westmont College in Santa Barbara, California. He is the author of a pair
of wilderness fantasies, *No Clock in the Forest* and *The Stolen River* (Avon
Books), and of a poetry chapbook, *Poison Oak* (Mille Grazie Press). Paul
wrote "Madulce Cabin" on a solo trip to one of the high wilderness ridges
behind Santa Barbara. These islands of old growth and snow and meadow,
rising out of the hot chaparral, are always a spiritual surprise. "Madulce
Cabin: A Fantasy" first appeared in *Cafe Solo* in 1992.

When you came back
I saw the mountains in your eyes.
Your arms swept out
like long full limbs of sugar pine,
glinting in the final sun. You sagged
on the step, lifting the laces
of your boots like cedar logs

from the forest floor, but still
your eyes spoke luminous heaven,
the miles and country they had seen
never to surprise again as now
received and known in secret.
You cannot tell me. I will not ask.
Your mouth tastes like melting snow.

IV

Animal Encounters

*I*n rare and private moments, our lives are graced by encounters with animals. Animals, particularly those that are not domesticated, possess an untainted wildness. They live in the world of nature and survive by their own instinct. Each creature has a unique way of adapting to wilderness—of locomotion, of eating, of communication, and of living—whether it be deer, bear, wolf, whale, loon, or skunk. In fact, there are systems of divination based on the particular habits and qualities of animals. Any time I come into unexpected contact with a large animal in the wilderness, I pay close attention, not only because of the joy of being witness to the presence of a magnificent creature, but because through the process of witnessing, some place of mystery is opened up to me.

This summer, I had the grace of seeing a bobcat and a black bear cub on two different occasions. In the brief spell of being near these mammals, I was riveted. It was hard to imagine that such beautiful, graceful, and noble beings still thrived in the wilds on the fringes of human activity, and yet here they were right before my eyes. Coming across both animals brought me immediately into an alert state.

Catching sight of the cub jumping out of an irrigation ditch, I thought that the mother must not be far behind. I had heard enough stories of the dangers of being near a mother bear and her cub. But the mother never did appear. The cub wandered ten feet past me and into the brush of a nearby river.

In the same manner, the bobcat, stocky, three feet long and two feet high (large enough to attack and kill me) appeared and disappeared. He was in clear view, walking across a piñon-covered hillside, and then he was gone.

For minutes after these two sightings, I was stunned and full of the wonder I had just witnessed. The memory of these encounters continues to remain vividly with me months later. I suspect I will frequently revisit and be nourished by these chance occurrences for years to come. Gradually, in the retelling of these events, their import will grow dimmer and dimmer. What was—and is—most real, satisfying, and electrifying was—and is—the actual encounter. The rest is only a shadow of memory.

Coming into contact with a wild animal is like this. It rips us open and brings our world into that of the animals. We feel ourselves looking back at ourselves through those wild eyes. It is as if we are the ones—covered in fur, feathers, and scales—gracefully and quietly moving through wilderness. In the peak of these unusual meetings, we recognize ourselves as kin to the very animal we are beholding. There is no separation between us and them; it is the meeting of two as one that stands out prominently in our mind's eye.

Many encounters are not so dramatic, but each has its own beauty and magic. Most of us know of the precious intimacy that is shared with pets. Tigger, a black miniature schnauzer, is clearly one of the most significant relationships in my life. We play. We go for walks. We sleep together. He is a dear friend and companion. We were both born and we will both die, and yet our lives come from and return to the same source. What is this mystery of life that he and I and all beings share? What is it that does not die? What is it that lives on beyond death?

In Wilderness

Joseph Bruchac

Joseph Bruchac is a storyteller and writer of Abenaki ancestry. Featured as a storyteller at festivals in New York, Vermont, Illinois, Missouri, Massachusetts, Nevada, and England, he was brought to Alaska in May 1987 by the Institute of Alaska Native Arts to work with native storytellers. He is the author of over sixty books, including *Iroquois Stories* (The Crossing Press), *The Faithful Hunter* (Bowman Books), and, with Michael Caduto, *Keepers of the Earth: American Stories and Environmental Activities for Children* (Fulcrum). "In Wilderness" was first published in the anthology *Near the Mountains*.

Last night the loon's cry
was thin as the edge
between mist and rain.

It wasn't full of the real world,
like the chickadee's flute note
or the throated chuck
of the anthracite grackle
in the birches where sand bank
breaks into beach
carrying small trees
down, a decades-swift
flow into current.

It might have been easy
to forget that call

if I were truly sure I heard it,
stirring past midnight in the thin tent,
cut by ghosts of dream.
It might have been only
the whine of a mosquito
slipped through netting,
the breath of one of
those sleepers with me.

Yet because there was
the chance of a loon,
it changed the night,
because it sounded twice
before I turned again to sleep,
because it was distant
as that place where river becomes lake,
because it was here—
far from lights, roads,
all the shaky foundations of certainty—
in wilderness.

Two Looks Away:
The Art of Seeing and Belonging

Fred Donaldson, Ph.D.

(for Jean, Sybil, and Jan)

Dr. Fred Donaldson has for many years studied what he calls "the old ways" as an expression of belonging to life on earth and has taught them in Yellowstone, Glacier, and North Cascades National Parks. He is a Native American craftsman and an aikidoist. Fred is also a play specialist, internationally recognized for his ongoing research and usage of play with children and animals. He is presently developing The Playmate Project, an international program designed to train adults to play (give and receive love) with the world's children. His book, *Playing by Heart*, published by Health Communications, Inc., was nominated for a Pulitzer in 1994.

The eye with which I see God is the same eye with which God sees me.
— MEISTER ECKHART

Not what the eye sees, but that which makes the eye see, that is the spirit.
— UPANISHADS

He gave him the steadiness, and he gave him the little uneasiness and the pressure that a young man can only get from an older man's eye.
— WENDELL BERRY

I've just been cleaning out the trunk of my car. I unzip an old green duffel bag. On top is a small quilled deerskin pouch. Packed underneath are a plaid shirt with frayed elbows and a torn pocket, worn Levis still embedded with wolf hair and smells, and a pair of hiking boots caked with dried mud and wolf scat. These palpable reminders draw me inward to rummage in my memories of Montana.

It is January in the northern Rocky Mountains, a time of white landscape and gray skies when the grizzly, the marmot and the willow bud are all snuggled under a deep blanket of snow, waiting for spring. It is a time when wolf howls echo from mountain peak to mountain peak, rolling down the valleys and the spines of any solitary human who might be out and about. Such is January, the time of the Wolf Moon, when cold pierces the lungs as deeply as the wolf's howl pierces the soul.

There are three of us here somewhere in the northern Rocky Mountains—Grandfather, myself and a wolf. In the play of firelight and shadows, his face, framed by two thin, gray braids, is deeply furrowed like the bark on an old cottonwood tree. He is mountain born, variable as the winter winds and, like the gnarled pine, seared gray by the wind and sun. His experience is more than his own, immutable, passed on as certainly as his silver hair and the cast of his quick, piercing eyes. His stature is reckoned by the distance he sees, which has nothing to do with horizons and eyes. Utterly synchronized to his place and time, his movements flow with the efficiency, ease and grace of a wolf's trot. When he stretches in the warmth of the morning sun, he does so as the earth creatures at the crests of their burrows. The mountains are for him charms, each animal, stream and cliff caressed first by his spirit, then his hands, and now by his memory, like silver tokens on a woman's bracelet.

Darkness rises around us, the campfire shoots its sparks aloft and it is as if his soul is revived. No words pass between us as we sit. He knows that translating one man's meaning to another is difficult and best done with as few words as possible. Our relationship has been fine-tuned during many long, quiet times together.

He sits quietly on his buffalo robe, aware of something that most would miss, lurking beyond the limits of logical sensibilities, where no image registers. Nodding toward the aspen grove, he whispers that he is afraid that like the wolf, the wisdom of belonging will disappear. His dancing eyes penetrate me as he tells me that I must keep the wisdom alive and pass it on to those who wish to share it.

I feel the wolf, but I don't see her. She waits, one look beyond my view, standing silently just inside the edge of the aspen grove, where the white radiance of the moonlight blends with the velvet black of the forest and makes a zone of almost ephemeral silver-blue where shadow and substance appear and vanish. She gazes from among the trees—solid, erect and purposeful. Her silver-gray body glides among the trees as a shadow. Her oversized paws move over the earth with the quietness of feathery snowflakes.

I've learned not to strain my eyes to see what Grandfather sees. I've been told about wolves being "two looks away": the first being eyesight, the second being insight. The old one whispers, "First, you learn to see the tree in front of you, then the rock behind the tree, then the wolf behind the rock behind the tree, then the spirit of the wolf." I'm still learning to see the tree in front of me.

Not only does Grandfather see differently, he belongs differently. He is as much a part of the northern Rockies as the wolf and the winter snows. This is not a matter of morality or ethics but of vision. His is of a different order of relationship in which earth, wolf, weather and self are of one root. I am a pupil of his memory and of those before him, and from this company of seers I discover a timeless vision of possibility.

"Grandfather, tell me about your wolf."

"When I was a young man my father and his father took me to a sacred place in our mountains. I sat alone, silently with my grandfather's wolf robe. During the night a wolf came to me and said, 'I am chief of the mountains and I respect you; therefore I am going to give you something that will preserve you and your path and take care of you in times of danger. You have a road within, the Wolf Road. If you keep your spirit on that road you will, at the end of your days, merge with the Wolf Trail in the sky.' Then she left, softly loping toward the horizon, seeming to become part of the night sky. When the sun rose in the east, I looked at the ground and lying in front of me was a gift.

"When grandfather and father came to get me we sat quietly while grandfather prepared the pipe. We smoked. I told them of my experience. Grandfather nodded his head and looked off for a moment then said, 'She gave her gift to you to be passed on so that the wolf-nature will not disappear.'"

He rises effortlessly, his sinewy old body still lithe and strong. He touches my shoulder in benediction and looks directly and ceremoniously into my eyes. With his eagle-feather fan he tidies my mind and sweeps my soul. He walks away softly, each step a prayer, into a nearby aspen grove.

He sits and sings an ancient melody, telling of a time when the world was woven together by grandfathers and grandmothers. There is something inherently sacred in the sound. His words wisp by me like aspen leaves carried with pride and gentleness on an autumn breeze—not meant to be caught and held but allowed to finish their natural journey to the earth. The stars dance and grow from pinpoints to blurs as sleep softly settles. He concentrates his mind and his spirit on the earth, a landscape he cherishes. We are together and yet he is alone, beyond my reach. I know that I will not see him again.

Awakened by an untroubled touch and the faraway warmth of the morning sun, I am aware of an immense stillness. I walk to his spot. Among the willows I find a quilled medicine pouch. I, in turn, am left with the gift of wolf-nature to pass on to those who follow me. What is this wolf-nature Grandfather received? He never said.

This story is about seeing and belonging in a way in which life's memory subsides in a person's spirit and is maintained at the simplest level through the sharing of gifts, sometimes a story, a touch or a craft but always a presence that fits like a well-tanned buckskin shirt. Grandfather never spoke to me about how he "fit." Like the wolf, snow and mountains, he belonged. His presence was his lesson. He had no doctrine to preach, only the gift of his own belonging to share. His impeccable regard radiated beyond him, so that it was impossible to say that nature ends there and human starts here.

Seeing the wolf in the night shadows was not just a matter of superior eyesight. Grandfather's sense of belonging informed his perceptions. Grandfather knew that he lived with and by a bounty not of his own making. His belonging to a particular place entailed the responsibility of sustaining the livability of that place for future generations. Through his rootedness in place he asserted his connections forward and backward in time. His lessons were both hallowed and haunted.

We are conceived belonging to the whole, completely in touch with and touched by our surroundings. To be a thread in this elegant tapestry is to be aware that one is sustained by and in turn sustains a much larger fabric woven with earnest meticulousness, whose strands are too durable and ancient, too delicate and intricate, too powerful and strong to be comprehended within the limits of one life.

Grandfather is part of all who came before and, through me, all who would come after.

WAITING AT THE SURFACE

Monica Woelfel

Monica Woelfel lived on an island in the Pacific Northwest for five years. Her short stories and articles have appeared in numerous publications including the *Writer's Forum,* the *North American Review,* and the Portland *Oregonian.* She currently lives on Orcas Island in Washington State, where she is completing the book, *Women's Stories of the Sea: A Journey in Search of the World's Fisherwomen,* interviews with fisherwomen from around the world.

Yesterday I sat on a granite cliff above Puget Sound. The direct sun warmed me, but drew no sweat. The channel stretched out from the cliff west to the dark bulk of Vancouver Island. White clouds clotted behind those black hills, but the channel was bright, etched with twisting lines where tide met tide. Kayaks made delicate marks on the shimmering plate. All was in shades of blue, all was liquid: the sky, the hills, the clouds, the sea. They drifted and mixed like watercolors running.

Then came the orcas. Satiny and black, they split the surface with audible grunts. From two hundred yards away, I heard their cavernous breaths come out in hoarse barks as the vapor spouted from their backs. The sound made my heart race. It gave tangible evidence of their great size, reverberating like an empty barrel—a huge drum. The fog from their lungs exploded out. In that one graceful arc, each sucked in fresh air and dove again.

A group of picnickers rushed to the water's edge. They jostled one another. Some laughed. One cursed. They all talked at once.

"Did you see that?"

"Could you see them?" As if only in community did their own vision exist. Had they seen it? If others had, then, yes, they had too. They had seen that sudden show of might and grace, the unexpected reward. And reward for what? For looking out to sea? For being born?

One little boy laughed with exhilaration, "I sure wouldn't want to be in one of those kayaks out there. Would you?"

The whales breached again. And the chorus went speechless in gasps. One tall fin traced a semicircle in the air. Two small ones followed. We had to imagine the rest of the huge animals — their dark eyes and propeller tails, the ice-white streaks along their flanks — but no one lacked that image. Their power and size were as evident as their flat black fins.

Once the whales passed, we were left in the wake of knowing that the channel's gleaming surface was merely the sky of another world below, a mysterious place where creatures the size of elephants flew and dove with the ease of swallows.

The tingling spreading up my backbone to the base of my skull had to do with more than that, though. I was touched by more than the sight of the orca, by more than its smooth motion through the water. The sight reached into my own knowledge of truth — into some place inside me that resonated with the ecstasy of beauty, grace, the unexpected knowledge of a monstrous depth beneath the opaque blue surface. Suddenly I felt a part of all that surrounded me, a part of the air, the clouds, the stone — just another liquid. I also understood more clearly — though I would be hard pressed to say exactly what it was I understood.

Did I see God?

"No," I respond, "just an orca." And I laugh. "Just an orca!" Of course, that is — in the metaphorical sense — everything. Yes, I saw what wise people call God. It was still an orca though — an orca and me.

When the wind ruffled the water where the whales had passed, the expanse appeared solid, a field of short blue grass tufts. I knew then that we humans are crust dwellers. All we see is all we believe in and that's why we are astonished to see something, *someone*, break the surface, and prove to us that there is more. Once the whale has sounded, we go back to believing in the surface, doubting the depth — just the way the ocean closes without a trace over the whale's body.

Sitting on that cliff above the Sound, in an act of faith, I hummed a melody and imagined that the whales' tender eardrums sensed my song.

MAKING MEDIA, NOT MAKING MEDIA

Jim Nollman

Jim Nollman is the founder and principal investigator of Interspecies, which promotes a better understanding of what can be communicated between humans and other animals. Jim is the author of *Why We Garden: Cultivating a Sense of Place, The Charged Border* (both by Henry Holt), *Spiritual Ecology* (Bantam Books), and *Dolphin Dreamtime* (Bantam Books), reissued as *The Man Who Talks to Whales* (Sentient Publications, 2002). He has also made recordings with wild animals—*Playing Music with Animals* (Smithsonian) and *Orca's Greatest Hits* (Interspecies). He lives on San Juan Island, Washington, with his wife, Katy, and daughters, Claire and Sasha, and continues to research musical communication around the world.

"Making Media, Not Making Media" is excerpted and edited from a longer version found in the *Interspecies Newsletter,* Winter 1991, printed quarterly by Interspecies Communication, Inc., a Washington State nonprofit organization.

In August 1989 the ABC Thursday night show, "Primetime Live," flew a crew up the coastline of British Columbia to film Interspecies Communication's annual Orca Project. The three crew members spent an entire week on-site with the six of us from IC, shooting many hours of film that captured the ambience of a wilderness camp of musicians busy developing a communication relationship with free-swimming orca whales.

We at IC have always asserted that the life and culture of our instant community is every bit as innovative as the vital rush of music that transpires when the whales drop by late at night to sing with us. The ABC crew seemed to acclimatize very quickly to the process of living in this wilderness community with the orcas as its guiding presence. Consequently, we were elated to notice that by their second day on-site, the crew had started focusing their cameras on the community itself, in an attempt to depict our "sense of place" on film.

The director, Rudy Bednat, also conducted lengthy interviews with each one of us. These sessions, sometimes focusing on individuals, sometimes on the entire group, were held around a campfire or on the bridge of our boat. Intriguingly, no matter what the initiated subject started out as, it always seemed to settle into a deeper discussion about our community serving, in some small way, as a prototype to help guide the entire culture away from its current exploitive relationship to nature. We all talked about developing an aesthetic and Gaian perception of nature.

It seemed almost too easy for us to find examples to elucidate this path. All we needed to do was point directly across the strait at the last virgin watershed on Vancouver Island, which was then in the process of being clear-cut. All we needed to do was point to the waterway itself, which used to be full of orcas at this time of year. But they were not there. Excessive net-fishing combined with a ballooning whale-watching industry had caused the whales to flee.

Rudy also asked us to describe how we had learned to distinguish between, first, orcas and humans merely making sounds simultaneously, and second, orcas and humans creating a musical dialogue in response to one another. In the grandest of terms, the difference between the two is the difference between delusion and communion. Rudy rephrased that same question ten different ways on five different days. Inevitably, by the fifth day, we had not only learned to give good concise answers, but we had also discovered the path each of us had taken to get to the very same place. In my own case, I described simultaneity in terms of the disconnected although concurrent conversations at a lively cocktail party. A dialogue, on the other hand, reveals the same sense of communion inherent in any good music making. As it refers to the objectives of our ongoing Orca Project, that warm glow of communion transforms anyone's connection to nature into something new and positive. Something downright revolutionary.

Every year the whales seem to disappear for longer and longer periods. Unfortunately, this year was the worst yet. The whales vanished for an entire week, starting just before the commencement of the filming process. It was the longest departure during the month of August that I have personally witnessed in twelve years working that coastline.

Thankfully, the orcas reappeared again on the last day of shooting. The crew kayaked down the coast and then spent the next hour paddling and filming the whales as they slowly swam toward our moored boat.

When the orcas finally reached the headland that defines the entrance to our cove, they were being closely followed by three large whale-watching boats. Did the boats have anything to do with the fact that the pod was so uncharacteristically silent? And whereas the orcas typically choose to make a sharp right-hand turn into our cove—presumably to visit our own anchored boat with its dangling array of underwater speakers and hydrophones—this time they decided to keep in the channel traveling due west.

Then came a dramatic change for the better. Just as the pod seemed on the verge of exiting the area altogether, the musicians on board our boat altered their tune from a dronal piece in a minor key to a very upbeat rhythm reminiscent of an old James Brown dance riff. Almost immediately, one of the whales turned 180 degrees and started heading right for us. It was A6, a large bull saddled with that improbable name by the local biologists. We know A6 well. Both he and his recently deceased mother, Nicola, had always been the most frequent cetacean visitors to our music-making camp. Not only does A6 possess the most wildly animated signature whistle of all the whales on this coast, but he also displays the most consistent interest in human music. These two traits cause me to reach the blatantly anthropomorphic conclusion that of all the whales in this strait, A6 is the master musician of his species. In fact, I have probable recordings of him interacting with my own music from as far back as 1978.

When A6 turned, we were jubilant. Only rarely has music ever diverted the whales once they are already committed to passing us by. Significantly, both A6's change in direction as well as the music that prompted that change had been caught on audio and videotape. This reversal was followed by two good minutes of interaction between the big bull orca and my own solo guitar. A6 swam within one hundred yards of our boat and then hung there for five minutes before turning back to rejoin his pod. He gave one last call, and then turned silent again.

Given the fact that orcas can vocalize underwater at the volume of a jet airplane at takeoff, one hundred yards felt quite adequate and even exciting by our own standards. However, in terms of the filmmaker's own visual needs, the distance proved a disaster. Whale and boat were simply too far apart, meaning that the predetermined "payoff" shot of the orcas swimming inside the same camera frame as our boat was never actually captured on film. And A6's reversal of direction that had seemed so stirring to all of us who have worked with the whales over the years looked like nothing at all when filtered through the camera lens.

A year and a half has passed since A6 surprised me by switching direction and "Primetime Live" still has not aired that segment. Several reasons were offered to us in explanation. Despite pre-production sessions spent deflating expectation levels that neither IC nor the whales would ever be able to meet, the folks back in New York City may have still ended up expecting a standard nature film full of breaching whales and scientists peering through binoculars. What they got instead was a boatload of non-expert, consciousness radicals: a pod of happy campers.

Incidents such as this have recurred enough times over the years to force us to come to grips with the entire genre of the TV nature film. Why doesn't it work for us? Or let's generalize the issue. Does it work for anyone?

In its stereotypical form, the nature film might be best symbolized by the redundant image of a field biologist lying close to the ground (or water) with binoculars hung around his or her neck. He or she is pointing, always pointing off into the distance at some animal species, while whispering, always whispering into the microphone so as not to scare the beast away.

Simultaneously, a sober narrator ostensibly transmits a sense of authority by reading from a script that describes the sobering facts concerning the particular human/nature cusp being depicted.

Perhaps no person has mined the nuances of the format more deeply and more successfully than Jacques Cousteau. But even Cousteau, whose underwater footage is so utterly breathtaking, places far too much show time on featuring some new and exotic technology. We are shown shot after shot of his manly crew unloading, constructing, maintaining, and finally using that new gadget in the romantic cause of "expanding the frontiers of our knowledge." It is a vision of nature as adventure, conceived and perpetrated by engineers.

Three key words finally emerge to describe the standard nature film: observation, expertise, and objectivity. In other words, the genre is based upon the exact same premises as field biology. Those terms also point to several good reasons why IC has never made a satisfying nature film. We tend to focus, instead, on cocreation and communion. The relationship we embrace is highly experiential and rejects the separation between observer and observed favored by both field biology and its filmic form of expression.

Also, IC may be unique in all the world as an organization that consistently sponsors artists instead of scientists to research animals and nature. This stated emphasis clearly signifies that the intent of our research is primarily aesthetic and therefore quite subjective. No wonder we have so much trouble when somebody else — especially an experienced film crew — tries to make an objective statement about our subjective work. Apples and oranges.

We at IC have taken that last statement to heart. We have concluded that the planet is a mess and that the old-style nature film has obviously failed to elicit the kinds of changes we need so badly. Perhaps the time is ripe to reinvent the nature film around the premise of Gaia.

IC walks that Gaian path. We do not encourage stereotypically masculine solutions based upon gadgetry and/or control. Nor do we promote visual images that express separation from our wild animal peers. We do not peek through binoculars very often, and certainly have little interest in depicting ourselves that way on film. In grand symbolic terms, we wonder if that old cliché simply magnifies the separation, while also accentuating mastery through technology. Likewise, we believe that whispering is a powerful metaphor for invisibility. But it's all a lie. Look around you. Humans are not invisible anywhere else but in nature films.

SWIMMING WITH LOONS

Howard Nelson

Howard Nelson has lived for thirty years in the Finger Lakes region of New York. He teaches at Cayuga Community College in Auburn, New York, and spends as much time as possible around lakes and creeks. He is the author of *Gorilla Blessing* (Falling Tree Press) and *Bone Music* (Nightshade Press), and the editor of *Earth, My Likeness: Nature Poems of Walt Whitman* (Wood Thrush Books, 2001).

I stroked out quietly,
not long past dawn,
naked in the chilly water,
the mist hovered
in the gray light,
a lake of silence,
and I eased close
to the two loons,
the tapered black swimmers,
low in the water.

And they didn't swim away
or dip under,
but drifted closer
until I could see
the white shimmer
of their breasts,

their black webs
paddling underneath,
and the waterdrops
on their beaks.

We were so close
I could have reached
my hand out
and touched them,
touched the perfect swimmers,
but instead I just floated
in the cold water
in the black grace
of being with them
in the dawn.

BLOODTIES

Ted Kerasote

Ted Kerasote has written about nature for a variety of publications,
including *Audubon, Outside,* and *Sports Afield,* where his "EcoWatch" column
has followed the many issues of wildlife and wilderness preservation. He is
also the author of *Navigations* (Stackpole, 1986), *Bloodties — Nature, Culture
and the Hunt* (Kodansha International, 1994), and *Heart of Home — Essays of
People and Wildlife* (Random House, 1997). He lives in northwestern
Wyoming. "Bloodties" is a condensed version of several chapters from his
book *Bloodties.*

My back fence happens to be the southeast border of Grand Teton National
Park. The boundary curves around our settlement of houses and corrals,
surrounds the village, and continues to the big bend of the Gros Ventre River,
where it meets the Teton Forest. We are an inholding — inheld within the
park, which is bounded by national forests, stretching north to Yellowstone
and beyond. Out my windows, I can see its southern boundary.

Marked by long, cold winters, high mountains and big mammals, it's a
natural order in which agriculture has been a recent arrival. Those who
lived here before me gathered roots and berries, and, of necessity, depended

on the flesh and blood and the hide and fur of animals to survive. Looking for a way to reduce my reliance on agriculture based on fossil fuels, and the inevitable costs that agribusiness incurs—wildlife lost from wellhead to oil spills, from combine to pesticides—I have tried to respect the knowledge of these hunter-gatherers.

In my freezer there's the meat of an elk, the being whom I consider the distillate of the country. As I defrost one of her steaks this February morning, the thermometer reading minus twenty two, a crystalline stratigraphy appears throughout her meat. It's as fine, and lovely, as the ice flowers on the kitchen windows. When thawed she smells faintly of what she ate last summer: grass and sedge, wildflowers, stream water. She smells of this place which, when I eat her, becomes an inholding within me. I guess to another I must smell of her, and of this place as well. We have joined and it's the hunting that creates the conjunction.

Putting a piece of the broiled steak into my mouth, I remember drifting among the pines, the just dawning air heavy with the scent of wapiti. Hearing the crunch of a footstep ahead of me, I wait to hear it again before taking a step of my own. Then I wait a few more minutes. Another crunch … I move a foot. Forty yards off stands an elk: its ruddy hindquarters and left flank facing me. When it raises its head, I see that it's a spike bull—a young male and illegal to shoot.

I stand while he paws the snow and grazes. A red squirrel scampers in a tree to my right but, inexplicably, this habitual watchman of the woods ignores me. Then I see another elk, perhaps filly yards off and to my right, appearing and reappearing along the forest edge as it grazes. It wears no antlers.

Waiting, I listen to the nearer elk chew. When he takes a step, crunching the snow, I take a step toward the cow. But slowly, ever so slowly, she recedes from me. I go to a knee, and try to sight on her. Fallen trees block my view. I stand again, move slightly left, which is even worse for a clear shot. I have to wait a long time before one of his footfalls lets me move back to the right. The cow is now screened by many thick branches.

Several minutes go by, the forest lightens, and I hear more elk in the distance … in the thicker trees descending steeply to the headwaters of the creek. But I see no way of getting closer to them. The spike bull is twenty-five yards off, and in another two steps I'll be within his circle of awareness. Moving only my eyes, I watch the cow elk reemerge from the trees. She is large and without calf.

Slowly, she angles away, down the steep north slope. In the many miles walked this fall, among all the elk seen, she has become the possible elk—the elk approached with care, the elk close to home, the elk seen far enough into the season so that soon the season will be over . . . the elk whom the morning, the snow, and the elk themselves have allowed me to approach. Only the asking remains.

"Mother elk," I say. "Please stop." I speak the words in my mind, sending them through the trees and into her sleek brown head. She crosses an opening in the forest, and there, for no reason I can understand, she pauses, her shoulder and flank visible.

It is a clear shot, though not a perfect one—I have to stand at full height to make it. But I know I can make it and I say, "Thank-you. I am sorry." Still I hesitate, for though I can lose myself in the hunting, I have never been able to stop thinking about its results—that I forget it's *this* elk rather than *that* elk who is about to die; that it's *this* creature whom I'm about to take from the world rather than some number in an equation proving the merits of wild food harvesting over being a supermarket vegetarian; that this being before me—who sees, who smells, who *knows*—will no longer be among us, so that I may go on living. And I don't know how to escape this incongruous pain out of which we grow, this unresolvable unfairness, other than saying that I would rather be caught in this lovely tragedy with those whom I love, whom the ground beneath my feet has created alongside me, than with those far away, whose deaths I cannot own. Not that I think all this. I know it in my hesitation.

Still she stands, strangely immobile. I raise the rifle, and still she stands, and still I wait, for there have been times that I have come to this final moment, and through the air the animal's spirit has flown into my heart, sending me its pride and defiance, or its beseeching, frightened voice, saying, "I am not for you." And I have watched them walk away. She sweeps her eye across the forest and begins to graze down the north slope, exposing her flank for one more instant, and allowing me to decide. I listen, hearing the air thrum with the ambivalence of our joining, about which I can only say, once again, "I am sorry." As she disappears from sight, I fire behind her left shoulder, the sound of the shot muffled by the forest.

She arches her back, and elk stream from the trees, run across a meadow, and disappear into the distant pines. I run to where she, too, fled and find her kneeling in the snow, her head turned over her left shoulder. She looks directly at me with her great brown eyes, utterly calm, and my heart tears apart.

I fire at her neck and she falls to her side. As she kicks her final shudders, I go to her and sit with my hip against her spine, my hand on her flank, feeling her warmth, her pulse, her life, changing states. She is enormous, and beautiful. Her right cheek lies on the snow; her nose is moist; her eye stares into the heaven. There isn't a speck of blood anywhere. My throat constricts with this loveliness going from the world.

After a few minutes I take off my pack, unload the rifle, and lean it against an aspen. With my knife, I slit the hide on her belly. Using my fingers under the knife as a shield, so as not to cut her viscera, I open her peritoneum and go inside her, up to my elbows. As I puncture her diaphragm, steam emerges around my shoulders with a gasp. Cutting away her heart, I feel hot blood bathe my arms, which is what the old hunter-gatherers knew when, in a cold, cold world, they found improbable warmth ... life ... in the bodies and blood of mammals.

THE NIGHT OF THE LIVING SKUNK

Doug Elliott

Doug Elliott is a naturalist, herbalist, storyteller, and musician. For more than two decades, he has traveled from the Canadian North to Central American jungles studying plant and animal life, and the wisdom of traditional peoples. He is the author of four books, including *Wildwoods Wisdom: Mythic Encounters with the Natural World* and *Wild Roots: A Forager's Guide to Edible and Medicinal Roots, Tubers, Corms and Rhizomes*. He also has a number of award-winning recordings and has published natural history articles in numerous magazines. He gives storytellings and lectures and leads workshops/hikes in natural settings. "The Night of the Living Skunk" is reproduced from Doug Elliott's book, *Wildwoods Wisdom* (Paragon House, Possum Productions, 1992).

One year, when I was teaching a course on edible and medicinal wild plants at a "holistic studies" center, a concurrent workshop on shamanism created a great deal of excitement around campus. The instructor had spent many years in the South American jungles and other remote parts of the world, studying the spiritual practices and psychic healing techniques of tribal cultures, and he was trying to teach these skills to modern Americans.

One of the initial steps in shamanic practice is acquiring an animal ally as a spirit guide. This animal becomes a source of power and strength that can be called upon in times of need, in everyday life as well as when one has embarked on a shamanic journey into other realms of reality.

During the first part of the week, the class members were involved in attempting to contact their individual spirit animals through meditation and guided imagery. Once the animal presented itself, each rookie shaman was to try to merge with the animal and become one with its spirit. This meant not only trying to learn the lessons that their creature had come to teach, but also becoming one with the physical body of their ally and learning its movements. The mellow meditative atmosphere of the campus was transformed that week as people got more and more in touch with their animal allies. There were soaring eagles, lumbering bears, prowling cats, howling wolves, dancing cranes, breaching whales, trumpeting elephants, and even a few seals flopping about on the ground. Some days the students would show up at the dining hall with painted faces and feathers in their hair. Other times, they could be seen stalking the woods singly or in packs. At night, ceremonial bonfires blazed with eerie chanting and feverish dancing, accompanied by the ever-present pulsing of the spirit drums.

Toward the end of the week one of the class members (whom I'll call Michael) took me aside. He seemed very preoccupied, and he had a wild look in his eyes. He said, "Doug, I know you have a strong feeling about animals and maybe you could give me some advice. I think I've gotten in touch with my spirit animal. I think it's a skunk. It came to me last night, I mean, I really saw one! Tell me what you think I should do. They talked in class about Native American shamans on a spiritual quest actually hunting down and taking the life of an animal to capture its spirit power. Do you think I should kill that skunk? Maybe I should make a medicine bag from its hide."

I agreed that a fresh skunk hide would certainly be powerful and probably would make some mighty strong medicine (phew!), but I suggested that perhaps he could be more creative than simply killing it. I told him it would seem much more in keeping with his quest to spend time with the animal, study its nature, and come to know its habits and ways. A live animal could probably teach him much more than a dead one. This advice seemed to resonate with him. He thanked me. That faraway, wild look returned to his eyes and he took off back into the woods.

I did not see Michael again for a couple of years. When our paths did cross, he seemed slightly less wild-eyed. He had the same excitement about life, but he seemed more centered and settled. When I referred to our last conversation about his skunk encounter, he said, "I never did tell you the whole story of what happened that night, did I?" And this is what he told me:

I was learning a lot in that shamanism class, but I was learning it in my head and not in my spirit. Whenever we'd do those meditations and try to call for our spirit animal, everybody else would get one, but nothing would come for me. I knew I had one out there somewhere, but I just couldn't make contact. I was starting to lose sleep over it and I couldn't figure out what to do. Well, one night (I guess it was the night before I talked to you) I was tossing and turning, so I got up for a walk. It was warm and cloudy, but the moon was nearly full so I could see pretty well. There was a mystical quality to the soft night air—like it was bearing secrets. I realized that this was the ideal time for me to ask again for my animal spirit ally to reveal itself. So I went to a secluded area down by the lake. I wanted to bare myself, body and soul, so I took off all my clothes and sat down with a straight spine and my legs crossed in a lotus position. I tried to quiet my mind and let my heart and spirit speak. "Hey God! ... Michael here. . . Yep, back again. Still tryin' to get in touch with my animal spirit guide. I think I'm ready, God. My heart's open, and I'll just be hanging out right here."

So there I sat, that moist night air caressing my skin, trying to keep my heart open and my mind quiet. Then I heard a noise in the bushes, a rustling in the leaves. It was some animal in there, and it was coming my way! My heart started pounding. "Uh, oh! Is this it, God? My spirit ally?" And sure enough, a little animal pokes its nose out of the bushes and looks around. It was a skunk. "Aw, come on, God. What is this, a joke? My spirit ally isn't really a skunk! ... IS IT?" Seemingly in answer to my question that skunk headed right toward me! I wanted to get out of there quick, but I had chosen a warrior's path and that was no way for a warrior to greet a potential spirit ally, even if it was a skunk. I took a deep breath and waited. That skunk walked right in front of me and paused. It dug in the grass, looked right at me, and then started waddling off. If that wasn't a sign, I don't know what was. I knew I had to follow, so I started off on my hands and knees, crawling behind that skunk, doing the best skunk walk I could. The skunk and I were making our way across the lawn, around some clumps of bushes and into some tall grass, when I heard a weird guttural moan. What was that? My heart was pounding. I could barely make it out, but there in the dusky moonlight up ahead of us was a large, light-colored, amorphous mass between two clumps of bushes. That thing was hissing ominously and undulating. The skunk was leading me right to it! I was disoriented and I was terrified, but I had chosen a warrior's path. I had to follow that skunk and face my destiny.

Closer and closer to that ghastly thing we crawled and it took my breath away when I got close enough to see it clearly. It was a man and a woman intertwined. They were on their own journey of spiritual union. Was I embarrassed! But that skunk was headed right for them. I had to warn them. So in a loud whisper I said, "Hey, you two! There's a skunk coming! . . . Hey! There's a skunk! It's heading right for you!"

Michael shook his head, "They didn't even hear me," he said. "They didn't miss a beat. That skunk walked right around 'em and off into the thicket. I carefully backed off and tiptoed away. That was enough destiny for one night!" Michael said that when he got home, he called one of his close friends and told him about the workshop. He said he had made contact with an animal spirit ally but it was pretty confusing. When his friend asked him what animal it was, Michael said, "Now don't laugh. It's a skunk."

His friend paused for a moment and said, "You know, Mike, that's a perfect animal for you, because you really are like a skunk. You are generally an easygoing, friendly guy, but you will let people get only so close. If anyone gets too close, you piss on 'em!" Michael thought about the events of his life, about his recent divorce, and about his other relationships. He realized that he really did have much to work out regarding issues of intimacy. When he had accepted that skunk as an ally, it took him on a journey to confront (quite literally) that which he feared most—the deep intimacy between a man and a woman.

Michael did a lot of personal work after that. He went for counseling and on vision quests. He worked hard with his ex-wife on healing some of the wounds left by their divorce. They might not be completely reconciled, but they do have a good understanding of each other and completely share the parenting of their child. He volunteers at his child's school and is probably more a part of his child's life than many married fathers.

Michael says he is learning to give of himself more deeply and is more willing to accept intimacy and closeness in his relationships. "But people who are close to me know," says Michael, "that sometimes my tail still goes up. And when it does, they'd better look out!"

INTERSECTION:
A Meeting with a Mountain Lion

Barbara Dean

Barbara Dean is executive editor at Island Press and the author of *Wellspring: A Story from the Deep Country* (Island Press, 1979). She lives in northern California. "Intersection: A Meeting with a Mountain Lion" was first published under the title "Lion" in *Northern Lights,* July 1988.

In January 1986, I dreamed of watching a mountain lion give birth. Six weeks later, on a Sunday morning in February, a mountain lion strolled through the oak trees behind my house.

I live in a wild, lightly populated part of the Coast Range of northern California: mountain lion habitat. But in fifteen years here, this is the first big cat I have seen.

I am sitting at my desk, when a movement out the back window catches my eye. The mountain lion is passing in front of my woodpile, crossing to where my car is parked. She (or he) is not as big as I imagined (though when I look in a book later, I discover that this cat is average size for the area: about 26" high and 7' long). Her tail looks exactly as it is supposed to: full, fluid, sweeping the ground.

I watch the lion cross over the path to a clump of manzanita bushes. Strong body, tawny color. A cat head. She moves gracefully, easily, right at home. No sign of nervousness at human habitation.

Nandi, my Rhodesian Ridgeback, catches the excitement and starts to bark (though more at me than at the lion). The lion seems not to notice. She pauses for a moment in the manzanita and then pushes off so I can see her powerful haunches. As she crosses from the manzanita around a shed and into the woods, the Steller's jays call out sharply. I can trace the cat's path for several minutes by listening to the shouts of the birds.

And then the lion is gone. The air comes together over her path, and I start to breathe again. Sun pours down on a hillside that seems suddenly translucent—and empty.

Those few minutes change the day. A half-hour later, I go outside to examine the ground to see if I can find tracks. But the lion seems to have stepped only on hard ground or meadow grass: no soft earth or mud in which to leave a big paw print.

Mid-afternoon, when Nandi and I go out for a walk, I discover that the hillside feels different to me. The lion's paw marks may not be visible, but her presence feels imprinted on this place. Hours later, her image still hangs in the air. As Nandi and I walk through the meadow and into the woods, I feel my skin on edge, my senses on alert. A big cat has been here, could be here now. From the safety of my house, seeing the cat had been a pure thrill; from out here in the woods, knowing that a lion might be nearby brings an undercurrent of nervousness.

The encounter triggered months of contemplation about wild animals — those in the mind and those in the flesh — and about what difference it makes whether or not wild animals actually inhabit the landscape. Until that Sunday, the mountain lion was the only big animal that shares these hills with me that I hadn't seen. In fifteen years here, I had encountered coyotes, foxes, raccoons, an occasional bear or bobcat, countless deer. But no mountain lion.

I had known that the big cats were around because of neighborhood news. A rancher to the south had a calf attacked by a big cat last summer, another neighbor to the north says a lion tried to carry off a newborn foal. People report sightings now and then — a big cat on a rock at the river, a mother and two cubs walking down the county road. More often, there are rumors, especially of the blood-curdling scream that some swear is a mountain lion's roar (whether or not the local cats really scream is a matter of some dispute).

In the absence of the grizzly bear (long extinct in this area), the mountain lion is the rarest animal that roams these hills. Sleek, shy of humans, almost completely nocturnal, the big cat is seldom seen. Even in the stories of calves killed by mountain lions, the cat itself appears, if at all, only as a glimpse.

The mountain-lion-in-my-mind before that Sunday was composed of other peoples' stories, intuitions of the cat's invisible presence, and the feelings that the word "lion" evokes in the human imagination. Mountain lions are this continent's "big cat," an animal that has stirred the human psyche for centuries. Listen to Laurens van der Post in his book *A Testament to the Wilderness*.

The lion, not only in the imagination of first man, but even in our day, is not the king of beasts for nothing. It is so chosen because, of all forms of animal life, it is the most many-sided, the most highly differentiated. It is powerful. It is swift. It is strong. It can see as well by night as by day. Its senses of smell and hearing are very good. It is very intelligent, and it doesn't abuse this formidable combination of powers. It has a sense of proportion, and does not kill except for food .... Above all, the lion is fundamentally the cat that walks alone. In other words, the lion is the individual; it is the symbol of the instinctive and royal individual self.

As vivid as my mental image of a mountain lion was before that Sunday, my response to the living, breathing cat in my backyard began not in my mind, but in my body.

At first glimpse of that tawny shape, my heart had begun to pound, my body to tense. In the long moment of recognition, knowledge seemed to come from below my conscious mind, as if my animal self named the mountain lion while my head was still processing information ("cat-head, bigger than a bobcat, long tail ..."). When my intellect finally made sense of the image, recognition resonated throughout my body: "Ah-ha. So this is a mountain lion. Of course."

What my imagination hadn't grasped was the cat's wildness. With the real animal before me, I realized that I hadn't fully understood "wild"; I hadn't understood the cat's raw power, the fact of its "otherness." This animal embodied a reality outside my experience or comprehension. An unknown. The real animal evoked a feeling that the animal in my mind hadn't, a feeling I hadn't expected: fear.

The Eskimos have a word for this kind of fear, according to Barry Lopez: it is "ilira," the fear that accompanies awe, as distinct from "kappia," the fear in the face of unpredictable violence. In *Arctic Dreams*, Lopez explains that ilira is what you feel while watching a polar bear; kappia is the fear of having to cross thin ice. That is a distinction made by people who, from living intimately with the powers of the natural world, know fear well enough to define its subtleties.

For me, ilira came when I walked in the woods later Sunday afternoon and knew that a mountain lion might be around. My rational mind understood that my chances of being attacked were slight. But in another, more primitive part of my psyche, I was sharply aware of the big cat's power, of her capacity to kill. The possibility of encountering a mountain lion was suddenly real and immediate. Before Sunday morning, my mental image of mountain lions tended toward the romantic. But the lion who crossed behind my house that day brought the real animal into focus, and corrected the distortions of my human imagination.

That was not the first time I had experienced such a shift. Five years ago, I was living in a yurt that was attacked by a bear on the full moon for three months in a row. I was away for the first encounter, but when I returned and saw what my ursine visitor had done to a tin can, my romantic notions of bears dissolved.

When I asked for advice, my old-timer neighbors without exception said: "Kill it. Once it has the taste of human garbage, it will never stop." My transplanted city friends said, also without exception: "Oh, how wonderful. A bear!"

My own emotions were torn between those extremes, and I had a terrible struggle deciding what to do. Over the next weeks, I wrestled with a relationship to the bear-in-my-mind that had suddenly become more complicated by the threat of this particular bear to my home. Until then, "bear" had meant to me the thrill of living in remote country, free of civilized constraints. The encounter with a real bear forced me to acknowledge the danger that a real wild animal can pose to human life, a danger that my mental image had lacked.

As it turned out, I moved a little earlier than intended to my present, more substantial house. And that summer my neighbors across the river killed five bears. I suspect that "mine" was among them, since he hasn't returned.

Sometimes a real encounter has provoked a psychic shift in another direction. My fear of rattlesnakes threatens to explode for a few weeks early each summer, when I know the snakes must be at large after their winter hibernation. In the month of June, I hardly take a step without expecting a snake to appear at the end of it. But when I do finally encounter the real animal, I see that it has not been lurking behind each rock, waiting to get me (as the snake in my head seems to do). The real encounter, in this case, tames my archetypal fear, and turns obsession into realistic caution.

The point is that an encounter with a real animal keeps the animals in the mind real, too. A face-to-face meeting with a wild lion or bear or snake prevents an anthropocentric world view: a real wild animal reaches beyond human experience, brings us in contact with an "other" beyond the reach of human control.

That matters because one of the functions of the animal-in-the-mind is precisely to mediate with the unknown, the unknowable. The animal links us with forces beyond human experience, by symbolizing capacities and ways of knowing and being that are foreign to human consciousness. As a symbol, the animal-in-the-mind brings us in contact with the stuff of our unconscious through dreams, daydreams, myth, literature, and popular culture.

Seeing a real mountain lion made me wonder what happens when the symbol loses its grounding in the real animal. If someone, somewhere, isn't encountering a real lion, it seems likely that the collective mind will eventually forget what a wild lion is really like. And as the symbol becomes slowly contained, humanized, stereotyped, then its function of mediating with the unknown that gives life its depth and power and mystery will surely be weakened.

The mountain-lion-in-my-mind was powerfully satisfying until I saw the real animal. I wonder what might be missing from our collective image of, say, a dinosaur or a pterodactyl. There's no way to know.

I have thought a lot about my fear—the Eskimo's ilira—because the feeling caught me by surprise, and I was embarrassed by it at first. Think of it: Here is a mountain lion, an animal I have hungered over for years, right behind my house—and I am afraid. The emotion seemed ungrateful.

As I reflected on the events of that Sunday, I wondered what difference it would have made if I had carried a gun with me on my afternoon walk. Would I have felt afraid? The gun would surely have altered my feeling of vulnerability, the sense I had of possibly encountering the big cat directly, creature to creature. If I had felt fear, it would have been a different kind.

The fear I experienced—fear of a creature more powerful than I—is probably more familiar to women, and may be akin to the feeling experienced by primitive hunters before the invention of guns. Through long years of evolution, that kind of fear surely had survival value, as long as it didn't degenerate into panic, because it sharpens the attention so successfully. I wondered if fear might play a similar role in our present moment of evolution, when the unknown from within often seems to be a greater threat than the unknown that is without. Certainly it was true that my unexpected fear startled me into alertness, not only for the big cat in the woods, but also for the meaning of what I had experienced.

I thought again of the Eskimos, whose culture evolved while they were hunting with knives and spears rather than with guns, and who know fear so well that they have more than one word for it. Like other totemic cultures, the Eskimos have a rich mythology, in which the animal is a teacher and friend whose help is petitioned through ritual and passed on in story. The Eskimos also have face-to-face encounters with the real animals. For totemic cultures, the relationship between a bear-in-the-mind and the bear-in-the-woods is fertile and fluid. The bear who is celebrated will also be hunted; the hunt may provide food for survival and it may also bring death for an unwary hunter.

Whatever happens, the hunt and the story are entwined, so that inner and outer flow in and out of one another. Ritual animal and real animal, human and nonhuman, mind and flesh are part of a single experience of life, joined in a pattern that embraces fear and purpose, hunger and longing.

In my dream of the mountain lion in January, the big cat was giving birth in a zoo. I was watching with my mother and a friend. We looked right into the cat's vagina, and we could see the folds of a uterus in contraction, struggling to give forth. The new life hadn't quite been born when the dream ended.

It was a powerful dream that has continued to live with me. I didn't understand the meaning of the mountain lion image until I came across the van der Post passage quoted above, but then I understood that the dream was really about my "royal, individual self" which was, indeed, struggling to be born, in many ways.

The week after the dream, I came upon a bobcat one night as I was driving home from town. The bobcat was caught in the headlights and so I watched him for several minutes before he went on across the road, in search of something. I wondered at the time if the encounter had been attracted through the power of the dream. If so, I was a little disappointed that it hadn't brought a real mountain lion, but I figured that was too much to hope for.

So when the mountain lion walked in front of my woodpile a month later, I was not exactly expecting her. But I was also aware of a certain feeling of nonsurprise, as if some secret part of me had, in fact, been awaiting such a visit since the night of my dream. I had no doubt that this cat had come for me. For me to be at my desk on a Sunday morning and to be looking out the window at the precise moment when a shy, seldom-seen, nocturnal predator appeared was too unusual for coincidence.

The synchronicity of having lived here for fifteen years without seeing a mountain lion—and then to dream of a big cat and to see one within six weeks brought my inner and outer worlds together with a force that left me literally tingling for hours. All day long, I turned over and over in my mind the figure of the cat, the feeling of my dream, the resonance within. I contemplated my startling inner certainty that this mountain lion came to make real the image in the dream: a real cat, not one in a zoo, coming to bring the symbol to life.

This, I understood, is the experience of living in a world in which inside and outside are one. This is "participation"—an experience that was commonplace for our most distant human ancestors, whose intimacy with the natural world combined with an innate sense of belonging to produce a feeling that personal destiny was linked with that of the natural world. Experiencing this feeling from the inside, as I did, courtesy of the mountain lion, is to know what it means to live in perfect accord with nature: as if all life, inner and outer, is engaged in a single revelation. It is a feeling of being known.

The Kalahari Bushmen say, "There is a dream dreaming us." My encounter with the mountain lion was an experience of living in such dream-time, where unlikely events come together in a pattern of personal meaning, in which my destiny was part of the destiny of the mountain lion and of the oak trees and of the sun-drenched hillside, on a Sunday morning in February.

So, then, it seems to me that animals-in-the-flesh are important because the animals-in-the-mind are not enough. Animals do live deep within us, unbidden; they emerge in dreams and stories, in the metaphors with which we speak. Animals-in-the-mind allow an intimacy that is not possible with the real animal. But we need the real animal to guard the "otherness," to keep the power full, to ensure that ilira is part of our understanding of a polar bear.

And—we need real wild animals in the world so that we might encounter the animals that inhabit our dreams.

It's impossible to know for sure, but I suspect that the first humans lived closer to the link between the world of spirit and the world of appearances. That intersection seems to me to be one of life's deepest mysteries, where matter and mind, flesh and spirit merge: the mystery of incarnation.

This, I think, is the real power of my experience with the mountain lion. The connection between my dream animal and this real animal—between mind and matter—was meaning. Meaning: the glue between the worlds, the intelligent, transcendent power of the universe: the pattern of God. As a friend said, upon hearing the story, "It makes it very easy to believe, doesn't it?"

Moments such as my encounter with the mountain lion are rare, to be sure. And the more estranged our inner and outer worlds become, the rarer they will be. This particular moment, for example, would not have occurred if mountain lions had disappeared from this mountain range, by loss of habitat or by planned extermination, a policy option that was being considered by California's Fish and Game Commission during the same week that the mountain lion appeared behind my house, as a way of "managing" the mountain lion population in an area near the North Fork of the Kings River in the Sierra National Forest.

Later that spring, the North Kings proposal was tabled, and it remains dormant two years later. But public concern about the health and viability of California's mountain lions persists because of the repeated attempts of the state Fish and Game Commission to open a "sport" hunting season on the big cats. The pursuit and killing of mountain lions for wall trophies has been and continues to be legal in many other Western states.

I find proposals that threaten the continued existence of mountain lions in their current habitat a chilling counterpoint to my personal reflections on big cats. Chilling and disquieting—because, although our understanding of the importance of large predators to the human psyche may be embryonic, knowledge of their importance to the ecosystem is well established. Ecological studies show clearly that any disturbance at the top of the food chain will affect all other life forms in ways that are unpredictable and profound. Without the presence of large predators in the wild, nature loses its biological complexity and balance; the quality and essence of life itself are diminished.

It is already unlikely, in modern America, that many people will encounter a mountain lion in the course of a day. But as long as these cats survive, it is possible that someone will—and perhaps the experience will register for us all through the shared mind of the deep unconscious. It seems desperately important to protect that possibility—for humanity and for all life.

MANDLOVU

Deena Metzger

Deena Metzger is a healer and writer who has always been concerned with the fate of the earth and the wild. Her books include *Writing for Your Life* (Harper San Francisco, 1992); *What Dinah Thought* (Viking), a novel; *Looking for the Faces of God* (Parallax Press, 1989); *A Sabbath among the Ruins* (Parallax Press, 1992); and her latest novel, *The Other Hand* (Red Hen Press, 2000). With Linda Hogan and Brenda Peterson, she edited *Between Species: The Bond between Women and Animals* (Ballantine, 1996). She and her husband, Michael Ortiz Hill, live at the end of the road in Topanga, California, with the wolves Akasha and Blue.

Mandlovu is the word the Ndebele people of Zimbabwe use for female elephant. It is connected in resonance with *MamboKadze*, the name for the deity that is both elephant, the Virgin Mary, and the Great Mother.

Suddenly, I am of a single mind extended
Across an unknown geography,
And imprinted, as if by a river, on the moment.
A mind held in unison by a large gray tribe
Meandering in reverent concert
among trees, feasting on leaves.
One great eye reflecting blue
From the turn inward
Toward the hidden sky that, again,
Like an underground stream
Continuously nourishes
What will appear after the dawn
Bleaches away the mystery in which we rock
Through the endless green dark.

I am drawn forward by the lattice,
By a concordance of light and intelligence
Constituted from the unceasing and consonant
Hum of cows and the inaudible bellow of bulls,
A web thrumming and gliding
Along the pathways we remember
Miles later or ages past.

I am, we are,
Who can distinguish us?
A gathering of souls, hulking and muddied,
Large enough—if there is a purpose—
To carry the accumulated joy of centuries
Walking thus within each other's
Particular knowing and delight.

This is our grace: To be a note
In the exact chord that animates creation,
The dissolve of all the rivers
That are both place and moment,
An ocean of mind moving
Forward and back,

Outside of any motion
Contained within it.

This is particle and wave. How simple.
The merest conversation between us
Becoming the essential drone
Into which we gladly disappear.
A common music, a singular heavy tread,
Ceaselessly carving a path,
For the waters tumbling invisibly
Beneath.

I have always wanted to be with them, with you, so.

KILLING THE BEAR

Judith Minty

Judith Minty's biography appears before her poem "Prowling the Ridge" in the previous section. "Killing the Bear" first appeared in the anthology *Talking Leaves: Contemporary Native American Short Stories*, edited by Craig Lesley (Bantam Doubleday Dell, 1991).

She has strung the hammock between two birch trees at the edge of the clearing. Now she drifts in and out of the light there and drowsily studies the pattern made by the rope's weaving and the flickering leaves.

When she had the dog, he stretched out beneath the hammock. Hackles raised, growling and nipping at flies, he'd meant to save her from shadows. In truth, he'd startled at noises, even at shifts in the wind, and she ended up more his protector than the other way around.

There were wolves at the little zoo when she was a child. She heard them howling from her aunt's kitchen and went to see them up close.

And a bear.

Three times she visited, slowly circling the bear pen, but he was always sleeping. He looked like a bundle of clothes by the dead tree. His fence was electrified and posted with signs, and she was afraid to touch the iron bars.

The wolves set off a chorus of neighborhood dogs. Their calling floated back and forth all that summer vacation.

She lies in the hammock every afternoon, her life in the rhythm of the woods. Up at dawn to the shrill pitch of blue jays. Logs tossed into the stove, match lit, breath steaming in the cabin's chill. Trip to the outhouse, coffee perking, bucket of water from the river. The rest of the morning, ping of nails driven into boards. Her porch is nearly done. One room and another room. Something inside and something out.

The afternoon silence and the sway of the hammock lull her and when she hears a low guttural, she thinks, at first, it is the dog. Then she remembers the dog is gone.

She struggles to sit up and makes the hammock sway crazily.

A bear stands beyond the pines—small jets of eyes, heavy black coat. He snuffles, then drops on all fours and weaves into the forest.

Her hands lift to cover her breasts.

Her favorite doll was a stuffed animal and she slept with it close to her heart. She was nine when her mother said, "Give me your bear for three months. Let's see if you can stop sucking your thumb."

She tried very hard to stop, and when the time was up, she asked for the bear again.

Her mother said, "Another month."

One day, as she sat in the kitchen watching a cake being stirred and poured into the pan and then put into the oven, it came to her that her bear was gone, that it had been thrown down the incinerator.

Only a few years ago, her mother told her, misspeaking even then, "I'm sorry for burning the animal in you."

Her hammer has stopped its thump and echo. The roof is laid. The porch smells of fresh paint. She has hauled the old sofa out and can sit there in the evenings, if she wants.

When the bear understood that she was alone, he came closer. The first time, she was reading in the hammock and heard something like a sigh. She knew it was him, even before she caught a glimpse of black gliding through the woods. The next time, he was so close she smelled him—a terrible, rancid odor. Without looking, she swung out of the hammock and walked to the cabin. Two days later, he stood next to the birch tree, breath rattling his throat. If she'd turned, she could have touched the bristles on his shoulders.

The Gilyak tribe honored him. They put his head on a stake outside their doors and made offerings to it. On Yezo Island, the Ainus thought he was a man trapped inside the body of a bear. If a hunter found a cub, he brought it to his wife who suckled it.

In Lapland he was King of Beasts. The men lived alone, purifying themselves, for three days after the hunt. At the funeral, after they had feasted, they put his bones back together in the ground.

Once she spent an evening with two Swedes. At dinner, their wine glasses held the tint of leaves. Ole, the painter, said, "You live in green light." Gunnar told magic tales. "When a woman meets a bear in the woods, she must lift her skirt. Then he will let her pass."

In the travelogue about Alaska, the Kodiak caught a salmon, his claws stretched out like fingers. When the second bear approached, he reared up. He looked soft and gentle, as if he were greeting a friend, until, with a sweep of his paw, he split open the head of the other.

In college, a classmate told about the summer he'd worked at Yellowstone and got too close. He never felt the nick, only knew when blood trickled down his forehead.

There was also the news story about the woman dragged from her tent in the middle of the night, crying, "He's killing me. Oh God, he's killing me." The bear carried the woman away, his claws tangled in her hair, ripping at her arm.

When she drove to town for supplies, she bought a secondhand rifle. She keeps it loaded now, propped against the doorjamb inside the cabin.

The clerk at the hardware store showed her how to fire it, how to aim along the sights. He winked and told her she could get a man with it at twenty yards. She said she didn't need a man, just wanted to do some hunting.

She misses the dog. She carries the gun awkwardly over her shoulder when she goes to the woodpile or to the river.

Her calendar hangs on the cabin wall, each day of summer marked with an X, the rest of the year clean and open. She turns up the wick on the lamp and starts to brush her hair, staring at her reflection in the windowpane.

She is thinking about leaving. She is thinking about driving out of the clearing.

When the scream begins, it breaks against the walls. It shudders in a moan, then rises. Everything, even the wind, holds its breath.

It is over so quickly she almost believes it didn't happen and raises the brush again, and barely recognizes herself in the glass. She runs to the lamp and blows out the flame, then to the window, hoping she will not see what must be there.

She did not shoot cleanly the first time. When he ripped the screen and tore the siding loose, she stood on the porch, gun leveled.

"Go away."

He was no more than ten feet from her when she fired. He spun around and fell to the ground, then raised himself up.

When she realized she had only wounded him, she ran into the cabin and turned the lock and leaned against the door. She could hear him thrashing and bellowing in the bushes and against the trees.

She knew she would have to step onto the porch again, go to the ripped screen, with nothing but night air between them. She would have to take aim and shoot again. And if that didn't stop him, she would have to slip the bolt and reload the rifle and stand there and shoot him again until he stopped bawling and weeping and falling down and getting up and lurching against the trees.

When they began this, she never thought she would have to kill him so slow. She never dreamed she would have to hurt him so much.

It is nearly dawn when he dies, when she gets up from her chair, when his groans stop pricking her skin. She takes the flashlight and goes out on the porch. She shines the beam around in the gray light and sees the blood dried on the new screen and on the fresh-painted sill and spattered on the leaves around the cabin. She sees the trampled bushes and broken branches and where he crawled into the weeds.

She shines the arc out, light bouncing on tree and log, until it lands on a black heap, huddled in the middle of the clearing.

As soon as the sun rises, she begins to dig, and by midafternoon she is through with it—the rope tied to him, the car backed up to the hole, the rifle and box of ammunition remembered and dropped in next to him, the musty soil put back, and branches over that.

Then she bathes with the last of the water from the river and sweeps the cabin floor, thinking that rain will wash away the blood and that, soon enough, snow will fall and cover it all.

It is dark when she gets to the state line. Next summer, she will dig him up to take the claws.

COMING HOME

Joseph Jastrab

Joseph Jastrab is a teacher, therapist, wilderness guide, and seasoned workshop leader who has been guiding vision quests since 1976 through his organization, Earth Rise Foundation. Joseph's men's vision quest work is featured in his book *Sacred Manhood, Sacred Earth* (HarperCollins, 1994). "Coming Home" is an edited excerpt from that book.

And the world cannot be discovered by a journey of miles, no matter how long, but only by a spiritual journey, a journey of one inch, very arduous and humbling and joyful, by which we arrive at the ground at our feet, and learn to be at home.
— WENDELL BERRY, "THE UNFORSEEN WILDERNESS"

This summer morning awakens like most in these forested valleys. The ground mist slowly disappears into the sky, birds sing their new song, the river flows as ever to the sea. But to this eternal choreography, we humans add the steps of our own colorful dance with life—steps created from our awareness of beginnings and of endings. This is just like all other mornings. Yet, it is also our last morning together in this place.

The drum signal normally used to call us together finds the group gathered around the camp medicine wheel, ready to begin the closing circle that will turn us toward the world we left behind. There is eagerness here similar to that present the morning we descended from the sunrise knoll and first faced this way. For we are soon to be on the trail that leads past Guardian Rock, and that trail always leads to adventure.

Our final council begins. We pass the Talking Staff around with the question: "What lives in your heart now?" This time the Staff will move in the direction contrary to what we've been accustomed to. This practice reflects our intention to unravel this circle and release this sacred vessel of brotherhood that a larger one may be formed. What is of most value is that which remains after the vessel is broken.

We say good-bye to the land and spirit that has served us well. We bid farewell to the men we have come to know as true brothers. We acknowledge gifts given and gifts received, and yearnings left unfulfilled. We may not know fully what societies embrace us now as kin, or what mysteries we have embodied with such abandon as to escape our knowing. Nonetheless, we are here. The forest recognizes us. The trees bend to hear our quiet conversation. The rocks have matched our will and tested our patience beyond what we could bear. And they are with us still.

The youngest member of our clan takes up the Talking Staff and speaks of the specific quality of manhood he admires in each of us present. He has stalked each man here closely and is grateful for the diverse modeling of manhood he has witnessed. Then the eldest man takes the Talking Staff and speaks of this journey as a ten-day contemplative prayer. He shares his delight in being able to celebrate his entry into elderhood. Another man grieves his failure to allow anything of importance to touch him here. The Talking Staff continues to move around the circle evoking poems, prayers, promises.

Suddenly the river's song changes. A man across the circle whispers, "Look … upstream!" His glance shows us where. For a moment our eyes struggle to penetrate the camouflage of foliage and the sparkles of sunlight glinting on the water. But then we see it: some creature, making its way down the center of the stream toward us.

It appears to be a fawn, a young spotted one, searching for something. Yet the stream has served up many apparitions during our time here: faces of departed loved ones, sounds of distant drumming, whispered callings of our names. This fawn—a visitor from this world or a reflection of some other?

It keeps coming, close enough now for our sight to confirm the deer-child as one of this world. Its slender legs find their way among the rocks and eddies. Its eyes are wide open, its ears upright and alert. The sudden appearance of this trembling creature has swept our minds clear of thought and brought our senses to full attention.

The fawn comes closer still, until it stops in the river directly alongside our circle. It turns to face us. Any remaining armor falls from our hearts. Then, without hesitation, the fawn walks toward the riverbank, toward us. Its spindly legs grapple for purchase on the gravel slope until it gains a foothold. Bounding up onto solid ground, the fawn walks to the edge of our circle, pauses briefly, then nudges its way between two men to stand at the center of our Medicine Wheel.

And the world stops. The fawn stands dripping wet, impossibly unafraid, in the center of our collective heart.

What the fawn is looking for we will never know. What it finds is a refuge safe enough to trust its trembling heart to. A world of men. Imperfect and wholehearted men. In our midst, a part of each of us stands revealed: our homelessness, our vulnerability, our searching, our gentleness and strength, our willingness to step into the unknown.

My mind, in a desperate attempt to reassert itself, races between the two worlds looking for one to host this event confidently. No use. A crack has appeared between the worlds, and this gentle creature has led me through that crack. I suddenly find myself in a universe in which I truly belong. Tears stream from my soul, releasing the sorrow that accumulates in taking life for granted—those waters, mixed with the tender light of my return to presence. I hear the word "epiphany" but I do not reach for it, for even its respectful tone forces this moment apart from all others. I feel in the fawn's vulnerable presence the invitation to hold to nothing, but to stand in the center of *every* moment with the open eyes and heart of this one. I let myself love outside of time for as long as I can bear before I reach out for that word once refused. In fear, I agree, this is an exceptional moment, apart from all others. In truth, the grace is unbearable.

And so I fall once again from the garden, from the moment that is all moments, from the immensity of the world—myself. But it lingers like a sweet fragrance. I can remember the full attention I gave to life and the full aliveness that life returned to me. I can remember the time I rested in the grace of the world and was free. I may not be able to live it fully, but I can remember it.

Call it vision, call it whatever you like—it is the experience of being fully alive. Not only as a receiver of life, but also as a giver of life. Somewhere within every man is a womb that bears life. Perhaps that womb is the heart. The world needs a man's heart. Life-bearing hearts. Hearts that choose to remember what they cannot yet fully live.

The fawn turns to face the woods beyond our circle. This refuge of belonging is not its final destination. It knows that it cannot live within a moment frozen in time. Neither can our pilgrimage.

The fawn slowly turns its head to look into eyes that will no longer hold it to this place, and then disappears into the forest.

Its journey homeward continues … as does ours.

V

Teaching in the Wild

*T*hese days, the common approach toward teaching in wilderness is one of inquiry into how things are put together and how they relate to one another. As part of our cultural legacy we possess many sciences—biology, geology, astronomy, chemistry, physics, and all of the more specific fields within these broader studies. I can recall, from my childhood education, dissecting frogs, learning about glaciation and the three different basic types of rocks, catching butterflies and putting pins through them, counting the rings of trees, and having my head stuffed with a lot of facts, obscure names, and jargon that I have mostly forgotten. While this type of education is valuable and has its place, to be sure, I am interested in approaching the subject of wilderness education from a different angle.

What is it that we have to learn from nature simply by being out on the land and letting the land come to us as it were? Through the acts of attention and receptivity, we discover facets of wilderness that cannot be taught in books or discovered through scientific inquiry. In a stance of openness, our relationship to nature becomes real, immediate, and personal. After all, it does not take any conceptual knowledge to be able to appreciate a stunning sunset.

If we relax our minds, open our hearts, and enter into quiet dialogue with the landscape that stands before us, our understanding will silently deepen of its own accord. Insight and clarity come naturally. Within a simple and singular approach, there is nothing to do and nothing to figure out. The purity of being, being with ourselves and being with nature, leads us to the experience of gratitude and of joy and of peace. There is no greater teaching than this.

RAIN'S SONG TO THE CEDAR:
Teaching in Wilderness

Saul Weisberg

Saul Weisberg is executive director of North Cascades Institute, a non-profit educational organization in Washington State. An ecologist, writer, and mountaineer, Saul is committed to using the power of wild lands in teaching and caring for the earth. He is the author of *From the Mountains to the Sea:* A *Guide to the Skagit River Watershed* and *North Cascades: The Story behind the Scenery.*

> *"You're going to get wet."*
> *"The wet's what it's all about."*
> —OVERHEARD DURING A SUMMER STORM
> AT A TRAILHEAD IN THE NORTH CASCADES

The group, some ahead of me, some far behind, moves slowly, silently. It's not the silence of quiet communion with the wilderness, but rather the footsore slogging of exhausted students. Our discussion on forest succession ended when gray clouds descended to the ground. Our camp is miles away. We move without speaking. I think of the many forms of water: clouds and rivers and lakes and rain and sleet. I'm wet and cold and tired. I'm also teaching.

Once, when I was new to this business, an old friend turned to me in the winter darkness of a Wyoming cabin and said, "You can't teach in the rain." That was years ago and miles removed from this green river valley deep in the North Cascades, but once again that thought returns.

You can teach in the rain, of course. But you teach differently, you learn differently. The wilderness is not merely a backdrop for this class — everything we do is placed in the context of wildness. The rain is an integral element of this wilderness place. And the place changes you. It reaches out and grabs your attention, demands to be noticed. In the North Cascades, rain is one way the wilderness says, "You're not in the classroom (or the city) anymore."

There are many people out there who identify wilderness as wide open spaces, deserts, the dryness of the Sierra or the Rockies. They often forget about this lush green land, yet 10 percent of Washington State is preserved as wilderness. Then there are the nonbelievers, people who feel you need drylands to run outdoor and environmental education programs. Nonsense. All it takes is a willingness to accept the rain as an essential element of place, to accept what the land is teaching you.

Rain is the signature of the North Cascades. It makes the land. Glaciers, mountains, rivers, and the inland sea we call Puget Sound are all molded by its wet embrace. If you come here, you're going to get wet. If you teach here, sooner or later you find yourself walking through a dripping forest with your socks down around your ankles.

I've been teaching in the Northwest wilderness for over fifteen years — the last six as director of the North Cascades Institute, a nonprofit environmental field school. Our classes bring people into direct contact with the land. My work with NCI has shown me that teaching outdoors in the Pacific Northwest means accepting the rain as an essential element, and, more important, accepting what the land is teaching you.

The crux of teaching, and learning, in the wilderness is using the power of place. Letting the rain teach. Letting wildlands speak for themselves, with minimal interpretation. Getting out of the way.

The elements of wilderness education are time, place, people, and something to talk about. The art lies in putting them together, then trusting yourself and the students enough to stand back and watch what happens. Immerse a small group of students in a powerful natural environment, give them something to sink their teeth into—be it alpine ecology or old growth forests—mix thoroughly, and let simmer for a few days, a few nights under the stars. The experience is deep, powerful and lasting.

Teaching in the rain involves more than just teaching. Living in the rain is hard. Wet clothes, wet sleeping bags, soggy granola, field guides that either fall apart or swell to twice their original volume. We can learn from the earlier native inhabitants. Did they stay inside their longhouses, sitting around a smoky fire, or did they put on their cedar-bark capes and go out to face the wet? After two or three days the rain stops being an outside force. Its presence is invasive, another being living with you, close to your skin. It becomes as familiar and natural as the wet wool that clings soggily to our backs.

Each time I am out with students and clouds roll in from the southwest, sink toward the ground, and begin spitting at us, I relearn the same lessons. At first I look for signs of clearing, delaying projects "until the weather changes." Eventually, there is nothing left but to continue. We gear up and move on toward the day's lesson. It's not always fun, but it is important. A good time to learn the lessons of microhabitats, to hunker down in protected crannies and watch alpine saxifrages hiding from the wind.

Teaching in wilderness is powerful, teaching for wilderness is infinitely more so. Teaching for wilderness implies listening to the voices of the land. It can change your life.

Our goal is no less than to change the world. Rain is one of the essential ingredients of place. A basic tenet of ecological truth here in the Pacific Northwest is that the land is the way it is—in shape, smell, texture, sound—because of the rain. It sings sweetly to the cedars. Our job is to learn to listen to its song.

THE STUDENTS OF ALBERT CAMP

John Miles

John Miles is Professor of Environmental Studies at Huxley College,
Western Washington University. A mountaineer, backcountry skier, and
wilderness nut who is a specialist in outdoor and environmental education,
John has written and edited five books, the most recent of which is
Adventure Programming, edited with Simon Priest (Venture, 1999). He is
currently writing a history of wilderness policy in American national parks.

On a warm, mid-May day in 1980, I struggled into Albert Camp with a
group of college students. The camp was not our destination—we intended
to use Horseshoe Basin two miles farther on as base for our explorations
of the area. But the trail was becoming increasingly difficult and forced a
change of plans. Four feet of rotting snow covered what we guessed was a
wide trail in summer. We had followed the clear and comfortable trail
easily lower down, but above six thousand feet it had disappeared and we
were forced to follow blazes on the trees. After hours of post-holing, falling through snow to our hips under heavy packs laden with two weeks'
worth of supplies and gear, we gave up any intention of going farther. We
happened to be at Albert Camp, and it would have to do.

There were twenty of us there, miles from the nearest source of news,
when Mount St. Helens blew its top. That was the first year of our wilderness education experience; each year since I have returned to Albert Camp
with a new group of adventurers. Snow lies deep over the eastern North
Cascades of Washington and we can find true wilderness and its solitude
there. Later in the season backpackers may wander through, but in wintry May we have the place to ourselves to practice the arts of wilderness
travel, and to explore and reflect without fear of intrusion.

There are several reasons to travel to Albert Camp each spring. The
original and always primary purpose is to find a wilderness setting from
which to learn. The young people traveling up the Albert Camp Trail with
me aspire to become outdoor educators and leaders. The trip to Albert Camp
is the final experience in a year-long study of environmental and outdoor
education. The group has examined the how and why of teaching about the
environment. Their reading has led them to Thoreau, Muir, Aldo Leopold,
the educational philosopher John Dewey and others. They have struggled
with curriculum design and have explored the educational potentials of

many learning sites from urban schoolyards to national parks. Wilderness, the least accessible yet richest environment for outdoor learning, is their final challenge and their reward.

The trip is inspirational. While some of our group have climbed and hiked in wildlands, they have usually done so with a goal orientation that has not allowed them to stop and reflect. Lacking time, because of peaks they must climb or miles they must travel, they miss the opportunity to "hear only the wind whispering among the reeds," as Thoreau described his plans when asked what he would do at Walden Pond. They do not take the time to look closely at the nature around them, to contrast wild nature with the world of human enterprise in which they spend most of their days. Wildlands have much to teach about the Self and the Other, but the lessons require concentration and effort. Even on one outing the "cultural value of wilderness," as Leopold called it, can be appreciated. The ability to see this value, he said, "boils down, in the last analysis, to a question of intellectual humility." Such humility is one of the ultimate goals of environmental education, and the trip to Albert Camp can be a revelation about the nature of this goal.

What do the students learn in their Albert Camp experience? Do they grow? Do they change? Are they transformed? I have never done any empirical research into these questions, but I have asked students, years after their experience, to testify about its effects on them. What follows is a small part of that testimony, drawn from letters, interviews and a questionnaire.

Mark

The 1984 Albert Camp visit stands out as the year of the moon. A full moon was reached exactly halfway through twelve clear, nearly cloudless days and nights. Snow lay four to five feet deep when we arrived and had flowed almost entirely away in roaring streams by our departure. Winter yielded to summer, missing spring altogether.

Mark's alias was "Rolling Thunder," bestowed upon him by his fellow travelers because of his enthusiastic discussion of a book about the Indian shaman. Rolling Thunder's understanding of the natural world and connections to it were exceptional, and Mark was excited at the possibilities for relating to nature revealed to him in the book. He could not wait for his solo, for the chance to try some Rolling Thunder methods.

"Spring Block was a quantum leap in my understanding of and appreciation for wild places, conservation and education," he told me. "It helped me put together many of the pieces of the puzzle I'd been mulling over for so many years. The writers like Muir and Leopold had, I discovered, written my very thoughts. The whole experience was like a revelation that I had been heading somewhere all along even though I had been only dimly aware of it....

"Solo was not a time of fear for me as it was for some of the others. I was ready for it. I had done brief solos before, but this time I was able to immerse myself in the spirit of the wild place like never before. Perhaps it was the reading, especially the Rolling Thunder, that prepared me."

The memory of the experience visibly raises Mark's excitement as he talks about it four years later. "The high point came one evening after a brief but intense snow shower put a dusting of powdery stuff over everything. It was brighter than ever—maybe the moon was full that night. I couldn't sleep. Prowling around I came across cougar tracks. I wasn't scared a bit. Instead, I set off tracking it, ignoring your rules and instructions about staying in the prescribed area. I was Rolling Thunder, Tom 'The Tracker' Brown—generations of wilderness trackers were in me. I lost the tracks after a while but roamed around all night, feeling an exultation that is still with me. My spiritual consciousness was at the most acute level I had ever experienced. I loved that wild place! The Pasayten experience—but especially that solo—was a rite of passage for me. I broke through to a deeper level of understanding of my commitment and dedication to wilderness and of my love for it. All doubt about my direction didn't disappear, but that night I found a powerful blaze telling me where the path lay."

Mark has pursued a career in environmental management, interpretation and environmental education. He is now classified as an "environmentalist" for Washington State Parks and battles with engineers and bureaucrats bent on developing "user-friendly" parks at the expense of natural park values. He regularly goes on solos to restore his vision and dedication.

Melanie

Mel, now a mother, teacher, and environmental educator with the U.S. Forest Service, made her trip to Albert Camp in 1983. A warm, friendly and highly independent person, Mel came away from her wilderness adventures with many impressions, which she recorded in her journal. Solo was especially meaningful to her.

Ah, this land is so very beautiful. . . . I close my eyes and tears roll slowly down my wind-blown cheeks. The drops cool with this blowing wind. I heard the same bird again, his song a series of two sessions…six notes in each, three per breath. High high twirlee, low low twirlee. I shall never see grays, blues and whites blending as I do now. An intricately woven blend; the sky, clouds, snow, mountaintops, so soft. My back and chest radiate the result of prolonged high altitude sun but the rest of me is bundled. … It is now neither night nor day, but that precious time between. Far below flows the river, ceaselessly, over hollow logs and dry, iridescent bark. Time, for a few minutes, stands still. Our earth is eternal and boundless.

Mel and her group set off on their wilderness expedition, which would take them over 8,384-foot Windy Peak. The trail disappeared beneath snow, wound upward into thick fog and cloud. The group was forced to camp. Mel survived, along with her three male companions, the rigors of six wilderness travel days, and arguments, and returned to Albert Camp. Her journal describes the homecoming:

Talk, talk, talk! Such big smiles and sun-colored faces, similar adventures through different eyes. A very emotional campfire, readings and emotions and groping hugs, private tears and a feeling of oneness so intense that my heart rips in departure. But how do you say so in meaningful words? A caress, a sigh, a faraway smile will be my only indicators. For what are words?

Jennifer

Occasionally, a student comes to Spring Block from another school. Jen came from the demanding academic environment of the Ivy League where she was studying history and education. She came for fun and adventure, to experience a different approach to teaching and learning, for a taste of the American West and, especially, because she thought the Block might bring her together with people of like interest. All of these would, she hoped, help clarify her direction. Jen wrote a long letter explaining what happened to her. Here are some excerpts:

I was in a group of four, and one woman was slow—a lot slower than the rest of us. I hiked behind with her… . The other two guys went up ahead—they weren't really getting along. The whole thing was so frustrating. I got to the top where we sat by a huge rock and cried about as hard as I've ever cried. Here I was in this tremendously beautiful place doing things I've always wanted to do—it felt as if I've always been doing them—and I felt miserable. I couldn't fix the situation either—I couldn't make Kate hike faster, Mark be less particular about things, Sam be less frustrated. I felt incredibly powerless compared to life and the mountains and sky. Crying was a great release. I want to remember that feeling of powerlessness. I think it's important not to feel in the center of the universe. Somehow—the problems we encountered as an expedition group were never resolved—I made it through the experience, did my best, accepted the rest, learned about going with the flow, bumping along, and that a cluster of tens of thousands of ladybugs on top of Windy Peak is absolutely wonderful.

We had extreme weather by my standards—two inches of snow one morning, 80 degrees and sunny the next, pouring rain the next, and so forth. I survived quite happily as long as I managed to stay relatively warm and dry. There was a real sense of freedom in just having to cope with the basics of life—food, water, shelter, etc. I was surprised at how much time these things actually took up. I was never bored. Quite an amazing thing when one lives in a world of distractions and entertainment to go into the wilderness and only have a pack and be basically self-sufficient. …

I have a picture of me sitting on Windy Peak with the whole Cascade Range in the background. It's on my desk and I glance at it lovingly quite often as I study away. It's amazing how much two short weeks stand out in my mind and how often I refer back to those memories… . Very little else has affected me that much.

The students of Albert Camp have made many discoveries, as these few testify. Separated from family, friends, home, patterns of daily living, the clock, pressures to perform and various responsibilities, they have reflected on direction, purpose and goals. Insights and personal power have come to them. Swinging rhythmically along a trail they have sometimes fallen into a meditative state and suddenly brought important thoughts to their consciousness, thoughts normally jammed by the interference of hectic daily schedules. Sitting quietly on solo they have encountered themselves and their surroundings more fully than usual. We have asked them to attempt this, to open up to their physical surroundings, to embrace this unusual opportunity to live fully in the present. They have been accountable only to themselves. Upon their return from solo they have been asked to explain what happened. What did they learn? They have written in journals, talked around campfires, probed their feelings about what happened. Years after leaving college they have told me that their wilderness experience was the most significant learning experience of their college career.

They say they have learned about humility. They have looked down from Albert Camp, reflected on their personal history, and taken a step toward greater self-knowledge. They have struggled with their fellow expeditioners and gained a sharpened awareness of how they relate to people generally. They have relinquished a bit of their compulsion to control their world—they could not control the Albert Camp world—and have seen their situation back "home" with new eyes. They have transferred their learnings to classroom, job, family. They have gained an especially keen awareness of how much there is to learn and have been energized to tackle the challenge of learning and growth. In short, Albert Camp, a wilderness place, became for the students a very significant extension of the university.

John Muir wrote, "The mountains are fountains of men as well as of rivers, of glaciers, of fertile soil ... able men whose thoughts and deeds have moved the world, have come down from the mountains—mountain dwellers who have grown strong there with the forest trees in Nature's work-shops." So it has been with the women and men—the students—of Albert Camp.

THOUGHTS ON THE
IDEA OF ADVENTURE

Bob Henderson

Bob Henderson teaches Outdoor Education at McMaster University in Hamilton, Ontario. His articles have appeared in such publications as *Pathways: The Ontario Journal of Outdoor Education, The Trumpeter,* and *The Journal of Experiential Education.*

Adventure-based learning seeks self-growth through challenging experiences that heighten relationships and promote greater self-competencies and self-awareness. Unfortunately, this broad notion of adventure learning as challenge, risk, uncertainty, change, can all too simply be funneled down to a conquest of self over obstacle as a means to greater self-concept. In outdoor pursuits and adventure travel, the obstacle is nature. This staging of nature as obstacle/opponent is proving to be all too common in the educational domain and personal experiences where underlying cultural assumptions and practices encourage detachment from environment.

However, this blind conquest of nature for gains in self-aggrandizement and character skills is an adventure orientation that ultimately is detrimental to self and counter to a slowly emerging cultural realization that we must forge for a naturally beneficial reconciliation with nature.

Culturally, we are learning that our collective conscious must seek an ecological frame of reference that is fundamentally *with* nature, not *against* nature. In the end we must discover, as Theodore Roszak has said, "that the needs of the person are the needs of the planet." This is a clear expression of "with."

Typically, there is the individual versus (read "against") nature idea, that so readily fits our cultural domain. Here we cover ground, take on rapids, peaks, and great distance, often in competitive, efficient high-tech teams. As the sense of self is enlarged to the excitement of the challenge arena itself, the self more and more seeks "to know" the rock, rapid, landscape in a subjective depth of identity. The self seeks beyond itself and, ultimately, out of this advances a third stage of adventure maturity, which is to be "with" rock, rapid, landscape.

The self can be freed as an extending of one's center into one's environment through direct experience, a direct meeting, face-to-face. We experience vitality in the sense that we are as a sponge, that we are in context to surroundings we experience directly, not mediated through a cultural context that fundamentally breeds individualism, consumption and objectivity. We experience integrity in that we are aware of a possible integration to place. Both of these qualities bring a healthiness, or even holiness to our vital self. One does not sing the praises of the awe of nature. Rather, one comes to see and accept one's place in a grand design at the level of the comforted soul. This is indeed a state of adventure.

While on a dog-sledding trip in northern Manitoba's "land of the little sticks," I was hoping to capture the timeless ways and enduring patterns of life of this quiet part of the North. One hears so often about "... the ways of the North." I continually seek my personal, albeit romantic, sensibility for this way. This particular North I seek seems to me to have maintained its authenticity through time. It was a cultural fit and a vague notion of biological fit with this landscape that I was after. I would chat with Chipewyan trappers. I would mush dogs for hours and blend into another time, and to the place itself direct, to meet the territory, not some cultural mapping/image of landscape.

I do not wish to dismiss totally the popular but narrow idea of adventure of the physical. But, as a result of a rather disheartening experience with a journalist about my notion of adventure in northern Manitoba, I am prompted to suggest further possibilities: possibilities that advance adventure education and one's personal travels to the thought of being genuinely "with place" as a central question of self-growth. Such possibilities, which address an adventure of the spirit, were obscured in this interview.

The adventure of spirit is easily denied and marginalized to conventional viewpoints. Such adventure is denied to writers and educators of adventure who might spark such reflexivity. I have been told more than once by editors: "A well-written trip report but not 'epic' enough"; "You have not covered enough ground [physical ground]"; "There is little hardship expressed"; "Where is the heightened perceived risk?" I have seen editors of adventure-travel magazines cut out the more reflexive "one with nature" sentiments to insidiously reinforce other comments of hardship and death-defying moments that may or may not exist in the text.

One easily becomes trapped in an interview to discuss hardship and physical fitness, distance covered and the accomplishments simply because these are the questions asked. While all the above might be downplayed by the interviewee, it is still reported in such a way that its presence dominates.

So it was with a comic sense of disappointment that I found my dog-sledding experience described in the frustratingly familiar limited context of adventure as "hardship," where one "lives to tell the tale" and, of course, "roughs it." I was struck with a realization that my attempts to communicate the adventure quest that is a "with" nature orientation and a living history ambience had actually reinforced that which I consciously did not wish to communicate. The against-nature phenomena so annoyingly common to adventure-travel journalism was so easily overlaid on my own staggeringly different orientation.

The writer was simply doing her job of writing a cute adventure piece to be consumed by the armchair traveler and to reinforce the convention of adventure-travel writing. Should I have expected her to want to challenge the readers with the notion of "blood racing" that I was attempting to convey to her? The magazine and journalist know their readership. Or do they? There is little challenge offered the reader. This perpetuates a simplistic, shallow, and detrimental context for humans' engagement with bush travel. Rather than the subtle and humble fit with environment achievable through a felt experience and a sensuous knowing of a place stripped of cultural mapping, my quiet quest became framed within the man-over-nature theme, self-aggrandizing, with even a consumer orientation of humans' options for engagement with nature. This bagging of another peak, river, or historic route exists as a trophy to be scratched from the shopping list. This is another type of engagement altogether.

Consider how "physical hardship," as conveyed in the interview, is an example of misrepresentation. It was a total joy to be out on the land, in a more aimless orientation. We were simply traveling around in caribou country, coming to know the place rather than covering ground. At the time, any hardship amounted only to our growing frustration with the number of fresh caribou tracks, yet no sightings of caribou. We all wanted simply to see caribou in winter. When we did see caribou, it was more a matter-of-factness than a conquest that we felt. The North simply is and it simply asks the same of us. That is simply, to be! Physical hardship did not play a part in any major concern on this trip. Hardship is Toronto, Chicago, Denver rush-hour traffic and getting familiar again to stifling-hot indoor temperatures upon return.

I did have one "popular" risk to physical well-being. It was my first moment on the sled while it was still tied to a small standing spruce. I was to keep up the rear. I watched the two other teams release their anchoring slip knot and head down the trail with wildly excited dogs expressing their relief to be on the trail again, free from their pent-up state in a dog box. (I'm sure we could all empathize with the dogs.) My anchor line and the tree itself were straining with all this excitement. Finally with the right spacing of teams, I yanked, but only tightened my apparent slip knot. Oh, an adventure, I thought. The dogs went into hysterics. They knew what was supposed to have happened. The tree now bent with newfound energy. Native town kids, who had gathered to see us off, laughed hysterically. The other teams were long gone. Seconds passed. I had to be calm and quick. This wasn't easy. I was testing many personal powers.

I was left with one option, to fidget with frantic line and knot with one hand while holding on to the sled with the other. Once freed the sled would fly out like a bull in a rodeo. This was normal, but the extra frustration I had unwittingly caused the dogs I knew would be felt by them. If I could only free this knot. There was a risk of injuring my hand in all this. My pride was long gone.

I was rational but comically in a panic when the dogs and my fidgeting worked together. We were all free. I had held on. The tree had not fared as well. I had survived an adventure.

There are questions of great relevance for adventure education. They are: How does the adventure educator teach a pedagogy that is to be "with" landscape? How can our being adventurous be advanced into a relational and ecological context of being? I think that it is best not to dwell on thoughts and deeds of physical hardship, distance covered, roughing it, "living to tell the tale," and physical fitness. This all seems sadly egotistical with emphasis on a hostile environment, where humanity has no place and "place," the territory, is not perceived as primary. Our challenge, in the closing years of twentieth-century adventure education, is to develop an ecological relationship to nature concerned with the adventure of the spirit.

KIDS' CAMP

Willy Whitefeather

Willy Whitefeather is a river guide and the author of an outdoor survival handbook for kids. He is a mixed-blood Cherokee who believes that if we learn from our heritage roots, we can create a more beautiful world for the next fourteen generations. He is currently teaching desert survival classes to the U.S. Army.

Carry-all Rover at the head of a whole line of cars and trucks snaking up the summer dusty mountain road.

BAM!
KABAM!
JANGLE ...
Laughter as they roll over the bumps and...
SKOOOWASH!
... each time they cross the creek.
Arrival, creek water dripping from axles.
Reevis Mountain School.
The Best. Peter Bigfoot, founder, greeter.
Kids, moms, dads, backpacks all unload.
Dinner together, everybody talks at once.
Sunset. A chorus of "Kumbayah."
Waves and good-byes as the caravan of moms and dads
    leaves.

Stars you can touch. Introductions around the campfire.
    Stories. Sleepy eyes stare into flickering coals.
Campfire-smoky kids crawl into sleeping bags.
Then it begins ...
Giggles.
"Hey, that's my flashlight."
"Naw, it's mine."
"Givvitback, nerdturd!"
"Oh yeah, sure, uh-huh, boogerbrain!"
Laughter.
"Hey, give it back or I'm tellin'!"
"Oh yeah, sure, fishface."
Louder laughter. Laughter from all tents.
"ALL RIGHT, YOU KIDS!" (Counselor Johnny)
    "KNOCK IT OFF! GO TO SLEEP!"
Dawn. Mountains glow. Creek chuckles and sings its
    greeting. Coyotes now quiet, bellies rabbit full.
Breakfast gong. Kids stir. Some pull sleeping bags over
    heads. Scorpions go back under rocks.
Second gonnnnnnnnggggg. Breakfast line ...
"Hey, get outta my way, fishface, I was here first."
"No, you weren't, lamebrain!"
"Was too, boogerhead!"
"HEY! HEY! HEY!" (Counselor) "Knock it off, or you go
    to the back of the line!"
I hear these verbal arrows piercing young spirits — city smog
    words polluting young minds.
ENOUGH! I say to myself.
I go get my shovel, and while they're eating breakfast, I dig a mud
    hole, big enough, and fill it with creek water. Ten paces away from
    my mud hole I put the first pole with feathers on top. Seven paces
    away the second pole goes into the ground.
I put on my swim trunks. I mix the red clay mud, making it thick,
    removing the rocks. Good mud.
I go get my small bag of turquoise stones.
Breakfast over. Bigfoot's teaching a wild plant class. Kids wander by.
"Whatcha doin', Willy?"
"You'll know soon," I reply.
Plant class over. Midday sun.

"HEYYYYY! HIYOHHH, OHHHHH SEEEEE OHHHHH, HIYOHHHH!" I shout. "You kids all gather round. Here is mud, and here is turquoise in this bag. I challenge you. Everyone who hits me with a mudball, I'm going to give a free piece of turquoise." (With a stick I draw a line on the ground.) "And don't step over this line while you throw, and just throw as I run between those two poles over there. You kids couldn't hit me if you tried!"

Twenty screaming kids.

Forty hands in mud, making big, round mudballs.

I run.

WHAP—WHAP—WHAP. Only three hits—an arm, a leg, and an ear. City kids, my luck, they don't know how to lead a moving target. I make a U-turn, running, and they all let loose at me.

Mud flies before my eyes.

"HA-HAH! You kids can't hit me!" I egg them on.

Mudballs fly past.

WHAP—WHAP. Two more hits. Still running, I make another U-turn.

Round three.

They're ready this time.

I clear the first pole.

WHAP— SPLOOK—WHAP—SPLAT! I get slaughtered. I circle round, covered in red clay.

"OKAY! WHO HIT ME?"

Twenty voices: "I DID!"

I hand out the turquoise.

Back to running, I pick up a beat-up old briefcase. I run with it, and screech to a stop between the two poles.

"STOP!" I shout. "Don't any of you kids dare to throw mud at me! You see this briefcase, it's full of important papers. If any mud touches them, I'll call your parents, I'll call the police, I'll put you on report!"

Silence. Some of the kids look unsure, mudballs on standby ready alert …

"YAHHHH!" I yell (tongue out, thumbs in my ears, fingers waggling). "YOU BOUGHT IT!"

I run—too late.

WHAP! SPLAT! WHAP! Me and the briefcase become dripping red clay.

The seventh time around I'm thinking, I'm getting too old for this, but this is a class city schools don't teach.

One more time around, then I stop.

"Okay," I say, "how many of you kids hit me and got free turquoise?"

Twenty hands go up, followed by a din of "I DID!"

"Okay," I say, as I reach into the mud hole and round out a mudball, "now you all get to run, and I get to throw!"

"NO WAY!" they shout. They try to give their turquoise away. There are no takers. They throw it on the ground. They start to walk away. You can cut the air with a knife …

"Okay," I say, "so I hear you kids calling each other 'lamebrain,' 'fishface,' 'boogerhead,' and lots of four-letter words. I did this mud run because I wanted you to know those words go through your skin and into your spirit and damage you for the rest of your life. This mud you threw at me is only on my skin, it washes off, it's fun. Since you won't run, it shows me YOU CAN DISH IT OUT, BUT YOU CAN'T TAKE IT!"

I walk away (pretending to be angry). Now you need a machete to cut the air.

About an hour later they come around to my tent and say sheepishly, "Hey, uh, Willy?"

"Yeah?" I say.

"We kinda, uh, well …"

"That's okay," I say. "No apologies needed. You guys wanna go backpackin' along the creek?"

"Yeah! All right!" And soon we head up the trail. Lesson learned.

A Note: I do the mud run because I feel kids today have a lot of stress and no outlet for their hostility and resentments. Spray-can painting on walls and shootings in restaurants are their release valve for anger and pent-up emotions—instead of mudballs, it's bullets, booze, and drugs.

Politicians with briefcases use the word "mudslinging," but that's all it is, just a word. Try throwing a real mudball at one of them and you'll do jail time. You can't throw mud at a grown man in this country without being beat up, shot, or jailed. They have lost joy. Mud is joy. Joy is laughing children throwing mudballs at you and forgetting the cutting words they use on each other, learned from grown-ups.

As for you, Dear Reader, you couldn't hit the broad side of a barn—YA-HAH!

REFLECTIONS ON AN OUTDOOR EDUCATION EXPERIENCE

J. Gary Knowles

J. Gary Knowles is a visiting professor at the Ontario Institute for Studies in Education at the University of Toronto. For over twelve years he worked as a secondary-school teacher and principal in South Pacific countries (including Australia, New Zealand, Fiji, and Papua New Guinea) with a focus on employing the out-of-doors as medium and vehicle for learning about history, geography, social and natural science, and a whole host of other topics. "Reflections on an Outdoor Education Experience" is edited and excerpted from the original, which first appeared in the May 1992 issue of the *Journal of Experiential Education.*

> *This sudden splash into pure wilderness—baptism in Nature's warm heart—how utterly happy it made us! Nature streaming into us, wooingly teaching her wonderful glowing lessons, so unlike the dismal grammar ashes and cinders so long thrashed into us. Here without knowing it we still were at school; every wild lesson a love lesson, not whipped but charmed into us.*
>
> —JOHN MUIR

The nights were getting cooler, the days shorter; winter would soon arrive. For the present, we were immersed in our outdoor "school" activities. The Auckland, New Zealand, high school was conducting its first week-long outdoor education program in a rural setting. The fifty students included Australians, Tongans, Samoans, Cook Island Maoris, Nuieans, and other Pacific Islanders, besides New Zealand Pakehas (whites) and Maoris. Their socioeconomic family environments were as diverse as their racial and ethnic origins, but in the camp setting they lived, worked and studied together with considerable harmony.

Situated on the shores of Lake Karipiro, the site of Camp Finlay provided a varied environment for the learning of outdoor pursuits and academic-based field activities. Considerable time was spent teaching the rudiments of canoeing and kayaking, and a cool autumn evening provided an opportunity for adventure.

The plan was simple. We were to paddle across Lake Karipiro to a small tributary stream. The hill moon, glowing in the clear sky, beckoned us. It was a perfect night for canoeing. The fifteen or so canoeists donned warm flannels, woolens, and life jackets. Each canoe, kayak, and paddler was linked with another according to a buddy system. With an instructor at the "bow" and "stern" of the flotilla, the aim was to keep the group tightly together.

Silence was the key. From the outset, there was to be no unnecessary audible communication—quite a task for thirteen- and fourteen-year-olds. There were waterfowl nesting on the far side of the lake we did not want to disturb, and, besides, if everyone kept silent, emergencies could readily be detected. We anxiously paddled across the expanse of water, our eyes straining to penetrate the darkness and interpret the eerie forms that loomed ahead. Soon, eyes became accustomed to the night and confidence soared. No longer were the timid secretly wishing to turn back. All we heard was a gentle swishing as each craft glided through the dark waters, the hooting of a morepork (a native owl), water dripping from paddle blades as alternating strokes were made, the occasional arrogant and indignant screech of pukeko, and the croaking of the ubiquitous frogs. It was a serene way to conclude a hectic day.

Soon we reached the tributary stream. We entered a narrow gorge with sheer cliffs on either side of the stream that seemed to stretch up to the heavens and topple in on us. We cowered, nearly enshrined by their mammoth size. The going was now considerably more difficult as the paddlers had to contend with the gentle yet persistent current as well as the numerous root snags and overhanging vegetation. The steep-sided banks were moist and cool and glistened with silvery heads of dew dancing on spiders' webs. Above us were the myriad stars of the Southern Hemisphere Milky Way and the warm, reassuring glow of the full moon.

We rounded a bend and I heard gasps and sighs, even squeals of delight. We had emerged upon an earthly Milky Way: There above us, and on either side, was the illumination from innumerable glow worms. It was breathtaking. Each tiny glow came from a single phosphorescent, light-emitting creature.

This tiny glow worm is a marvel of creation. At the end of its caterpillar-like body, a luminous light is produced. Glow worms feed by producing what appears to be a long thread of silk on which hang a series of mucous droplets, giving the appearance of a pearl-like string of beads. In the darkness, small flies and midges are drawn to the glow worms' light, only to become ensnared in the sticky droplets of mucous. Quickly the glow worms draw up the fishing line and eat their prey.

Suspended like delicate jewels, these larvae of the fungus gnat had emerged to feed, their diffused glow reflecting on the faces of the exuberant students. Once before I had seen faint green glows on the faces of fellow night explorers and that was the occasion of a shimmering southern lights (aurora australis) display. Here, we had our own display, which could be lost in an instant, for if we made excessive noise, the glowing lights would extinguish as if we had some great invisible switch at our fingertips. With the gentle hooting of a morepork far in the distance, the canoeists and kayakers quietly continued upstream, without a hint of conversation. Soon the gorge opened up like the mouth of a great whale, and we left the glow worms behind.

We gathered our craft together at the large bend in the stream. It was appropriate to rest a moment, and, in the serenity of the night, we laid open our thoughts. Alternately, we listened intently to the night and to each other. I was silent, allowing Nature to speak—and speak She did. The occasional echo of bleating ewes and lambs was heard and a family of sparrows in the scrub seemed to have their feathers ruffled about something. We spoke our thoughts about the week's activities, our paddling exploits, the glow worms, and the simple beauty and serenity of the place. We marveled at the organization and design of Nature's panoramic night display. Heads poured out expressions of wonder and praise for the tiny glow worm. For the first time, many students felt the power and beauty of nature.

We huddled together, afloat on the ever-so-gentle eddies in the middle of the stream. The night was colder now, but we hardly noticed in our awe and praise for the night's revelation. It was almost midnight, several hours since we began our journey. Young Joni's mother would have had "fits" if she had known. And Ngaire's mother—would she have slept? Regretfully, we maneuvered our craft for the journey back through the gorge and across the lake. We reverently glided past the glow worms. When we entered the lake, the lights from the camp stood out like lone beacons, drawing us, just as the glow worms had, but these were ever so paled, as human efforts always seem next to those of Nature.

Wearily, the night venturers beached their craft and reluctantly climbed the hill to camp, sad to have left the glow worms' place. But an inkling of joy also bubbled beneath the surface, for they had an experience to share and, like the glow from the fungus gnats, it was plain to see. From that time on, the journey to the glow worm grotto was the sought-after peak experience at Karipiro Camp.

To have huddled on the river in the gently swirling flow of the stream nearly two decades ago was extremely important to me. For most of the students, it was a peak experience. Several parents and students have attested to the lasting impressions that were formed. While the description I have portrayed is clearly my perception of the night, my role as the person responsible for the school's outdoor education venture was intertwined with the students' perspectives. Thus, the event became central to my thinking about the benefits of experiential learning. I was an integral member of the group, yet the facilitator and a mute leader. Upon reflection, it was my greatest teaching moment. I was silent.

No longer did I feel uncomfortable with silence in the outdoor classroom. There were other forces that could teach. Nor was I shackled to the conventions of the formal classroom like so many of my fellow teachers. I now wanted them to have an experience like mine, to feel the gentle strength of the eddies, the enticement of the glowing fishermen, the invitation of the Milky Way, and the recognition that awareness of self does not necessarily come at the hands of teachers, but rather as the result of some empowering situation. My silence in the classroom was contrasted by my eager talk of the event afterward. How could I be silent about such an experience? The towering cliffs, the bush, the glow worms, the bend in the stream—these were all elements of a place that came to be sacred in my thinking.

I had often wondered what real spirituality would be like. I grew up in a nominal Christian environment, went to Sunday School, and later in my life, sought greater meaning in seeking to know God, but with relatively sterile results. Later I worked in a Christian private school, yet often found myself defeating one of the purposes of the school—to make God more meaningful to students. In my mind, and in the minds of several students, on that night a sacred place was established. It was the site of a special event, a place, if you will, where individuals united with the powers of Nature. And, for the first time in my career, the meaning of my teaching mission became clear.

For two years prior to this event, I had grappled with philosophical questions concerning the value of the exclusive use of classroom settings for children's learning. Why were so many teachers bound to the four walls of the conventional classroom? Why the emphasis on vicarious and artificial learning from textbooks and other media forms? Why were teachers unable to place greater responsibility for learning on the shoulders of the students themselves? What happened to children's sense of wonder and excitement so evident in their curiosity before they enter school? The answers to these and a host of other questions were illuminated as I reflected that night, and later, upon earlier events and the outdoor education activities of the week.

On leaving the glow worms that autumn night, I knew where to direct my future energies. I understood more about the relevance and value of learning in the out-of-doors. But more important, that night I believed in what I saw and felt. It was possible to seek the development of the complete child—intellectually, physically, emotionally, and spiritually. The out-of-doors could provide an important vehicle for learning. While not all students would benefit in the same kinds of ways from the use of outdoor environments, using the outdoors would make possible the satisfaction of a greater number of children's needs than is often possible in more confining settings. To be sure, outdoor education would be no panacea for educational ills, but it could go a long way in the hands of sensitive teachers— the kind I wanted to be.

As the students and I discovered, adolescents can benefit from spontaneous, out-of-doors learning experiences. By opening the doors on the confines of the classroom, teachers may open up vast opportunities to students for whom school has had little meaning. Through the experience of discovering their own sacred places—genuine, uncontrived experiences, not preplanned events—students may come to better know themselves. By discovering new perspectives on knowing, and experiencing successes in the out-of-doors, students may begin to perceive their own personal potential for success back in the environs of the formal classroom. And perhaps most important, through learning and exploring the natural world, the potential for developing the whole individual is awakened. As Muir spoke of his youthful experience, I contend that more students need to experience Nature's "wonderful glowing lessons," not to escape from reality, but rather to enter into it more fully, with a keener sense of place and self, and a sound base for experiencing life.

WILDERNESS REVISITED:
The Twilight's Last Gleaming

Michael J. Cohen

Michael J. Cohen, Ed.D., coordinates Project NatureConnect, an environmental activities training division of The University of Global Education. Michael conceived, founded, and, for twenty-seven years, directed the National Audubon Society Expedition Institute. He is the author of seven books, including *Well Mind, Well Earth; How Nature Works;* and *Reconnecting with Nature*. "Wilderness Revisited: The Twilight's Last Gleaming" is adapted from Dr. Cohen's articles in the *Proceedings* of the 1991 national conference of the North American Association for Environmental Education.

> *The senses, being the explorers of the world, open the way to knowledge.*
> —MARIA MONTESSORI

Deep in the bowels of Grand Canyon National Park, a spectacle of color and towering cliffs marks the place where Bright Angel Creek joins the Colorado River. There, in 1966, a thunderstorm on a broiling August day cracked my twentieth-century prejudices about life and the land.

To keep cool in this desert country, I hiked shirtless. Occasionally, I munched potato chips to maintain my body's salt level. As I crossed the bridge spanning the muddy Colorado, my hand touched my surprisingly icy stomach. My years of scientific training went to work: *This is a cooling mechanism. Evaporating sweat molecules carry away excess body heat, leaving this residue of salt on my skin.* It never occurred to me that miracles, not just molecules, keep my body temperate while the sun scorches the world about me.

Thunderclouds moved in from the southwest. "Now you're going to see something amazing," I told the twenty expedition members who accompanied me. "As the thunderstorm rains, the heat evaporates the raindrops. We'll see the rain fall, but we won't get wet down here." We were a mile below the rim.

I knew this would happen. It had happened almost every year on this outdoor learning trek, which I inaugurated in 1959. The expedition students looked skeptical, but the prospect of a "dry" storm excited them. The dark clouds rolled in and poured torrents, drenching us while we stood agape.

"Hey, look everybody, I'm really dry," taunted one soaked girl, while smirking group members scurried for cover, gleefully mumbling, "Oh sure, Mike, it *never* rains in the Grand Canyon."

But the skies opened up and rain it did. Quickly the canyon cooled. Like soap suds rinsed from shampooed hair, the red sands and clays of the Grand Canyon sloshed over the thousand-foot inner gorge walls that loomed above us. Everywhere, blood-red water cascaded and the roaring river turned from tan to murky maroon. The trembling canyon felt like a vein gathering and carrying blood. For a moment, I sensed we were in a gigantic organism's bloodstream. The flowing landscape seemed alive. And just like my evaporating sweat had cooled me, evaporating rain now cooled the canyon, furthering this sense of aliveness.

As I watched Grand Canyon salts run downriver to the sea, I wondered, *Why does the sea never become too salty, or the land never too hot for life?* It was then I first sensed Planet Earth as a living organism, which knows how to survive. To survive, the wilderness and I must deal with becoming too hot, cold, salty or toxified. The living planet's biology, geology and chemistry are its metabolism; night-day, night-day, night-day its heartbeat. Warm evaporating inland seas serve as kidneys; air and water are plasma. In congress, all aspects of Earth compose a planet-size intelligence, a wise gigantic self-regulating plant cell whose life approaches perfection. The cell knows how to organize, preserve and regenerate itself and how to create its diverse life without pollution, war or insanity.

Self-doubt possessed me. This was 1966, sixteen years before I heard of the Gaia hypothesis, three years before James Lovelock even conceived it. My understanding of Gaia grew as I learned that every eighty million years the salt content of the sea doubles, but the sea never becomes more saline; Mars and Venus, the two planets surrounding Earth, become warmer as the sun gets hotter, but Earth's temperature stays within the limits necessary for life's existence; and our atmosphere maintains oxygen in amounts neither too great nor too small for all life to survive.

Scientific findings continue to validate what I sensed that day in the Grand Canyon. They show that life will succumb to overwhelming chemical and physical forces without regulation and regeneration. Recent findings indicate that Planet Earth's biology, physiology and geology are tightly linked into a single indivisible process. "Organism Earth" shows every sign of life. That's why this idea lives within me.

Learning by Sensing

In the fall of 1969, one of my wilderness fantasies became reality. On that day, my modified yellow school bus, carrying outdoor equipment and a small library, picked up twenty college students and headed for an extraordinary campus. Fueled by a passion to live and teach close to the land, wild America became our classroom and textbook. We spent an intimate, challenging school year camping out across the United States. In consultation with experts from many disciplines, we immersed ourselves in the natural world. Cradled in consensus decisions and intense encounters, we created a unique accredited education. I have lived, researched, and taught outdoors continuously ever since and the most practical skill I've learned is the secret of how to let wilderness teach us about itself. My nature-connecting activities share that secret with anyone.

Our prevalent social and environmental irresponsibility confirms that what is called civilization is bewildered, meaning "strayed from the wilderness." To sense this, I asked my students to visit an attractive natural area and place a thick mitten on one of their hands, then blow on their hands, kiss them, pinch them, sprinkle them with soil, cry on them. They touched the dew on a wildflower and softly stroked plants and rocks. One participant said, "The gloved hand was warmer and more protected, but it felt very little or not at all." Another: "It sensed things differently than did the bare hand; it was numb to texture, form, motions, pain and touch."

This exercise helps us sense how major problems might result from a person living the first twenty years of their life in a mitten or a closet. Studies indicate that Americans, on average, spend over 95 percent of their time indoors. Even when we're outside, we mostly act, think and believe in cultural ways, ways foreign to Nature's sentient callings. We often do not pay attention to the natural world's callings because we are not in tune with them. Wilderness is "the environment," "outside." It is not us. Predictably, our problems result from our extreme sensory separation from our origins and lifestream.

Our wilderness-separated thinking has become excessive and runaway. For example, we legally require that 18,000 childhood hours be spent closeted indoors in public schools, strengthening "the three R's." As our problems increase, many believe even more such isolated hours are needed. We cannot see that through excessive indoor schooling and indoor relationships, we learn to disown our wilderness senses. Unlike more balanced societies, our upbringing seldom exercises or validates our earthy senses because we find them rude and uncivilized. *We subtly learn that Nature is our illiterate enemy. Nature is to be conquered, not extolled.* This belief is why we feel free to excessively and guiltlessly bomb, bulldoze, poison, cut, exploit and destroy wilderness. We condone the process as intelligent survival, improvement, progress. We negate our natural outcries as we negate other natural things, such as other species, indigenous cultures, people of color, women, children and caring, sensitive men. Senses are not materials so they are immaterial; they are not matter so they don't matter. Note that Satan, the biblical explanation for our problems, is Nature: he has fur, horns, claws, scales, forked hoofs and a tail, he's found in the wilderness and he's seldom a white person.

Antidotes

Too often we forget that Nature's congress of senses is intelligent. In exactly the same way that it has the wisdom to heal an injured landscape, it also knows how to heal our cuts, burns and emotional wounds. This may account for the success of wilderness, indigenous and holistic therapies. I find that when modern people connect with wilderness, they feel more intensely and cooperate more easily. As wilderness activities awaken our sensory roots, they therapeutically ground us to Nature's peace.

Imagine a group of citizens, picnic baskets in hand, walking into a cathedral and chopping up the pews for firewood, roasting hot dogs on the holy candles, strewing litter throughout the sacred areas, carving graffiti, firing bullets and throwing hatchets into the columns, excreting in the holy water before washing their dishes in it, and then telling the Archbishop to clean up the mess. No citizen would do this, because the very nature of sacred places awakens senses that prevent this from happening. Even in war, we seldom bomb enemy cathedrals. People who treasure their natural senses develop a similar reverence for wilderness. Wilderness becomes sacred, their cathedral, their spirituality, and they actively protect it.

For me, hope arises from outdoor activities that empower people to incorporate Nature's wisdom into their lives. These activities act as responsible rituals and therapy. They mandate that our honed senses of reason and language awaken, enjoy, trust, celebrate, integrate and act off our many other natural senses. They catalyze lasting bonds to the global community. They help us unashamedly love wildness, Earth and each other, because balanced life feels good.

VI

In Mourning, Defense, and Celebration of the Earth

*F*oremost in my mind, in gathering this anthology, was the need to convey the broader spirit of the human and personal relationship—not politically motivated—that we all share with nature. I have intentionally not gathered a lot of emotionally charged essays that moralize about how we *should* protect wild areas, *should* become active in saving endangered species, and *should* educate and campaign the masses about the complex and troubling issues that we face environmentally. And yet, at the same time, it is clearly important to see the seriousness of the current damage our planet is experiencing and to meet the challenges we face regarding wilderness preservation and protection.

Of all the book's chapters, this one is the most political in its tone. Within the grief, anger, and despair we feel about the current status of the natural world, I hope to liberate, celebrate, and name the joy and peace we experience as a result of contact with wildness. It is my belief that the most effective and thoughtful political action ultimately comes from joy and gratitude, and not from shortsighted and impulsive reactions.

However, I suspect that even outright monkey wrenching—violent acts against perceived threats to wilderness—has its place. Extreme behavior and political actions serve to get our attention and to remind us of what is important to us and why we value wilderness. Without extremist wilderness advocates, some of us more complacent moderates might not become active and encourage change—educating ourselves about the environmentally sensitive issues in our neck of the woods, writing our congresspeople, attending town meetings, and casting our votes on important environmental bills and for political representatives with whom we agree on environmental issues.

Some of these essays are politically colored in their content, but they are also deeply personal, born out of a strongly felt love of nature and of wild creatures. As a way of balancing the intensity of such views, I have built the overall mood of this section around the theme of celebration of the earth, reflecting the entire anthology as a full-on festive and triumphant praising of wildness.

The Peace of Wild Things

Wendell Berry

An essayist, novelist, and poet, Wendell Berry is the author of more than thirty books. He has received numerous awards, including, most recently, the T. S. Eliot Award, the Lyndhurst Prize, and the Aitken-Taylor Award for Poetry from *The Sewanee Review*. He lives and works with his wife, Tanya Berry, in Kentucky.

> When despair for the world grows in me
> and I wake in the night at the least sound
> in fear of what my life and my children's lives may be,
> I go and lie down where the wood drake
> rests in his beauty on the water, and the great heron feeds.
> I come into the peace of wild things
> who do not tax their lives with forethought
> of grief. I come into the presence of still water.
> And I feel above me the day-blind stars
> waiting with their light. For a time
> I rest in the grace of the world, and am free.

In the Eye of the Hurricane:
An Interview with John Seed

Kaia Svien

John Seed is founder and director of the Rainforest Information Centre in Australia. Since 1979, he has participated in campaigns and direct action that have resulted in the protection of many rain forests throughout the world. With Joanna Macy, he cocreated the "Council of All Beings" workshop and coauthored the book, *Thinking Like a Mountain — Towards a Council of All Beings* (New Society Publishers, 1988). He coproduced the film, *Earth First*, for ABC TV, the story of how the Australian rain forests were saved. In 1995, he was awarded the Order of Australia medal by the Australian government for services to the conservation of nature.

Kaia Svien is a mindfulness instructor, a writer, and a community activist. She writes, speaks about, and makes ceremony from the Ancient Wisdom of Europe as a means to connect European Americans with their nature-based spiritual roots. She was inspired to interview John Seed because of his ability to articulate and personalize the vision that is the foundation of some powerful experiential work that helps humans to recognize their bonds to other species. "In the Eye of the Hurricane" is edited and excerpted from an original transcript that was first printed in the Winter 1992/1993 issue of *Reconciliation International*.

KAIA SVIEN: John, many people consider you the world's most outspoken rain forest advocate. The *Christian Science Monitor* refers to you as "the town crier of the global village." How do you think of yourself and how does your story as an activist begin?

JOHN SEED: I am a global environmentalist, an activist, a singer, a workshop leader, an organizer. I use all the resources I have to inform people about the condition of the environment and then to inspire them to do something to change it.

It started for me in 1979 when I was living in the hills outside Lismore, Australia, practicing Buddhism and, along with my community, growing a wide variety of fruit trees and veggies for our sustenance. Then, about six miles away, the Forestry Commission decided to log the last remaining rain forest in our area. Before long, the sounds of chain saws were cutting through my daily meditations. Standing on that intense line where humankind meets the wild, I found myself not with the humans with their chain saws and bulldozers, but, rather, I stood with the trees and critters, facing the humans and saying stop! Here, after the years of sitting [meditation], of turning inward, the forest deemed me ripe and plucked my heart so I could hear the cries of the earth within me, so that I could feel my ancient roots in this forest, and pushed me back "out" among the world of nature, the world of politics. Though, of course, this is all "in" as well.

KAIA: Which precepts of Buddhism guide your philosophy now?

JOHN: I try to be harmless to all living things, I practice compassion and insight and, of course, practice nonattachment to the fruits as I watch forest after forest disappear, and live with the knowledge that even those that are saved are only saved very temporarily, for unless the atmosphere, the hydrological cycle, the soil and all the life-support systems are saved, unless the planet is saved, nothing is saved at all.

KAIA: The work that you are probably best known for, at least in the United States, is the Council of All Beings. The essence of this workshop is ritual. Why do you think that rituals are so important?

JOHN: Well, it is only in the so-called civilized world that humans have ever thought we were able to dispense with ritual and that somehow our brain, our reason, was sufficient to look after us. And yet you only have to look to see where that has got us. We know everything, but we don't know enough to stop destroying the biological fabric out of which we are woven. Now this generation is about to oversee the destruction of that biological fabric. I believe that this destruction has a lot to do with the sense that "we know everything, we're so wise, we're so rational, we've passed through the Age of Enlightenment" and so on. The incredible arrogance of this culture that believes it can conquer even nature! I think that our belief that we can conquer nature as though we are not a part of nature ourselves is part of the same process as our starting to relegate rituals to the position of mere superstition.

Every culture other than ours finds the necessity to have ritual and ceremony at the very center of their social lives — occasions where people get the chance to affirm and nourish that sense of interconnectedness, and to push back the sense of alienation and the illusion of separation from nature that modern humans are so prone to. Having done away with ritual, we now believe in this illusion and believe that we are separate from nature and so we are about to destroy nature altogether.

KAIA: Do you think it is because people feel separate from the earth that they seem to be unconcerned about environmental destruction?

JOHN: I think so. This is another area where we are very foolish in our culture. We deny our feelings about what has happened to earth. Most people are unwilling to acknowledge and to honor the feelings of grief and rage considering what is happening to our planet. Or we may allow ourselves to know about it, but we won't allow ourselves to feel it. And denial of this feeling, first of all, takes up a tremendous amount of energy, and so we have no energy left to struggle. It also takes away a lot of our intelligence because we imagine that our intelligence is somehow limited to our cerebral cortex and we won't acknowledge the fact that our feelings are an important part of intelligence.

KAIA: It seems to me that you are able to hover over a place of joy and connection. How do you move through grief and outrage to get there?

JOHN: I'm not sure that it is a particular piece of bad news that I somehow turn into joy. It's more the fact that I involve various levels of ritual and ceremony that express acknowledgment of the sacredness of the earth and my interconnectedness with the earth. The Council of All Beings is the place where I can most easily let myself feel what's really happening to the earth. I allow myself to open up to all my feelings, to let them come up fully. Then I feel my roots go down deep into the earth for certain kinds of nourishment. Certain kinds of wisdom become accessible to me. I am re-assured that the world as a whole is OK. The earth doesn't lose it and become hysterical. I am part of that earth; I can manifest that same calm. When joy wells up, I feel the connection between all beings. I know, once again, that the truth doesn't hurt us. Truth saves us and however pleasant or unpleasant that truth, if we can cleave to the truth, joy and enormous creativity will always be part of that.

It's important to remember that we ourselves are natural. When we put a lot of blame on ourselves, saying, "Oh, we are cancer destroying the earth," it's good to recall that cancer is natural. Even we, in our denial and our destructiveness, are part of the whole. There are obviously a number of possible scenarios for our future but all of them leave us guilt-free in the end because we are just an expression of the earth. If we are destroying the earth, then we are an expression of the earth destroying itself and that's quite a noble task. Let's say that the earth is dead already. Then we could be the maggots that are now chewing on the world. So whatever it is that is happening, we're doing exactly what we're meant to be doing and that may or may not include evolving to a higher consciousness. What we call more complex life may be about to disappear from the earth or it may be that we are about to undergo some transformation in our human commu-nity that—in the nick of time—is going to prevent that from happening. But whatever our future is, it's a totally natural outcome, the unfolding of an organic network of which we are part. We can see, then, that the lament, "Oh, I am so worthless, I am destroying the earth," is part of the false separation. To take all of that blame, that sickness, into ourselves is to buy the concept of separation that first got humankind into this crisis. We are part of the earth. We eat the earth, we drink the earth, our bodies come out of the earth and return to the earth. If there is something wrong with us, it means that there is something wrong with the earth.

KAIA: John, it sounds to me like you have moved to a place of acceptance of whatever will be, including the possibility that higher mammals may not roam the earth fifty years from now. I don't hear outrage at other humans; you have just said that blaming ourselves is part of the illness of alienation. And yet, you have not given up. On the contrary, you seem to have given yourself quite fully to the possibility that humans will awaken to this crisis. You craft your life around that likelihood, moving from land to land, singing, reporting on the destruction, giving workshops. Your face lines tell that you grin a lot, your body says it's relaxed. Where are you, John?

JOHN: I'm here with you, a being who feels her connection to the planet. I'm sitting close to another amazing being with strong, rough bark for skin and tendrils so delicate they suck nutrients from the soil and I hear another winged being trilling between our words. So, in every moment, I am surrounded by wonder and beauty in myriad forms. I am also in the eye of the hurricane. Yes, I look as clearly as I can at the reports of destruction. I release all my hopes and pleas that such things are not so. With that release, tremendous energy is freed up for me to calmly accept the state of things as they are and to create passionately and lovingly all that I can to change the flow. I stay in touch with my wild love for beings of all kinds as much as possible so as to nourish myself and so as to model for others that it is safe here. You can open your eyes to what is happening and not go crazy or you can lose yourself in endless depression. It is good here. I am present to as much of earth as I can be. I am awake to my life.

ONE BY ONE

Constance Perenyi

Constance Perenyi has written and illustrated two children's books, *Growing Wild: Inviting Wildlife into Your Back Yard* (Beyond Words, 1991) and *Wild Wild West* (Sasquatch Books, 1993). In addition to her ongoing volunteer commitment at oil-spill clinics, she has worked for two years at HOWL Wildlife Rehabilitation Clinic near Seattle. Constance's experiences with wildlife reinforce for her the importance of preserving habitat, be it an old tree in a city park or a pristine mountain meadow. "One by One" originally appeared in *Living Bird*, the quarterly publication of Cornell University's Laboratory of Ornithology.

It wasn't until I worked at an emergency oil-spill clinic that I stopped observing animals at a distance. Surrounded by injured birds, I could not separate myself from their vulnerability. I was sickened by the oil on their feathers, evidence of human insensitivity to the environment. At the same time, I was heartened by the actions of my fellow volunteers. Once state agencies or local wildlife rehabilitation experts set up a clinic, it is primarily the volunteers who keep it afloat by donating supplies and energy. Most volunteers hear about an accident on news broadcasts and decide to help for a few hours, days, or weeks. Many arrive without animal-handling skills, but all come with a commitment to learn.

Looking back at three clinics I've worked at, I recall different lessons from each. My first clinic, in a gymnasium thirty-nine miles north of Seattle, seemed like an adventure—a chance to practice what I had learned as a keeper's aide in the waterfowl unit at the Seattle Zoo. Because I had pertinent training, or thought I did, the coordinator asked me to force-feed a group of buffleheads and goldeneyes. They were small birds, I had small hands, so it seemed logical.

I immediately realized how unprepared I was to pick up a wild creature. I reminded myself that no one, not even a veterinarian or professional trainer, knew instinctively how to handle animals. These skills are learned. After several hesitant attempts, I grabbed a bufflehead, pried open its beak, and pushed a dab of moistened food down its throat with my little linger. I worked to perfect my technique, trying to move quickly without further stressing the bewildered birds. To this day, I smile when I think of those dozens of tiny duck tongues.

In contrast to the pleasant memories of that first spill, my memory of the most recent one is colored by desperation. Two days before Christmas '88, a tugboat rammed a tanker near Gray's Harbor, southwest of Seattle. Oil soon spread south to Oregon and north to British Columbia. Officials initially underestimated the gravity of the worst accident in Washington history, and they were reluctant to enlist aid. First asking for help only from experienced volunteers, the Washington Department of Ecology later enlisted less-experienced people who traveled from as far away as California and Canada to help.

By the time the first wave of volunteers arrived, three critical days had passed. Inadequate supplies of hot water at a temporary clinic hampered washing efforts. Some of the rarer birds, such as a rhinoceros auklet and a few loons, were washed immediately after recovery from the beach, but hundreds of common murres, pigeon guillemots, western grebes, and various scoters sat in oil for nearly a week. As the birds anxiously preened, they swallowed the toxic oil coating their feathers. Each day without a clinic bath lessened their already slim chances of survival.

I joined other volunteers trying to keep the unwashed birds fed and hydrated until we could move them to better facilities. Exhausted after my first day at the clinic, I checked into the motel, tried to rest, and awoke abruptly. I looked around the room and thought I saw shadows of murres and guillemots on the floor. They broke in dark waves against the bed, vanishing every time I reached out. I forced myself to go back to sleep, and then dreamed about a small white-winged scoter I had held during the day. Unlike the other birds, this one was quiet. I stared at the soiled feathers on her back and sheltered her head with my hand. As I rocked her, her heartbeat weakened and I repeated, "I'm sorry, I'm so sorry." For weeks afterward, I fought to rid myself of this nightmare and often woke in tears.

Time has passed. The dreams have faded, but not the scars on my hands. These commemorate the feisty energy of the murres and my often unsuccessful attempts to catch them without getting caught first. Jousting with one after another, I learned to respect their tenacity. Even weak birds could be formidable. During my final days at Gray's Harbor, I overheard a coordinator instructing new recruits in the art of handling western grebes. He believed the longer-necked, sharply beaked species to be the most dangerous and difficult to control.

"Just be grateful we don't have any cormorants," he concluded. "They're the worst."

On the dawn of another Christmas, in 1985, I took a ferry from Seattle to the Olympic Peninsula and signed the volunteer roster in Port Angeles, where a spill had just occurred. All morning I prepared birds to be washed. Before the first rinse, each bird received preliminary veterinary care: antibiotic injections, protective salve for its eyes, and a careful beak swabbing to remove residual oil from its mouth. Then the tedious scrubbing process began, with volunteers carrying birds back and forth from sudsy washtubs to the showers until every feather was rinsed clean.

Volunteers at emergency spill clinics are generally divided into two groups: feeders who work with clean birds and washers who are confined to the locker rooms. The people with the oiliest clothes work with the dirtiest birds and pass them on to cleaner volunteers as the washing progresses. At Port Angeles, I started with dirty birds; by noon sticky oil had chewed holes through my rubberized overalls. Here was proof of the corrosive properties of petrochemicals. While I could not see the oil's long-term effect inside the birds, I knew the oil on their feathers was deadly. Unwashed, these creatures were helpless—they could not fly, they could not float, they could not stay warm.

I, at least, could take off my useless overalls. Once I had peeled to a cleaner layer, the washroom coordinator handed me a double-crested cormorant that had been de-oiled. My task was specific: to clean each feather on its head with a water-pik. For hours I sat on a folding chair with the bird balanced between my legs and the pik humming on a table next to us. With one hand, I supported the cormorant's neck. With the other, I focused the water and combed the feathers in short methodical strokes.

I began the process cautiously, watching the bird while it noted my every move. Earlier, a veterinary technician had closed its sharp beak so the bird could not bite or spear its handlers. But when the cormorant began to blow bubbles through its elongated nostrils, I removed the band. It instantly relaxed and seemed more curious than dangerous.

At once I realized that this was an extraordinary opportunity. I had handled captive birds at the zoo, and wild ones at other clinics, but I had never examined one so closely. I had relied on mounted specimens and photographs for details. I had filled my head with facts and could, for example, recite the range of avian body temperature. But until that day, the figures had remained abstract. As I sensed the cormorant's damp body heat radiating through my clothes, I experienced warm-bloodedness in a new way. The bird and I exchanged body heat everywhere we touched. I could feel impressions of webbed feet on my legs and feather marks all along the inside of my arms.

Unlike others around us, this bird appeared healthy and unafraid. As it looked around the room, the cormorant seemed to watch the day unfold as a spectacle rather than a trauma. It was calm and seemed willing to cooperate, which enabled me to consider every feather tract I cleaned. The more I contemplated the depth of its blackness, the more detail I perceived. Points of turquoise outlined pale green eyes. Burnt-orange skin marked the bird's throat in colorful, featherless contrast. Against my skin, its snaky neck and armored feet felt reptilian. I could even feel its small flexible gular pouch.

As the afternoon unfolded, the bird became my sole focus. Earlier in the day, I had yielded to every distraction, watching other people, even checking the clock. But as I worked with the cormorant, I became oblivious to the hectic activity around us. I shut out the noise to concentrate on my task, and soon it seemed as if the bird and I were the only beings in the room.

Outside, a few miles down the beach, state ecologists surveyed the oil slick and assessed its impact on a large population of over-wintering birds. None of us could reverse the damage, but I knew that by working on the problem at its most elemental level, I had found a way to make amends with a single bird.

For five hours I had enjoyed the company of another creature and I regretted ending our time together. Reluctantly, I lowered the cormorant into a pool with other birds. This was the final test: if it could float, its feathers were oil free. The bird swam off and the washroom volunteers cheered. The cormorant looked strong, and after it regained energy and natural oils, other volunteers would release it on a clean shoreline miles from where it had been found.

Release was weeks away, and I realized I would never know this cormorant's fate. The mortality rate of animals rescued from oil spills is depressingly high. Even if they outlive capture and cleaning, many later succumb to lethal doses of ingested oil. And of those released, few remain capable of reproduction. On that day, I did not dwell on the statistics. I like to think that the cormorant is alive. If a bird can be said to express a will to live, this one seemed to do so.

It is the hope of saving even a few animals that motivates volunteers at an oil-spill clinic. Confronted by death, we work hard to preserve life. We do what we can and in the process we are changed. Like other volunteers, I have returned home with a stronger commitment to conservation and a new appreciation of life. In the end, I realize my efforts with the birds have helped me more than I could ever hope to help the birds.

THE PASAR BURUNG

Eric Paul Shaffer

Eric Paul Shaffer, long an accidentally expatriate writer of poetry, fiction, and nonfiction, currently teaches American literature and English composition on Maui. *Portable Planet* (Leaping Dog Press, 2000), poems of his eight years in Okinawa, Japan, Indonesia, and America, explores what defines particular places, what it means to be native, how to participate in the spirit of a place, and how to leave no traces as he celebrates wildness and wilderness. He is also the author of *Living at the Monastery, Working in the Kitchen* (Leaping Dog Press, 2001), a book of poems, and the editor of *How I Read Gertrude Stein* (Grey Fox Press, 1996), a study of the works of Stein by Lew Welch.

Was Hell on Earth, stifling, hot, crowded with cages
shit all over the sidewalks, urchins and old men
crouched in dark stalls, cocks stalking
the dirty narrow paths, crowing at cocks
behind bars, puppies puking in wooden boxes too small
to turn around, bellies bulging below like little balls
of Buddha, whining or staring at walls too close to noses, birds
crying every conceivable call, parrot screech, sparrow
twitter, myna mocking, the windy song of the Zebra Dove
    hung high
in the dark thatch above, cat and kitten panting, left
in the dusty sun without water—this I could not stand,
    moving them
to the shade, the boy running up grabbing my hand yelling,
"Dua-ribu enamratus rupiah"—laughter of men behind me, jokes
in a language I barely know, commotions, scuffle, angry shouts
on the other side of the stinking pen of a goat standing in a week
of manure; the sudden blue, white, black of a Javan Sparrow,
red bill, yes, two bouncing from bar to bar to bar in a square cage,
    singing crazy, singing a way out.
The Javan Sparrows cost 13,000 rupiahs, almost nothing
but noise carrying the bamboo cage away
through the maze of beggars, merchants, and buyers
intent on fingering the merchandise and ignoring
the merchant's encouraging words, only asking at last
    the price.

To the slope of *Tangkuban Prahu,* the quiet volcano
we live on, a couple thousand feet above the city
steaming and brown with dust below. We set the cage on the grass
by the bamboo grove leaning over the steep ravine
running with the water we drink every day, open the tiny door,
    the rush and flash of wings.
The birds fly to the bamboo perching
where the tops turn down, sitting silent, and then diving
straight down, out of sight, to the water
we can hear coming clear down the mountain
from the constant clouds above.

Bald Mountain Vigil

Lou Gold

Lou Gold dropped out of a career teaching urban politics at Oberlin College and the University of Illinois and metamorphosed into being the caretaker of Bald Mountain and a forest activist. His travels with a popular Ancient Forest slide show have earned him the title of "the hermit with the most frequent flyer miles." Louis is a founding member of the Siskiyou Regional Education Project, a grassroots group in southwestern Oregon set up to help with the protection of Ancient Forests. "Bald Mountain Vigil" is excerpted and edited from two earlier articles that originally appeared in *Siskiyou Country,* Vols. 8 and 15.

We sat in the yurt at Cedar Gulch listening to the sounds of the swollen creek and the heavy rain. Karin, who was visiting from Germany, spoke of how over half the Douglas fir forest in her homeland was dying from the effects of acid rain. Pablo talked about growing up in Madrid and never seeing a true wilderness forest. I told the story of my fifty-six-day vigil on Bald Mountain the summer before and the ongoing struggle to protect Oregon's North Kalmiopsis Wilderness.

For days we had been making preparations for my second summer on the mountain. A series of sweat lodge ceremonies had been conducted to purify our minds and bodies. The Takilma Peace Circle had dedicated Bald Mountain as a special sanctuary to pray for world peace. A group of friends had formed a support group to deliver food to the trailhead throughout the summer. Everything was ready: we were anxious to go, but the storm continued.

Waiting is difficult—it makes me think too much. I thought about the so-called "Wilderness Bill," which had just released over two million acres of Oregon's roadless areas to the timber industry. I thought about the threat now posed to the great old growth forest that still flourishes on the slopes above Silver and Indigo Creeks. I thought about the senseless greed and destructiveness of today's world. Nearly half of all the forests on earth have been cut down since 1950.

Like the rain, my wondering continued. What sense does it make to ask a society that discards its old people to save its old trees? What sense does it make to ask a society that regularly abuses its children to preserve the forest for our great-great grandchildren? What sense does it make to ask a government, which is continually preparing for war, to maintain the peacefulness of the natural world? And what was I doing hiking up to Bald Mountain with people from distant lands, to maintain a forest sanctuary in the middle of nowhere?

My vigil on the mountain began over a year ago when I was arrested for blockading a bulldozer with eight other people. The court made our probation conditional on not reentering National Forest land for one year. Less than a week later I was back in the Kalmiopsis declaring, "My purpose is peaceful and religious. I shall remain to bear witness to the present attack upon the forest and pray for its safety."

My camp was near the top of the mountain, next to a crystal-clear spring that bubbled out from under a rock. The young ferns, miner's lettuce, and violets growing around it provided a ready supply of fresh salad greens. A great Douglas fir, ten feet in diameter, created a thick carpet of needles, and its branches shielded my tent from wind and rain.

Within a few days of my arrival I began to sense a growing trust among my new neighbors. The local squirrels, blue jays, and juncos were now content merely to announce my presence rather than scold my every move. Deer began to travel the trail through my camp in daylight. The mouse family, which lived in a nearby stump, scampered across my feet as I sat by the fire at night. One afternoon, as I basked in the warm sun, a hummingbird lighted on my shoulder and I knew that I had arrived at some sort of harmony with my relations in the natural world.

My life on the mountain became magical in many ways. Occasional visits from folks bringing supplies felt like a combination of Christmas and family reunion. This kind of experience was not limited to my friends or "support people." Total strangers, just hiking through, found themselves hanging out, camping overnight, or readjusting their plans. Sometimes the reaction was extraordinary, as in the case of an Ashland man who made a special return trip to bring me two weeks' worth of provisions. Nearly everyone tried to offer some kind of assistance: extra food or reading material or a clean pair of socks. Best of all was just watching people fall in love with the mountain.

The top of Bald Mountain is like Friar Tuck's head, a flat, barren area about thirty feet in diameter, with a view of the untouched North Kalmiopsis. It is a holy place: good for seeing the four directions, for touching the four winds, for sleeping under the stars, and for talking to God. The overall ambiance of the mountain is more "old growth forest" than "mountain." Decaying remains of ancestral trees still feed the soil and house creepy-crawlers. Grandmother and grandfather trees, the old living ones, stand proudly as secure anchors on steep, fragile slopes. All around there is a feeling of connection with earth and critters and vibrant growing energy. Wendell Berry, in one of his poems, describes feeling "the earth's empowering brew rise in root and branch." Yes, it was like that.

My daily routine was simple. Gather wood, prepare meals, keep warm and dry, hike down to watch the illegal construction on the Bald Mountain Road, and explore the forest. Walking was a good time for prayer and I often found myself reciting a traditional Navajo chant—

In beauty I walk.
With beauty before me, I walk.
With beauty behind me, I walk.
With beauty above me, I walk.
With beauty below me, I walk.
With beauty all around me, I walk.

This was not ritual. It was simple appreciation.

One day, as I was returning from a morning of road watching, I found a beautiful Knobcone Pine branch, which seemed to have potential for a walking stick. As I passed through a high meadow about a quarter mile from my camp, however, I plunged the stick into the ground. I had found my meditation spot.

The view from this south-facing slope overlooked seven mountain ridges, which seemed to drift off into the ocean some fifty miles away. Often the ridges rose through low, misty clouds, looking like Oriental paintings. For centuries, Buddhist monks have chosen places like my meditation spot to sit and contemplate the impermanence of worldly things. It was a good place to unburden my mind.

During those early days on the mountain, perhaps as a reaction to aloneness, my mind often got terribly busy. I found myself concocting great dramas, holding arguments with the logging industry or delivering self-righteous lectures to the Josephine County Court. This wasn't why I had come to the mountain—my purpose was "peaceful and religious"— and these mental debates were making me feel furious and angry.

I meditated and watched my own thoughts come and go like the clouds. I saw that I had no perfect solutions to offer. As my mind emptied, I remembered the awe with which I had, as a child, watched the clouds; I could see that we are all innocent as we attempt to confront the problems of our modern world. For the future of our planet will not turn on our ability to produce the "right solution" as much as on our fundamental values toward life. As the Native American religions tell us, "The two-leggeds have been given a choice."

After my meditation, I would cross over the ridge and drop into the deep, dense forest on the north slope. While the south side was mountains and sunlight and thoughts, here it was dark and cool. Dewy ferns and decaying branches commingled on the forest floor in an eternal dance of life and death while huge firs rose to form a protective canopy. I could feel the tremendous surge of Mother Earth as the forest enveloped me like a giant womb.

Sometimes I would talk to the trees. I would tell them that a government had drawn a line along the ridge and declared one side of the forest protected, the other side not ... tell them I was just a little guy who wanted to help, who was foolish enough to think that my being there might matter. I would ask the trees to temper my folly with their wisdom, to guide me toward whatever might help them. Each day, without fail, a particular tree or spot would emerge and grip my consciousness. "Just be here," it would say. "Live in harmony with us and you will learn whatever you need to know."

Going down to the road was full of another kind of unavoidable reality. The roar of diesel engines and blasting could be heard throughout the forest and reached up to my camp. Hikers told of hearing road work all the way from Pine Flat, which was 2,500 feet below along the Illinois River to Polar Spring Camp, six miles beyond on the other side of Bald Mountain. As I walked down the trail the grunts and sighs of machines became louder, and the air filled with anxiety.

I watched from a high vantage point about a mile away. From there I could see the full length of the road up to the clearcuts and barren slopes near its beginning on Flat Top. The places directly on the ridge where the trail and road nearly touched each other seemed especially battle-scarred. Freshly felled trees, oozing stumps, deep wounds in the earth and giant equipment all made me shudder.

One day, while sitting there with a visitor, I said, "Perhaps I'm exaggerating, but that looks like a road bringing warfare into a peaceful area."

The visitor told me about working on a Forest Service survey crew on Flat Top several years earlier. His supervisor looked out over the Wilderness area and said, "Those trees are protected now, but some day we will get them."

The Illinois River Trail formed the northern boundary of the Kalmiopsis Wilderness and the Forest Service had posted many signs. On the road side of the trail the signs read: ROAD CLOSED—NO TRESSPASSING—BY ORDER OF USFS. On the other side: WILDERNESS AREA—NO MOTORIZED

VEHICLES OR EQUIPMENT—VIOLATIONS PUNISHABLE. The trail felt like a demilitarized zone between warring armies.

I remembered some lines from the 74th Psalm:

> *The enemy has damaged everything*
> *within the sanctuary;*
> *Thine adversaries have roared in*
> *the midst of Thy meeting place;*
> *They have set up their own*
> *standards for signs.*
> *It seems as if one had lifted up*
> *his axe in a forest of trees.*

My first reaction was anger—I wanted to tear down all the signs. Instead, I carved a sign of my own, and hung it on a tree farther down the trail. It read: BALD MOUNTAIN SANCTUARY—FOLLOW THE BEAUTY TRAIL—COME IN PEACE.

I wanted to stay on Bald Mountain as long as the forest was threatened, but the coming of winter forced me off. I had kept my vigil for fifty-six days. Now, nine months later, I was ready to return.

The storm broke in the night and Karin, Pablo and I left for the trailhead early the next morning. The first few miles of the trail snake upward along perilously steep cliffs high above the Illinois River. My body soon registered the effects of my long rainy season hibernation. As my muscles screamed, every questionable item I had put into my pack danced in front of my mind and grew in size and weight. To make things worse, the clouds had reformed and we were soon putting on our rain gear. This was not going to be an easy hike. The combined burden of a heavy pack and bad weather left little space for my weighty thoughts of the day before. I was forced to set aside all my "wondering" and concentrate on taking one step at a time. When we reached our campsite, the clouds scattered and sunlight began to play across the forest floor. The last storm of spring had ended. Sore and tired, I cast off my pack and felt somehow younger, as if inner burdens born of the world below had been released.

I was excited to visit familiar spots in the forest and led the group on a whirlwind tour. The forest was full of the dense green lushness of late spring and the air was heady with the smells of new growth. The local blue jays, juncos and pine squirrels chattered at us and I wondered if they remembered me. I felt like an enthusiastic child bringing new friends home.

Last summer I had done much of my praying on my hands and knees, picking up bits of broken glass and rusty nails left years ago when the Forest Service had burned down the old lookout. Before leaving the mountain I had constructed a traditional American Indian Medicine Wheel—a prayer circle with flagpoles marking the four directions, the sky and the earth—and the mountaintop was reasonably clean. Now the flagpoles were bent over and a whole new layer of glass and debris had been uncovered by nine months of fierce winds, rain and snow.

Karin, Pablo and I committed ourselves to a regular routine of mountaintop cleanup. Restoring the Medicine Wheel for the approaching Summer Solstice became our most important task. The activity evolved into a meditation—we were not only cleaning up the mountain, but clearing away the thoughts and emotional debris that had been cluttering up our minds. Sometimes one of us would treat a particular piece of glass or rusty nail as a special treasure, seriously discussing its peculiar properties until there was nothing left to do but throw it away. In the humor of the situation, we also faced many of the meanings and absurdities within our own lives.

There were times during those mountaintop cleanup sessions when we'd laugh hard enough to send tears rolling down our cheeks. Then, cleansed by laughter, we'd sit quietly listening to the song of the Hermit Thrush—who we named the "Sunsinger"—and watch the sun sink slowly into the ocean beyond the distant ridgeline. Lighthearted and giddy, we'd stumble down the trail toward hot chocolate and stories around the campfire before sleep.

It was over a week until the first group of hikers came through, a 4-H Club outing from Brookings. The leaders of the group, two middle-aged women tired from the long hike up, looked at our piles of neatly stacked kindling and asked, "Are you planning to stay here all summer?" They were obviously disappointed that their hoped-for camping spot was occupied. I thought about the Forest Service fourteen-day camping limitation and responded evasively, "We'll stay as long as we're supposed to."

Fortunately, there was another campsite nearby with a good source of water and excellent forage for their pack animals. I told them about our mountaintop cleanup project and invited them to join us. About an hour later, three boys—Clint, Adam and Jay—came running up the trail. They turned trash gathering into a competitive game and soon several more buckets of glass were dumped into burlap sacks.

At sunset, Pablo, Karin and I sat quietly in the prayer circle, but the boys couldn't stop laughing. Jay and Adam would try to hold back, as if in church, but Clint's infectious giggle would soon get them started up again. Finally I said, "Go ahead and laugh. That happens to us all the time," and we joined together in a circle hug of laughter. In that moment, the sound of laughing children seemed like the finest prayer. Listening, I imagined a future full of old trees and happy children and knew then, with a deep certainty, why I was maintaining a wilderness sanctuary on top of Bald Mountain.

The next morning Clint organized another cleanup party at sunrise. We were just rolling out of our sleeping bags when the boys came down from the mountaintop. Clint looked at me with a wink and said, "We left a present for you up there." They had filled seven sacks, over 350 pounds of glass and nails. The cleanup task had been completed and I wished for a way to get it all off the mountain.

A few days later the Forest Service trail maintenance supervisor, Harvey Timeus, visited our camp. I offered him some fresh-brewed coffee. When he asked how long we were planning to stay, I responded, matter-of-factly, "All summer, if the food keeps coming." He frowned, mentioned the fourteen-day rule, and said he would have to do something if there were complaints. I wondered if the leaders of the 4-H Club outing had already produced some. Our conversation reached an impasse. After a long silence, Harvey said, "By the way, we'll pay our trail-maintenance crew to pack out all that trash you picked up. If you went to all that trouble, the least we can do is get it out of here." My wish had been granted.

The next day we were again visited by the Forest Service, this time by District Ranger Bill Butler. We talked about the wilderness values of the area and some of the hard decisions that lay ahead. I waited for him to raise the issue of the fourteen-day rule but, instead, he asked if I would like some volunteer work and mentioned brushing out an old trail. I said, "As long as the work doesn't carry me too far from the mountaintop." He said, "Fine, I'll send in some tools."

A week later Harvey returned with tools and an "Agreement for Voluntary Services." The agreement called for me to maintain the Bald Mountain Lookout Loop Trail. "Wow, that sort of makes me the caretaker of the Bald Mountain Sanctuary, doesn't it?" I said. He smiled and his son, who had come along for the hike, gave me a wink. Harvey's son was Clint, the boy from the 4-H Club outing.

By Solstice, the Medicine Wheel had been fully restored. Brightly colored flags waved in the strong breeze and fresh strings of tobacco ties decorated the flagpoles. On Solstice we spent twenty-four hours within the prayer circle, fasting and remaining in silence. The night before, we had gone to sleep blanketed by wet clouds that hovered about the mountaintop. At dawn a patch of blue sky opened directly above us. All day we watched as the sun burned off the moisture, and mountain ridges rose out of the low-lying fog and the clear sky spread toward the coast. It felt as if a light or energy was radiating outward from Bald Mountain.

Everything had a quality of sacredness on that longest day. We walked the circle, casting tobacco to the winds. We burned cedar and sage in the fire pit near the center pole. We prayed for the trees, gave thanks for the many wonders of this existence, and thought of loved ones near and far. The circle was complete: we stood humbly in the midst of a great natural harmony and the world, for the moment, seemed in order. Then I had a vision of many prayer circles, forest and mountain shrines throughout our region—places of power and renewal, of peace and pilgrimage. They would be, like Bald Mountain, safe spots in confusing times, rallying points and sanctuaries for those who love this earth and her peoples.

THE GIFT OF SILENCE

Anne LaBastille

Anne LaBastille, Ph.D., is an ecologist and author internationally recognized as an advocate of wildlife and wildland conservation. Her six books include *Woodswoman, Women and Wilderness,* and *The Wilderness World of Anne LaBastille.* She has also written over 150 articles and scientific papers and lectures widely. Anne was a Commissioner of New York State's Adirondack Park Agency for over seventeen years and has received numerous conservation awards. "The Gilt of Silence" originally appeared in her book *The Wilderness World of Anne LaBastille* (West of the Wind Publications, 1992).

Silence is an invisible, intangible, exquisitely fragile natural resource that is rarely thought about. No one makes an effort to save it, and no one donates to preserve it. There is no Citizens Group to Save Silence, no Coalition to Reduce Loud Man-Made Sounds in the Environment.

Silence is an integral part of every climbing, camping, or canoeing trip. It is the heart and soul of the wilderness experience. It is the perfect prescription for a good night's sleep, and the oldest remedy for stress. It may also be a partial cure for workers who are subjected to high noise levels in factories and who are prone to increased heart disease and nervous disorders.

Once silence stretched over the Adirondack Mountains from peak to peak like a velvet mantle. It was broken by wind soughing through great white pines, by August thunderstorms and February blizzards. It was disrupted by trout splashing, deer snorting, owls hooting, and coyotes yipping. These sounds melded and molded with silence, and have been there for ten thousand years and more.

With the invention of gunpowder, steam and electric engines, and gasoline motors, the erosion of silence began. This erosion has accelerated dramatically in the last ten to twenty years.

Now on a typical Adirondack Park summer day, an inhabitant or tourist may hear the following: around 7:00 A.M., the noise of vehicular traffic increases as workers and tourists take to the roads. Then outboard and inboard motorboats start cruising the lakes. From 9:00 to 10:00, mail trucks and mail boats cover their routes. Seaplanes fly over, carrying fishermen or sightseers. Or an F-16 makes a sonic boom while A-10s roar above the treetops on military training flights. Camp owners make repairs with electric skill saws, drills, and wrenches. At intervals, commercial jetliners pass high overhead. As the day warms, water-skiers and jet-skiers streak up and down the lakes. (In the winter, it's snowmobilers.) In the afternoon, chain saws rev up as firewood is cut. By twilight, most man-made noises diminish. A few late cars and boats go by. Finally, night sounds can preside, except for those infernal bug whackers!

Who among us today can say that they have spent a day totally free of sounds generated by motors, engines, and guns? Only the deaf, those in solitary confinement, and dedicated wilderness campers can claim this. The disappearance of silence in the Adirondacks, in America, and in every other First World country has been gradual, invasive, and continual. It will get worse as our materialistic society produces more and more mechanized products and gadgets.

The Adirondack Park and National Parks still offer substantial time blocks of silence. With it come those blessed feelings of solitude, contemplation, and creativity. Silence in the natural world has inspired humans as diverse as the biblical prophets, famous poets and musicians, and conservationists such as John Muir, Teddy Roosevelt, Sigurd Olson, and Aldo Leopold.

We need silence. We need it to be reminded of the vastness of the stars and space that surround our tiny planet. Of the awesome beauty of wilderness. Of the implacability of Nature's laws. In short, silence helps put us in our place. It makes humans humble and reverent.

Here and now, I consider it a gift to spend a summer's night with only the sound of a loon's tremolo on a silent lake. And to walk through the flaming leaves of autumn with the chorus of wild geese migrating overhead. And to lie for a moment at midnight on an icebound lake, wondering at the aurora borealis, and hear nothing but the trees cracking in the cold.

I fear the gift of silence will become even more precious and rare as we enter the twenty-first century.

OCEAN SONG

Robin Boyd

Robin Boyd lives and writes on a small land trust in Jaffrey, New Hampshire. Her work has appeared in *Green Fuse, Yankee, Calliope, Zone 3*, and other magazines. She wrote "Ocean Song" one foggy dawn while visiting an organic farm in Sonoma County, California, as a graduate student with the Audubon Expedition Institute.

Morning.
The sun licks at the heels
of the mist as it settles along
the folded valleys that trace
these old brown hills.
When the wind is right
we can hear the breath
of the ocean as it rises
and falls in liquid sighs.
The fog is the color of mussel shells —
a shade so right the soul ceases
to question itself for just a moment
and rests.
I want to wrap myself
in the stillness of this blue,
wear it like a robe
and walk before the sun, my hem
ablaze in fiery lace.

Shadow of the dawn,
dreamer of the surf,
my song would be a whispered breeze
and the silence of closed eyes.
I would ask what kingdoms
these clouds conceal.
And who needs to see
in a world so soft?

Bringing Nature and Grace Together Again

Matthew Fox

Matthew Fox is the director of the Institute in Culture and Creation
Spirituality and the author of *Creation Spirituality: Liberating Gifts for the
Peoples of the Earth* (HarperCollins, 1991) and some fourteen other books on
spirituality and the interconnectedness of all life. He is a former Dominican
priest and now an Episcopalian priest. Matthew was given the International
New Thought Alliance Humanitarian Award in 1992. "Bringing Nature and
Grace Together Again" was excerpted from a talk that he gave at the Voices
of the Earth Conference held in Boulder, Colorado, during the summer of
1994. The title of the overall lecture was "The Greening of Spirituality."

In the fourth century, there was a Western theologian, named Saint Au-
gustine, who set apart nature from grace, and this split has haunted Western consciousness for sixteen hundred years. Now, there are people who
came along like Hildegarde [von Bingen], and [Meister] Eckhart and others, who tried to heal the breach — [Thomas] Aquinas, too, another — but
essentially, we've been stuck with this war between nature and grace. It is
a great wound that exists in our Western consciousness, and I think it has
everything to do with ecological crisis, because if you separate nature from
grace, then nature is something to be afraid of. And the European Chris-
tians, when they came over here (to the Americas) in the fifteenth and
sixteenth centuries, having separated nature from grace, and seeing people
close to nature here ... this repression of nature as grace came up unconsciously and was projected upon the Indian people, not only in this land,

but others. This is how Frederick Turner writes about it: "That genocide was due to a misappropriated spirituality, a spirituality that thought you had to separate nature from grace."

And so, we set nature up to be destroyed—and people who are closer to nature than we are—if we separate nature from grace. And, in fact, religious fascism and political fascism then, which are controlled ideologies—and authoritarianism, which is a controlled ideology—take over because the whole purpose is to control this beast called "nature."

In addition, when we separate nature from grace there is a great scarcity of grace. There is a rationing of grace and you have these trickle-down theologies, theologies of trickle-down grace, as if there is only so much grace to go around, and it is going to be handed out through the spigot of some ordained system that will give you some if you get far enough down on your knees. This is not the way I see creation at all. Meister Eckhart healed it in one short sentence, in the fourth century, when he said, "Nature is Grace."

We are graced by the events on Jupiter. We were graced by the supernova explosion five-and-a-half billion years ago. We were graced by the fireball fourteen billion years ago, that set things going, that made our stories possible. We are graced every day the sun comes up, and every day a tiger smiles at you, and every day a whale winks at us. We are graced constantly by nature! Grace is nature, and if we would get that right, we would be green again, because there is plenty of grace to go around. Don't let them fool you. There's plenty of grace to go around. It's our problem that we are not receptive to all the grace we are swimming in, day in and day out.

Kabir, the wonderful Eastern mystic, says, "I laugh at the fish in the water who tells me he is thirsty!" That's us folks! We are fish in water. We think we are thirsty for grace. The water is the divine light. We're breathing it in, and breathing it out, just like a fish. Wake up. "Wake up!"—as Kabir says—"You have been sleeping for hundreds of millions of years."

ALPINE POND, CEDAR BREAKS

David Lee

David Lee's new poetry book, *My Town*, published by Copper Canyon Press, won the Western United States Book Award for 1995. In 1994, he received the Utah Governor's Award for Lifetime Achievement in the Arts; and in the same year a thirty-minute PBS documentary based on his work, *The Pig Poet,* was released and won first place at the Rocky Mountain Film Festival and at several other film festivals. David lives quietly in St. George, Utah, with Jan, Jon, and Jodee, where he scribbles, coaches youth athletics, and runs the county roads and trails, all at about the same rate and pace. "Alpine Pond" is taken from a larger unpublished manuscript of poems for his deceased father, tentatively titled *Penance in Desert.*

> *Joy, fair spark of the gods*
> *Daughter of Elysium!*
> *Drunk with fiery rapture, goddess,*
> *We approach thy shrine!*
> — FRIEDRICH SCHILLER

Just before dawn the sky darkens. Barely
perceptible. At times on the ocean or great plains
a green flash follows. Prelude. Or anthem.
And then sun. Up again, spilling through
this maze of pine and aspen
into the free sculpture of fluted ridges, hoodoos
and weathered earth. Below me a breastbone
for the winds, cirque rising out of cirque
until the small pond beneath the rim
loosely holding the essence of blue. Shadows
seep a red darkness as colors awaken.

The pond is still, so I make the sound of water.
All around me a trickle. A gurgle from the snowfield.
I lay on a frail summer grass. A splash
from the creek I etch on the west wall then
move down toward broken sandstone.
Pinnacles, spires and glowing rock.
The juxtaposition of two worlds
demands trumpets, strings, timpani, a
flood of grandeur. Allegro ma non troppo; Presto.
And the soaring of human voice, the fountainhead.
Deliverance through joy. Music pours
over the breaks, symphony and chorale:

Freude, schöner Götterfunken
Dawn spreads the high country. Day breaks.

Behind, a shrill whistle. A fat marmot
stands on his boulder, watching. Tiny paws
clasped before his chest, dark eyes glistening.
A grey camp robber clatters from its spruce perch.
The venerable hotai stiffens, lifts his chin,
whistles again. I whistle back. Almost, I see
him smile aha! you silly! almost, bow. I nod
for the both of us. Once more for the bird.
The marmot turns away. Disappears
in broken ground. No sound from the trees.
A slow shissh as dawnwind clambers over
the breaks. I go on sitting still as the old
sun makes its way. For the moment
no inclination toward moving anywhere.

THE BEAUTY OF THE WILD

John Daniel

John Daniel's biography appears with his poem "In Praise" in the first
section. "The Beauty of the Wild" derives from a longer essay, "Toward
Wild Heartlands," published in *Audubon* (1994). In its present form, the
essay has appeared in *Timeline* (1995) and in *Resurgence* (England, 1995).

Though we Americans flock by the millions to the landscape splendors of
our national parks and other natural areas, it seems to me that our experience of natural beauty is for the most part rote and passionless. I feel only
a dull grade of pleasure when I stop at a scenic overlook, and I rarely see
enthusiasm or even animation in the other watchers—I see bored children
and impassive parents showing the scenery to their cameras and video
recorders. Though drawn to nature, we are somehow insensible to it. Our
lives are so far removed from the wild land that it's become just a picture,
an image to be captured and taken home. As tourists we may not damage
the land as mining or timber corporations would, but in one sense we do
what they do: we value the land for one of its extractable qualities. We

have reduced natural beauty to postcard prettiness, another commodity to be consumed in our dogged pursuit of happiness.

There's a different beauty of the land, a deeper and far more lively beauty, that we have largely forfeited. To know this beauty requires more than eyes alone and can't be done at a distance. It takes legs and sweat, hard breathing and time. It requires that we approach the land on its own terms, that we enter it respectfully and yield ourselves to its presence. The beauty I mean is not prettiness or sublimity, not grace or loveliness of form necessarily, but simply the land as it is in its singular wholeness, as nature made it and is making it now. The *beauty* whose derivation relates it to *bounty* and ultimately to the Sanskrit *duvas,* meaning "gift" or "reverence." The beauty of the given world. All of us feel some stirring for it, some twitch or flood of yearning. On film or in words like these, it fades and cheapens. Only the wild land itself can give us its full measure, and renew our love for it, and show us how it lives within ourselves.

Wilderness, the word, shares roots with *willfulness,* the condition of being ungovernable, beyond authority and control. When I ask myself what wilderness most truly is, what its beauty is most made of, willfulness is what I find—a vast, unconscious willfulness that bodies forth mountains from seas of magma, dreams the dark chaos of soil into forests of spiring trees, fashions meadowlarks and black bears from the long weaving strands of evolutionary time. In this willfulness I am something small, rightfully small, refreshingly small. Out of my house and vehicle, away from typewriter and telephone and buildings and roads, removed from the busyness and trappings both worthy and worthless that compel our attention and delude us that our human affairs are of paramount importance, in the wild I experience myself and my kind in something like actual scale. And except perhaps for a few willful mosquitoes or one paramount pebble beneath my sleeping bag, I am happy.

In our restless sightseeing of nature, skimming down the highway from one view to another, we see much more than we can absorb. In wilderness, we absorb much more than we see. We walk to rhythms longer than the conscious mind can know—the rhythm of sequoias rising, the Escalante carving its canyon, the slow titanic stirring of this crust of Earth that bears us. The rhythm of the wild carries through shimmering aspen leaves and the blast of Mount St. Helens, through the boom of surf at Cape Perpetua and the hoarse whistle of a red-tailed hawk adrift in the summer sky. Life and death both dance to it: the deer browsing, the cougar snapping the deer's neck and ripping its belly, the carrion eaters transforming the cougar. The beauty of the wild is the long gesture of life in time. The beauty of skin and fur and feathers, the beauty of blood, the beauty of old bones sinking into grass.

In removing ourselves from the wholeness of nature we have become rich with power and possessions, but we have also impoverished ourselves. We can only observe the beauty we once belonged to, the wild matrix that gave birth to us and sustains us even in our distance and contempt. We won't be members of the wild again, but the wild was our first teacher, and if we could stop ourselves from destroying it and approach it with humility, it could again be our teacher. There is much we could learn from old-growth forest, how its diverse and vigorous community conserves and recycles its wealth, balances its growth and death, and so sustains itself through time. Much we could learn from wild salmon, who leap the rapids with a faithfulness to home we have scarcely begun to imagine for ourselves. We might learn patience from the bristlecones, fortitude from monarch butterflies, the dignity of space and breathing room from ponderosa pines and saguaros.

When I spend too many hours reading newspapers or watching television, too many weeks breathing city air and hardening my ears to city noises, I don't believe we as a people are capable of learning anything more than how to operate the next machine. But wilderness, as Wallace Stegner wrote, is the geography of hope. When I'm able to pry myself out of town and let the land inform me, an unreasonable optimism comes over me. The land lets me feel no other way. The land has been getting by for a long time, after all. The land is in no hurry and no alarm. It goes on with its endless work of making itself—and if I am unable to take joy in that, what joy can I take in anything?

"Talk of mysteries!" wrote Thoreau. "Think of our life in nature—daily to be shown matter, to come in contact with it,—rocks, trees, wind on our cheeks! the *solid* earth! the *actual* world!" If you follow the physicists, the actual world is composed of willful little particles with names like quark and gluon that dodge into and out of existence, enlivening a universe born billions of years ago from a single source, a form-seeking universe that has made itself into nebulas, stars, planets, and Thoreau with wind on his cheeks. If you follow others, you get other accounts. There are many good books, but even the book you most believe in can tell no more than a glancing passage of the actual story of being—the story that spirals through DNA and the snail's shell and the chambered nautilus, through the grain of junipers and the great spinning storms and the swirling arms of the Milky Way, and so joins itself to the infinite.

We are privileged beyond measure to be part of the story, and twice-privileged to be conscious in some small way of the orders of being we are joined to. We can't see far. What we call Nature, meaning all that the cosmos brings to birth, will forever elude the grasp of our science and philosophy and poetry. We belong to a mystery that does not belong to us, yet it is freely available to all who desire it. Though we distance ourselves and fail to see it, it is granted everywhere and all the time. It does not fail us. To rest on a mesa still warm with sun and watch the stars brighten to their fierce glitter, a little wind stirring with the smell of sage, and far away a coyote giving up his cry ... In this beauty, this mystery, I am glad to be alive. This beautiful mystery makes me whole.

ALONE IN THE FOREST

David Whyte

David Whyte's biography appears before his poem, "Ten Years Later" in the first section. "Alone in the Forest" is reprinted from *Songs for Coming Home* (Many Rivers Press, 1989).

It is only in the forest that I realize how many rooted structures exist inside of me, and it is in the forest now, with my breath lifting in billowing spirals in the cold air, that I am suddenly released into the miracle of small things;—a bird's movement on a branch, the sound of water still dripping from yesterday's rainstorm. In the forest everything in the mind can be given away, so that the heart can be open to the intense concentration that natural objects demand. Through this concentration where nothing exists but the object itself, enormous energy opens out through the woodland silhouette. By allowing this silence, nothing is held in the mind beyond the time in which it happens: the undergrowth rustles without judgment, the marsh can sleep undisturbed by comparison or memory. Out of this emerges an energy that can only be described as *praise*; and as this intensifies, even this must give way like the distant call in the forest, so that this energy opens up a void in the center of all things. At this point the praise suddenly becomes mutual and I stand revealed ... and even this in no way
diminishes this luxuriant moss-covered log which creaks,
scattering the birds as I sit on it.

VII

Extra-Ordinary
Wilderness

Yesterday, I went for a walk about a half-mile outside of town. I came across a woman and her massive male husky. He was vibrant, jumping in and out of bushes and tall grasses, running through the open fields, sniffing here and there, and chasing deer across a hillside. This gorgeous animal was completely in his element. It brought me great joy to observe him. It opened my heart. My thinking came to a halt.

In the fading light of day, I sat down in the hummocks of grass and began to *really* take in the beauty around me. The pine trees glowed. The foothills, dying shrubbery, and all the undergrowth were radiant and crisp. I saw a coyote come over the crest of a hill, traverse downward, stop, lift his white neck, and howl into the air of the setting sun. Down the valley, another coyote replied with great enthusiasm. The sharpness of their voices struck a deep place of resonance inside me and encouraged me to notice several varieties of birds calling back and forth to one another and to hear the crickets chirping. During this long stretch of time, it was as if I was not even there; I was everywhere—in the coyotes' song, in the crispness, and in the rich and living landscape. A deep peace, stillness, and bliss overcame me. And curiously, and amazingly, there was no "I" to experience this, only the omnipresence of God.

This is what might classically be called a mystical experience and yet it happened in a pause at the end of my day, in the midst of a very busy time, within a mile of my house. Similar experiences are a commonplace occurrence in my life recently. Not that they are common in the sense of being dull and routine, but common in the sense that they are becoming ordinary to my life, and in that, extraordinary. In the neutrality of nature, I open up to a presence that is both in me and far beyond me, a presence that reaches out into the infinite unknown of the sky and the material world before me. The recognition of this bounty of presence is becoming such an integral fabric of my life, both in and out of so-called wilderness, that what is starting to seem more unusual and strange are the times when I am not experiencing this openness. It is an inherent and integral part of who I am—and of who we are—to experience wonder, joy, and abundance.

The selections in this chapter point to the magic found in wilderness, from vast experiences of the mystical and transpersonal found in remote and wild places, to the simplicity, richness, and mystery discovered in our backyards, gardens, and city parks. It is my experience that there is no place nature and magic cannot be found. Wherever we go we find wilderness—even within the walls of our homes, where we are confronted with the unexplainable mystery and beauty of our own living. Wilderness has no walls; I have deliberately combined radically different ends of the spectrum of experienced wilderness to emphasize this point.

Seeing the smallness of our human lives against the unrestrained expanse of nature into which we have been born, we are deeply and gratefully humbled. Through this seeing, our attention may be turned away from the confines of our humanness and toward the depths of our nature, and in this act we grow immeasurably. We no longer perceive nature as something out there that we periodically visit, but as something that we carry inside of us wherever we are.

THE PRACTICE OF THE PRESENCE OF THE WILD

David Oates

David Oates lives in Portland, Oregon. He develops environmental curriculum and teaches English at Clark College, Vancouver. His book of poetry, *Peace in Exile*, was published in 1992 by Oyster River Press (Santa Barbara). In 1989, Oregon State University Press published his exploration of environmentalist worldviews, *Earth Rising: Ecological Belief in an Age of Science*. A follow-up to that book, entitled *Paradise Peeled: Myths of American Nature*, is forthcoming. It picks up some of the wildness in this essay and runs with it in unexpected directions. "The Practice of the Presence of the Wild" first appeared in the Winter 1990 issue of *EarthLight: Spirituality and Ecology*.

When I returned to live in Los Angeles, I began participating with a curious group of misfits and visionaries. They added a dimension to my life that, immersed in the sprawling city, I sorely needed. They gathered at an appointed hour each week and simply sat in silence "in the manner of Friends" (they were Quakers, following a meditative tradition dating to the seventeenth century). Out of this silence, someone would occasionally speak or sometimes not. But the silence, even when long continued, was a surprisingly full silence, rich with an unexpected depth and connectedness.

I was also taking hikes by myself in the Sierra Nevada Mountains. They varied from a few days to a few weeks in duration, and from easy strolls to arduous explorations up high, beyond trails and signposts.

Eventually I began to understand that the two experiences, seemingly so unlike, shared something essential. It was wildness: the uncontrolled and uncontrollable. Alone on a mountainside it is an obvious meditation to recognize how big the world is, and how much bigger the cosmos beyond it, and beyond that how encompassingly small the little life is that holds the beholding mind. Small and easily damaged.

In a silent meeting there sometimes comes a similar recognition. Out of the dark into which the mind descends, a becoming humility settles over. There is much in that dark silence, much that is not understood or understandable. But some of it emerges during a well-gathered meeting, either to stir an individual with unexpected intuitions or to impel someone to stand and speak words that are just a little truer than his ordinary talk.

The silence is wild. No one controls it or measures it. Without this silence, Quaker meetings would be shallow talk-societies. In the silence are the depth and the profundity. In it one encounters the truth: a person is a small bit of intellectualizing jetsam afloat on a mighty and incomprehensible stream.

This is distressing news to the Faust in us. Which is precisely why it is such important news.

Typical city folk today apparently believe that if anything goes wrong, it must be someone's fault. They suppose that we humans control all: if someone is hurt, some official must have screwed up. It can never just be the fact that humans are mortal, and life dangerous. Skiers who run into trees blame resort operators rather than the laws of physics. Earthquakes are followed by lawsuits.

Civilized life fosters this delusion. City lights blot out the starry sky, that insult to mortal pride. Day and night can be ignored. Weather is minimized. Edges are rounded. Health care is good enough, with a little luck, for one to go for months and years without an obviously unsolvable problem.

What losses these comforts are! What a revelation simple hunger can be — how sharpening to the senses, how bracing to the mind. What sleepy, deluded, dull people we turn into under such a regimen of toasty quilts and surfeit. What a silly theory it is to think that all hazards are, or ought to be, marked with red triangles and registered with the appropriate authorities. How badly we need a sharp pinch now and then to bring back to us the reality: Though we try to provide for our needs, life is nevertheless both uncertain and painful. Best not to forget it.

The common thread in all these urban delusions is denial of nature as an independent and superior reality. Our handling of wilderness is symptomatic of this denial; we label it "natural resource" and chop it up for raw materials. Where human desire is the measure of all things, all the world is a consumable commodity, a playpen for the infantile appetite.

But nature is present all the while. It is undeterred by our silly denial. Sickness, accident, old age, and death remind us, eventually, if nothing else does. But the systematic loss of awareness of this reality leaves us unable to comprehend. We think there must be some mistake. It is the urban/civilized lie that humans can control all, much, or even an important part of life. Most of what counts is far beyond our reach. By limiting our focus to those few trivial elements that we can manipulate, we shrink our lives to pitiable smallness. And all the rest of the cosmos goes unnoticed. It is a high price to pay for the illusion of safety.

If the reality of nature is as present as all that, then we do not have far to look for deliverance. Which is not to say there is no need for plain old outdoor trees-and-mountains wilderness. Contact with the real wilderness of uncivilized nature is an unmatched vehicle for awakening and deepening the mind. In many non-Western cultures, one leaves the village to encounter the natural world alone and in its full reality—and to gain the depth and serenity that encounter brings. The modern world needs wild places for this reason along with all the other good reasons.

But even right now, in the dregs of the Dark Ages of the twentieth century, in the middle of the city, opportunities for encounter surround us. The wild is everywhere, despite the city-lie. Wildness is the medium in which we swim, as near as the night sky, a brush with death on the freeway, a dream. By learning to welcome the unplannable, the uncontrollable, and the incomprehensible as nature itself, we can refresh and renew ourselves daily. Thoreau knew what he was saying—that in wildness (not wilderness) is the preservation of the world. Tracts of unexplored land are wonderful: but the wild is within us, as well.

A few places to look:

Silence

Thoreau again, from his 1841 journal: "I have been breaking silence these twenty-three years and have hardly made a rent in it. Silence has no end: speech is but the beginning of it. My friend thinks I keep silence, who am only choked with letting it out so fast. Does he forget that new mines of secrecy are constantly opening within me?"

The Body

Almost everything about it defies will and intention. Health and ill health, equally, are mysteries. I get spooked when I so much as lay abed for a day with a cold: it makes me think of dying and of the frailty of my daily happiness. These are good thoughts. A little exercise feels as good as a walk in the woods. It is me in my body, this amazing, difficult, recalcitrant, biological marvel. Myself my own zoo.

And sex, too. What a roller-coaster it is, and how far from rational control! It seems a perfect wilderness to me, a place where one goes along for the ride and is grateful for it.

The Mind

Our cultural theory, derived from Descartes, holds that the mind alone is free and apart from nature. This is baloney: The mind itself ranges far beyond our civilized control. It is a wild place, as every night's dreams prove. Even what we call "reason" is hidden from us. Try to trace how a conclusion arises! A sensible owner of a mind would welcome the whole thing, reason and unreason, waking and dreaming, bound and loose, known and mysterious. To explore it is, I think, to go on a vision quest.

Language

How could this most human of artifices also be wild? Because it is an organic process that operates by its own logic. Because it uses us as much as the other way around. Because our thought and our sense of reality are built as much out of language as out of our own perceptions. And because it comes to us unbidden and uncontrolled. "Language is simply alive, like an organism," suggests Lewis Thomas, a student of both biology and language.

Poetry

And all the other arts, no doubt. The reason they refresh us is precisely that they go beyond the merely measured and calculated response. To dive into a poem is to go places you cannot predict or control. That is what makes it a poem. Its resonances are wacky, like those in a cavern. It talks back to you from the strangest angles.

No matter how reasoned and clipped and formalized their above-ground manifestations, mind and language possess a deep tap-root of wildness. The poet who wishes to explore there must perform an act of awful courage: he must abandon the control our waking lives are based on. She must loosen the strings that tie together the personality and make the world safe and comprehensible. He must allow the carefully made whole to fragment. No one who has even fleetingly experienced the vortex of the unreasoning mind will underestimate the attempt.

The creative journey is perilous because it encounters the unknown and uncontrolled forces of nature residing deep within us. It is for this very reason that the creations of art, literature, and music are renewing and redemptive.

Failure

By my accounting, the little death. The ego comes crashing down. Plans fall apart. Goals recede, unreached and perhaps forever unreachable. Shame and embarrassment crowd out the mellow feelings of social worth and acceptance. Bereft of the social clothing, one is reduced to the basics—a poor, naked, forked animal. A beast that eats, sleeps, and thinks beneath the sun and the seasons. No longer a Controller of Destiny; now just an inhabitant, wandering among the marvels and dangers. It's an experience we all need, periodically, lest we forget.

There are, no doubt, many more of these potential encounters, many ways to catch sight of the wild. They are the antidote to the accelerating madness of our war-making, wall-building, money-hoarding culture. What craziness is produced by unacknowledged fear, by the mad attempt to control all, whether in the group mind of civilization or the private mind of individuals. What bliss when the doors are opened, the sweet fresh air blows through, and all that energy of denial is released for peaceful, productive, and happy pursuits.

The human spirit is refreshed as it looks straight into the realities. In the presence of nature itself, the fantasy of control and the neurosis of denial fall away. The open palm replaces the clenched fist. A sojourn in the wilderness is the primal way to learn this lesson (and to learn it again and again, as we must). But in between trips to the high country, the open sea, the desert, one can daily restore the vital balance of action and acceptance, planning and improvisation. One can always take a moment for the practice of the presence of the wild.

A Lake in the Mind

Deena Metzger

Deena Metzger's biography appears before her poem "Mandlovu" in the
section "Animal Encounters."

for Michael

What's essential is a lake in the mind,
and then this wind freshening, blowing through the windows, insistent
with the
assurance of morning,
but now the shimmer of the first moon
on the waters and the blue glimmer of the night sky alive with invisible
stars
and such a long draught of silence —
the water clear and coming from a source
which is either
at the very core of the earth
or somewhere far beyond earth in the heavens —
that we speak of it in the only language we know,

the early morning or midnight of the lake, the first streak of birdsong
across the waters, the way the moonlight breaks,

this language, being the only language for what it is we wish to speak
about without
saying a word,

the early morning or midnight of the lake and the first streak of birdsong
and
the wind blowing across the surface of the mind like a bell.

DEEP ECOLOGY AND WONDER:
Notes of a Sleight-of-Hand Sorcerer

David Abram

David Abram, cultural ecologist and philosopher, is the author of *The Spell
of the Sensuous: Perception and Language in a More-than-Human World* (Vintage,
1997), for which he was awarded the Lannan Literary Award for Nonfiction. An accomplished sleight-of-hand magician who has lived with
indigenous sorcerers in Indonesia, Nepal, and the Americas, his writings
have appeared both in academic journals and in such publications as *The
Ecologist, Tikkun, Orion, Utne Reader, Wild Earth, Resurgence, Parabola,* and
Environmental Ethics, as well as in a host of anthologies. His work focuses upon
the intertwined mysteries of perception and language—the way in which
these two dimensions modulate the relation between humankind and the
animate earth. Dr. Abram lectures and teaches widely on several continents,
and has been the recipient of numerous fellowships; in 1995, he was named by
the *Utne Reader* as one of a hundred leading visionaries currently transforming
the world. Nomadic by nature, David and his wife, naturalist Grietje Laga,
circulate between the high desert of northern New Mexico and the coastal
Northwest. A passionate spokesperson for night-herons, cedars, and storm
clouds, he maintains a strong interest in interspecies communication and in
the rejuvenation of oral culture. "Deep Ecology and Wonder: Notes of a
Sleight-of-Hand Sorcerer" first appeared in *Earth First!* under the title "Deep
Ecology and Magic: Notes of a Sleight-of-Hand Sorcerer."

These are dark times for magic. Few people in North America believe in
magic anymore, and no one has contributed to this sad state more than the
magicians themselves—those sleekly suspicious characters who perform
at our gatherings and bedazzle us on TV, making things vanish and appear amidst a flurry of sequined assistants. Since the days of vaudeville,
our magic has become an increasingly secular craft, forgetful of its origins
in initiation, in communion and secret communication with nature, and in
trance. Today, having mislaid the original significance of the rites they
perform, my fellow magicians prefer to call themselves "illusionists." For
although they sense something great and mysterious in the work they do,
the rational language and world-view of our time fails to provide any way
to acknowledge that mystery. "Your magic," say the scientists, "is really just

an illusion set up to fool our perceptions, for the real world is not magic."

And yet there are a handful of magicians who still believe in the magic. As sleight-of-hand practitioners, we know that we are connected to an ancient tradition by the fact that we work with the sacred mysteries of perception, the same mysteries that were studied and taught by our progenitors, the tribal shamans and sorcerers. Magicians, whether witch doctors or warlocks, have always been those individuals chosen to follow the way of the incarnate or earthly powers. As a result of their deep trust in bodily or sensual experience, these individuals became adept at activating the imagination of the senses. It was by tapping this wild, perceptual creativity in others that the tribal sorcerer was able to effect numerous transformations and remarkable cures.

But the role of the sacred magician has shifted with the rise of civilization. Through the progressive domestication of tribal humanity, through the spread of institutional religion and urban logic, our species has all but lost its native ability to smell, to hear, to see deeply. Today's magician has the great task, then, of reawakening the deep creativity of perception. Through the use of sleights and subterfuges, the magician endeavors to trick the senses free from their static holding patterns. If and when he or she is successful, we find ourselves abruptly immersed in a perceptual world far more vivid and wild than our tame definitions of reality.

In 1980, I received a generous fellowship from the Watson Foundation to support a year's research into modes of perception utilized by traditional sorcerers in the equatorial islands of Indonesia and the mountains of Nepal. One aspect of this grant was especially unique: I was to journey into rural Asia not as an anthropologist but rather as a magician in my own right, in hopes of gaining more direct access to native practitioners. By presenting myself not as an academic researcher but as a magician from the West, I would be able to explore from the inside the relation between these traditional magicians and their magic. My unorthodox approach was ultimately successful; my magical skills brought me into the company of several exceedingly powerful and bizarre individuals of the sort known as *dukun*s in Indonesia or *djankri*s in Nepal. Indeed, it was while staying in the household of one of these *djankri*s that I experienced a unique shift in my own sensory awareness.

On one of our first walks along the narrow cliff trails that wind out from his village high in the Himalayas of eastern Nepal, my host casually pointed out a certain boulder that he had "danced" on before attempting some especially difficult cures. It was a large rock which thrust out several feet beyond the cliff's edge, its surface alive with pale white and red lichens. Two days later, when hiking back alone to the village from the yak pastures above, I climbed onto the rock to sit and gaze at the snow-covered mountains across the valley. It was a sparkling blue Himalayan morning. Between gleaming peaks, two Lammergeier Vultures floated, wings out-stretched, riding invisible currents. Without thinking, I took a silver coin out of my pocket and began an aimless sleight-of-hand exercise, rolling the coin over the knuckles of my right hand. One of the huge birds swerved away from the snow peaks and began gliding over the valley, heading in my direction. I stopped rolling the coin and stared. At that moment the Lammergeier halted its flight and hung motionless for a moment against the peaks, then wheeled around and headed back toward its partner in the distance. I pondered for several seconds, then, on impulse, began rolling the coin down my knuckles once again, letting its silver surface catch the sunlight as it turned, reflecting the rays back into the sky. Instantly the bird swung out from its path and soared back in a wide arc. As I watched it approach, my skin began to crawl and come alive, like a community of bees in motion. The creature loomed larger—a sort of humming grew loud in my ears—and larger still, until it was there: an immense silhouette hovering just above my head, huge wing feathers rustling ever so slightly as they mastered the breeze. My fingers were frozen, unable to move—the coin dropped out of my hand. And then I felt myself stripped naked by an alien intelligence ten times more lucid than my own. I do not know for how long I was transfixed. I only know that I felt the air streaming past naked knees and heard the breeze whispering in my feathers long after the Other had departed.

It was dusk before I returned to the village, stunned and wondering at this strange initiation. Elements of my own magic (the coin-rolling exercise) and the *djankri*'s magic (the sacred boulder) had been woven together by the sunlight into an unlikely meeting, an experience that suggested that the deepest magic has its source not in humanity itself but in the meeting, the encounter of the human with what is not human. I had had intimations of this teaching many times in the past, but I had never felt its implications as clearly as I did that evening, and as I have ever since. After a dinner of potatoes dipped in salt and ground peppers, I took out my field notes and began to write. The following is excerpted from my research notes written in the Thami Valley, eastern Nepal:

> I have made progress in the task, set for me months ago by a Javanese witch, of thinking sensually—thinking, that is, with the senses, or sensing with the thoughts. It is a sort of clairvoy-ance, really, since we usually imagine thoughts to take place in

some interior space (we say that we think thoughts inside or that we are being "inward" when we are thinking) while the senses are in direct contact with the exterior world. But to have one's thoughts in direct contact with an exterior, open space—thoughts not just processing and interpreting data from the other senses, but thoughts which themselves are feeling their way through the shifting contours of an open world—how is this possible?

Perhaps it is best to begin with this fact: There is, indeed, an interior into which I commonly close myself when I think, but it is not inside my particular body or brain. It is, rather, the "inside" which my brain shares with all other brains that think in the same fashion. This interior is a sort of cave which has been formed among the sounds of the world, an auditory hollow that continues to define its limits and to isolate itself. It is, in other words, this verbal space, the house of human language, this one region of the world which is inhabited strictly by us humans, and which we therefore feel to be an "inside" or an "interior" in relation to the "outside" world. We readily perceive that this planet has given birth to many species, to many styles of awareness and ways of being, yet our everyday thoughts as humans currently inscribe themselves within a region of awareness that seems strictly our own and that presumptively shuts out all other styles of consciousness. Today we see and hear the rest of the planet only in terms of this privileged space—all the other animals, all trees and oceans, rocks and storms, all that lack a human tongue including Earth itself, we view from our insiders' space of purely human discourse. "If it cannot be put into words, then it does not exist," we say, efficiently banishing all other types of awareness. What arrogance! That to be human is a unique thing is quite certain, but surely it is also unique to be a crow, or a frog, or a night-blooming cereus. To be able to think with words is a neat power indeed—but that crow can actually fly!

By way of analogy: A person who is gifted with a certain type of intelligence is not thereby rendered unable to understand, empathize, and communicate with the rest of humanity. If he chooses to shut himself within his particular sensitivity, and to communicate solely with those few who share his gift, then so much the worse for him and his potentially wondrous sensitivity, which will become swollen and distorted. In a like manner, our collective gifts as Homo "Sapiens" hold wonderful promise, but we betray that promise when we hide behind those gifts and use them as a barrier between ourselves and all else that lives. We have such potentially grand powers for empathy and communication, since there is something in us of every animal, and also something of plants and stones and seas, for we are woven of the same fabric as everything on Earth and our textures and rhythms are those of the planet itself.

Yet we have staked out and established a space that contains only what we believe is unique and privileged in ourselves. All who cannot speak our type of language are necessarily dumb, not really alive; nothing is mindful but ourselves—all else is inert, determined, and therefore fit only for our observation and manipulation. We have closed ourselves into a universe of human verbiage.

How strange this is, and sad. And how clear it is why we have come to a crisis in our particular history, which is also a great crisis for the planet: How can we ever become fully human when we have forgotten how to be genuine animals?

The magicians I have traded with during the last nine months—like the monsoon magician of the rice paddies, or this mountain shaman whose medicineless cures are so remarkably successful—are persons who struggle to regain those memories. That is what sets the magician's path apart from that of the mystic; while others seek to move out of their bodies, the magician fights to return to her/his body, to recover a place in this material world from which s/he feels somehow cut off and estranged. Thus the successful sorcerer is hardly a transcendent being—he is an animal, human, a creature of Earth. His magic, far from being a supernatural power, grows out of an almost proto-human attentiveness to nature itself—out of his ability to listen not only with his verbal mind, but with his animal mind, his plant mind, his soil, rock, river, and deep Earth mind. For the sorcerer knows that the verbal space, this human gift, only makes sense for those who have learned how to enter that space, how to grow into it out of the silence, how to grow into the head from the body itself.

Yet there are many people these days who speak of communication with supernatural powers and other, a-physical worlds, many who write that our destiny as conscious beings lies not with the planet, but elsewhere, on other, more spiritual worlds or in other dimensions. The New Age lecture halls resound with such assertions, backed up with accounts of profound mystical experiences, of deeply spiritual sensations, of magic. I have an elegant intuition about all this, an intuition born from certain sensations experienced as a boy drawn to the study of conjuring, and then again, here, among the shamans of Asia. I, too, have had some extraordinary mystical experiences in my life, some powerful bursts of oceanic awareness. But somehow these shifted states were always caught up in the material world that surrounds; they did not take me out of this world into that purely spiritual region of disembodied freedom and light about which so many of my cohorts speak. No, as a young magician those experiences always revolved around a heightened and clarified awareness of the organic world that enveloped me. Far from drawing me out-side of this domain, my "spiritual" or "ecstatic" experiences never failed to make me startlingly aware of my corporeal presence, here, in the depths of a mysteriously shifting but none-the-less thoroughly physical world. So there grew in me steadily a sense that the so-called spirit is really the breath of the material world; indeed, there is no spirit more spiritual than the dance of light on the water's surface or the wind rustling in the leaves. What the conjuror is ever straining to express with his vanishing coins and color-changing cards is that the world of the most mysterious and mystical transformations is this world, right here, under our noses. And yet still I am confronted by news of another world, more eternal than this one (can it be?), an utterly transcendent, non-physical realm to which all "truly" mystical revelations give us access. From this I am forced to conclude either that my own ecstasies have nothing to do with the genuinely religious path, that they are, in fact, false ecstasies and unreal revelations still basely "attached" to the "physical plane," or else that there is some sort of mundane clarity in my own ecstatic experiences, which is lacking in the experience of those who feel the need to postulate the existence of some other wholly transcendent source.

Which brings me back to my aforementioned intuition about all our mystical encounters and revelations from elsewhere. Can it be that such experiences are, indeed, intimations of another, larger world than the one we usually inhabit with our everyday thoughts and perceptions, but that the larger world to which we thus gain access is none other than this very Earth, this very sphere within which we move, seen clearly now for the first time?

Is it possible that at such times we actually do break out of a limited, constricted world, although that limited world is not the material landscape that surrounds us, but is, rather, our limited and prejudiced human way of perceiving these surroundings, that stuffy house into which we lock our sensibilities by considering all other forms of life and existence to be without consciousness, inert, and determined? I wish to ask, finally, if it is possible that our ecstatic or mystical experiences grow precisely out of our receptivity to solicitations not from some other non-material world but from the rest of this world, from that part of our own sphere which our linguistic prejudices keep us from really seeing, hearing, and feeling—from, that is, the entire non-human world of life and awareness, from the sphere of whales with their incredible alien intelligence, of goats and apes and the fantastically organized insect colonies of flowers and hurricanes and volcanoes. It is the living, breathing, conscious Earth of creatures who are being bred and "harvested" as meat in our mechanized farms, of schools of fish choking in polluted waters, of whole rainforest universes, whole intercommunicating systems of elements, insects, plants and animals that are falling apart and dying from our fear, our species-amnesia, our refusal to recognize awareness anywhere outside our own brains.

The other animals have given us much, and they have been patient with us, as have the plants, the rivers, and the land itself. Many creatures have donated their lives to our quest. Many have undergone excruciating pain in our laboratories before being "sacrificed." The fish find it more and more difficult to swim in the stinging waters, while the passage upstream is blocked by dams. Birds spin through the chemical breeze, hunting in circles for that patch of forest that had been their home. They are not alone in their dizziness, for things are worsening throughout the biosphere. Naturally, then, the mountains, the creatures, the entire non-human world is struggling to make contact with us. The plants we eat are trying to ask us what we are up to; the animals are signaling to us in our dreams or from the forests. The whole Earth is rumbling and straining to remind us that we are of it, that this planet is our own flesh, that the grass is our hair and the trees are our hands and the rivers our own blood—that the Earth is our real body and that it is alive. And so, everywhere now, our "interior" space of strictly human discourse begins to spring leaks as other styles of communication make themselves heard, or seen, or felt. All over, in so many different ways, we feel intimations of a wholeness that is somehow foreign to us, and we see the traceries of another reality. It is indeed a time for magic, a magic time. But it is no supernatural thing, this magic. We are simply awakening to our own world for the first time, and hearing the myriad voices of Earth.

VOICES OF THE FOREST

Serge King

Serge Kahili King is the adopted grandson of Joseph Kahili, a *kahuna kupua* (master shaman) of Hawaii. Raised and trained in this tradition, he also has a Ph.D. in psychology and is the author of many works, including *Urban Shaman, Kahuna Healing,* and *Earth Energies,* related to the Hawaiian esoteric wisdom of Huna. As executive director of Aloha International, a worldwide network of Huna teachers and practitioners, Dr. King lives on the island of Kauai and travels extensively to teach Huna and to promote the spirit of aloha. "Voices of the Forest" is the epilogue from his book, *Kahuna Healing* (The Theosophical Publishing House, 1983).

What follows is the account of an experience I had, which now seems almost like it happened to someone else. I wrote this account shortly after it happened, and, looking back from the perspective of quite a few intervening years, I'm almost embarrassed by the fervor and improbability of it, and by the fact that I've not lived up to the task assigned me. But it did happen, and I'm still trying, and the name Kaula now evokes a kind of "future self" who helps me to help others. This was a mystical experience in physical surroundings, the kind that cannot help but change a person's life.

On August 30, 1975, I was camping with my family and several friends at the foot of Mount Able in Los Padres National Forest. We had all enjoyed the brilliance of the stars and the great number of meteors that flashed through the sky that evening. However, the cold soon forced us to retreat to the comfort of sleeping bags.

In the fullness of night I was awakened by a voice from within. Checking my watch I saw that it was nearly 2 A.M. The voice was urging me to get dressed and go outside, which I found myself doing without hesitation. The night was clear and warmer than it had been when we went to bed. The stars seemed even brighter, and there was still no moon. The air was undulating with a peculiar wave motion, which indicates a field of mana, and I was aware of a deep humming sound that seemed to vibrate through everything. It was nothing mechanical, but rather a living pulsation. The inner voice urged me to hike up the road to Mount Able, which I did, passing the sleeping figures of my companions.

Later I learned that they, too, had heard the humming, felt the power in the air, and had been called by an inner voice. But being unfamiliar with the area they thought it more prudent to remain in camp.

I walked for a long time, aware only of the humming and the mana, until my inner voice told me to stop and sit on a point overlooking the valley to the west. As I sat, I looked up at the stars. They were moving in large, irregular circles all over the sky. I blinked my eyes and shook my head, thinking it was an optical illusion, but they kept moving. Then suddenly the humming increased, a tingling went through my body, and a scintillating rainbow appeared before me, hanging in midair beyond the edge of the cliff. In the same moment I began to hear the murmuring of millions upon millions of voices from all around me and even inside me, from the stars, the air, the plants, the earth, from cells, molecules and atoms. Gradually I was able to perceive that all these myriad sounds were speaking as One, in unison. And they were speaking to me, calling me by my initiatory name.

"Kaula, Kaula, know that I AM, always, everywhere, everything. I AM the Nameless One of many names, the Soundless One of many voices. Kaula, be my prophet, my warrior of Light, my emissary, my Child of the Rainbow. Gather my children and help them experience My Presence. Teach Love, Kaula, for Love is the key to all. Love is the Path, Love is the Secret. Teach Love, Kaula, and Love Me."

Unable to speak, I sent out a feeling of love to the whole universe and was instantly flooded with a return flow so great that I entered a timeless, spaceless state of pure bliss. All conscious thought disappeared. I was myself, and yet I was All. I was a blade of grass, vibrating with tremendous inner strength as I slowly and inexorably pushed aside a rock thousands of times heavier and harder than myself. I was the rock, locked in a strange crystalline life cycle attuned to galactic time. I was a bird, warm and cozy under my ruffled feathers, asleep and dreaming my own unsharable dreams. And a tree, a coyote, an ant, a house, a comet, a cloud, the universe entire, one at a time and all at once. And I was I. At some point I passed into unconsciousness. When I awoke I was alone in the stillness, and as the new dawn broke I made my way back to camp.

"THE TREE IN WINTER IS LIKE"

Nancy Wood

Nancy Wood is a poet, novelist, and photographer. She is the recipient
of numerous awards, including a literature fellowship from the NEA.
She lives with her husband in Santa Fe and in Pagosa Springs, Colorado.
"The tree in winter is like" was originally published in *Many Winters*
(Doubleday, 1974).

> The tree in winter is like
> The lines upon my father's face
> Or like the paths I tried to take
> When I was young searching
> For one clear way to understanding.
> In every branch I found
> A smaller branch leading me
> Toward many ends and many sorrows.
> Too fragile to bear my weight,
> All my branches broke
> And I fell to the earth confused.
> I saw the tree in winter
> Reaching toward the sky
> With bare branches tangled
> Like so many paths and yet
> Each path had a purpose,
> Leading back to the roots of the tree.

FUSION:
The Soul Is Composed of the External World

Roger Dunsmore

Roger Dunsmore continues to teach Liberal Studies and Wilderness
Studies at the University of Montana, where he has been since 1963. He
was "Scholar in Residence" for the Arizona Humanities Council at the
largest Indian high school in the United States, on the Navajo reservation

in 1988–89. His book *Earth's Mind: Essays in Native Literature* was published by the University of New Mexico Press in 1997. Both in 1996 and again in 1997, he was the exchange fellow from the University of Montana to Shanghai International Studies University in mainland China. A manuscript of poems, *Tiger Hill,* from these experiences, has been completed. He has published two volumes of poems and three chapbooks.

> *The soul is composed of the external world.*
> — WALLACE STEVENS

The local, external world — the land and all the life forms that rise up from it — is internalized as a matter of survival necessity by native peoples. And it is just this internalization that gives to native peoples their power and beauty, the rightness of their existence. We call this inner/outer fusion, "harmony with the natural world." But the terms internal and external are themselves already the product of the separated consciousness that characterizes Western civilization — and civilization in general. It is as accurate to say that native peoples are called out of themselves by the beauty and diversity of the natural world as it is to say that they internalize it.

Rather than internalization or externalization, let us say that native peoples, Kalahari Bushmen, say, are the desert, as it articulates itself through human form and culture. And the desert is the Bushman as he articulates himself through natural form. They *are* together. They are one. They partake of the same is or being. They do not make sense in separation from each other. The desert without its Bushman, every bit as much as the Bushman without his desert, is emptied, reduced in its capacity to express itself, to be itself. This is not to say that the other desert life forms are insignificant — they too are the desert, are the Bushmen. But there is a human way of being of the desert that fulfills the being of the desert, every bit as much as there is a desert way of being human that fulfills the human being.

All that one really need know in order to understand the lives and cultures of native peoples lies in the meaning of the small word "of." If one understands at a deep level what it means to be *of* the desert, or *of* the Arctic, or *of* the bison or deer or salmon or reeds, one understands native peoples and this fusion between them and local place.

Laurens van der Post's *The Heart of the Hunter* contains a powerful account of native people being "of" the desert. With the help of an invincible steenbuck, a Bushman woman and child, an old Bushman grandfather, and the Kalahari Desert, van der Post takes us *inside* the deep interpenetration between Bushman and desert that is the underlying power of their existence. Van der Post is on his way out of the Kalahari after spending some days with a small band of Bushmen at a place named the "sip wells." It is a day in which van der Post experiences "the magic of the steenbuck," emptying the magazine of his rifle at a fine specimen not twenty yards away without hitting it, and spends the first night in his life actually camped amongst a group of "wild" Bushmen in the desert. At night, away from the campfire, he stumbles onto a lone woman holding her child high above her head, and singing something, with her own face lifted to the sky. He's told by Dab, his Bushman interpreter, that "the stars up there have heart in plenty and are great hunters. She is asking them to take from her little child his little heart and to give him the heart of a hunter." The woman greets him and Dab, and takes them to her fire; he makes the rounds of other fires as well until he comes to an old couple having some "man's talk" with their grandchildren. And van der Post, too, stays for some man's talk. Van der Post, true Western European that he is, has questions: "Was it true that the stars were hunters?" "Did the little steenbuck really possess great magic, and if so, what sort of magic?" His questions are met with a long silence. (We must imagine this silence. It appears in all true accounts of questioning exchange between those from European backgrounds and those from native backgrounds and is inseparable from the contents of any answers that are forthcoming. It is like the silence of the night that contains the language of the stars.)

The old man finally begins to speak. Yes, it is true, the stars are all hunters, but some are greater than others. The old man points to the brightest star in the Great Dipper and says it is:

> a great hunter who hunted in far away dangerous places in the shape of a lion. Could I not see how fierce its eye shone and hear the distant murmur of its roar? . . . The greatest hunter was not there yet. It hunted in the darkest and most dangerous places of all, so far away that we could not see it yet. We could see it only in the early morning when it came nearer on its way home. There, there was a hunter for you! The old father made a lively whistling sound of wonder at the greatness of the hunter. Yes, just before dawn one could see him striding over the horizon, his eye bold and shining, an arrow ready in his bow. When he appeared, the night whisked around to make way for him, the red dust spurting at its black heels. He broke off and shook his grey old head, as he once more uttered that sound of wonder, before ask-

ing as if the thought had just come to him: "But can't you hear for
yourself the cries of the hunt going on up there?"

The first time I read this passage, I was moved by its beauty, but my
skepticism was also aroused: I had not heard the stars. I suppose I considered it poetically quaint that the Bushmen should "project" their hunting
concerns onto the stars. It was just such accounts as this, I thought, that
had led to the rejection or romanticizing of native peoples and their experience. Native peoples appear to be naively animistic, or to anthropomor-
phize nature without knowing it. Stars neither speak nor hunt, I thought.
They will never truly understand the stars until they disengage from this
projecting of their own concerns onto them, etc. But my skepticism, too,
was not satisfying, for it expressed a kind of closure on a world that was
real, was there in the experience of native peoples, and I wanted to understand that world, that experience of the world. As I taught the book, more
than one student spoke of experiencing the stars speaking while sleeping
out in natural places. I began to ponder about meaning, about how things
come to mean what they do, about the shape meaning has for us. At some
point, my skepticism began to dissolve, or at least to become unimportant
in comparison to the world-experience I was trying to understand. The
skepticism was not wrong, but it was blocking. As a man from Euro-
American civilization, not as a Bushman—which I could never be—I came
to understand these pages in the following manner.

Meaning must occur in terms that make sense to us, in terms that have
to do with our actual life conditions. Meaning does not occur either in
some sort of experiential vacuum, or in terms that are divorced from our
actual concerns and condition. To the extent that this is so, we must be
cautious about labeling as "projections" those experiences of other peoples
that are expressed in terms suitable to *their* circumstances—that the stars
are great hunters is an appropriate response from a hunting-gathering
culture in a desert where sky is as vast and powerful as any ocean.

If survival for native peoples necessitated, as I believe it does, the dis-
solving of the borders between inner and outer worlds, necessitated becoming radically "of" the desert or the deer, then the means par excellence
of establishing this linkage, the means of becoming "of" particular places
and species, of creating a fusion between inner and outer worlds as every
Bushman carries the whole Kalahari Desert in its minute particulars within
him, is storytelling. The story that takes up with the place or other life
form in ways that relate the humans to the place or life form, that ex-
presses the human being's condition, concerns, circumstances, is the most

precious cultural creation there is. And such storytelling is neither mere personification nor subjectivity nor projection. It is based on sheer survival necessity through creating meaning out of one's relationship to the world. Without this creation of meaningful story as the literal fabric or flesh of one's interrelationship with the world, one is set adrift and either does not survive, or survives in despair, depression, anxiety, wantonness, or, I'm tempted to say, skepticism, which, yes, has its own story. What it means to be of the desert is to have so opened one's being or spirit to all the particulars of that place that the events of the desert take place within oneself every bit as much as out there in the natural world. Van der Post states it exactly:

> When one has lived as close to nature for as long as we had done,
> one is not tempted to commit the metropolitan error of assuming
> that the sun rises and sets, the day burns out and the night falls,
> in a world outside oneself. These are great and reciprocal events,
> which occur also in ourselves.

And so, the story about the stars as hunters.

When human beings are "of" their local world, centered in and by it, their stories are filled with experiences of star hunters, deer people, rain people, insect allies. They have found, there in their particular place in the world, those with whom to compose and nourish their souls. They have established or participated in the great, ongoing dialogue or conversation of everything with everything in their place.

We do not hear the stars. In the words of Martin Heidegger, things don't "thing" for us. The noise of our own society and central nervous system fills the airwaves—all else is jammed, like Radio Free Europe. We talk incessantly because we have forgotten how much there is to hear. A student once told my class that her grandfather always said the reason we had two ears but only one tongue was because we're supposed to listen at least twice as much as we talk.

If one pursues the imagery of the stars as hunters of the Bushman grandfather, one discovers that a large part of the power of the stars, for the Bushman, is their capacity to endure darkness and distance. Those who hunt in the darkest parts of the sky, and so far off it is nearly dawn when they return, are the bravest hunters. The sun has the power to vanquish darkness, but the stars must accept it as their medium; they are mere splinters of light flung out into the vast darkness of deep space. The Bushmen attribute to them great courage for their ability to maintain the pure intensity of their light in the midst of this dark ocean. To ask that the heart of one's own child be exchanged with the heart of a star—not only will the child be a great hunter, possessed of the courage to endure darkness and distance, but its own heart resides among the stars, establishing the supportive linkage with the universe that will see him through many a far, dark night. What a gift to have as an example of how to be—the bright star in the darkest sky—and to know that one's own heart is of these stars, of this sky, the simple, clear, always-available star presence in the desert night. To live with a star's heart in oneself—to know one's own heart shines in the night sky, to be the child of such an exchange. "The soul is composed of the external world." What comparable examples of sustaining linkage to the natural world does modern civilization offer to its children?

Personification. Projection. Animism. Myth. These are precisely the vehicles for establishing meaningful linkage between human beings and the universe.

Back-Home Pilgrimage

Elan Shapiro

Elan Shapiro, M.A., an ecopsychology educator and counselor, bioregionalist, and sustainable communities consultant, has trained in a wide variety of healing and ecological disciplines. He is coparenting and helping build a second cohousing neighborhood at EcoVillage at Ithaca, where he is the educational director. He is currently building partnerships for sustainability between EcoVillage at Ithaca, the local universities, and the local communities in the Cayuga Lake Watershed. "Back-Home Pilgrimage" was originally published in *Creation* magazine.

Returning from an extended pilgrimage in the wilderness to an everyday world that seems stripped of soul is often a shock. We may feel a sense of alienation, depression, and even violation. Eventually, as the high gears start whirring, we adjust to our thickly scheduled lives by allowing the wilderness experience—that interpenetration of self and place—to fade into the background. Sometimes, weeks later, we wake up to realize that we have almost fully lost the sense of connection we so treasured on our pilgrimage.

After many years of wilderness journeys—and recurrent bouts of postpilgrimage shock syndrome—I realized that the next stage of my sacred questing needed to be closer to home. So close to home, in fact, that it would necessarily restructure the very matrix of my everyday life, rather than collide with it.

The excursions I wanted to undertake could not replace the expansiveness, the primal nurturing and the rebalancing provided by an extended pilgrimage. They could, however, perform the equally vital role of re-establishing the sacred connection between my deep self and the whole of creation where I live—in this body, in this neighborhood, with these friends and neighbors, through this houseplant or pet. And they could help me locate the seeds of personal and planetary transformation in the quality of my moment-to-moment encounters with my surroundings and my companions, not later on, but today.

Tuesday, early morning. I pick a little bouquet of flowering thyme from the garden, drive to the nearby park without turning on the radio, and walk with even steps on a trail part-way up a little mountain. I find a particularly cozy spot overlooking a valley of oak and hay trees and bask in its bountiful green energy. I scatter the sprigs of thyme here—my corny ritual way of bringing a gift of appreciation to the place, a gift that says, "Of course I have time to visit you. See here, I have lots of thyme." Forty minutes from starting, I bring home two fresh, shiny bay leaves from the mountain and put one in the bean stew and the other on the pilgrimage altar on my desk. I make a few notes about the encounter in my journal, then start making business calls.

Wednesday, late afternoon. Both compost buckets are full and their contents are liquefying. I can't get to my friend's house where I would usually contribute them to her heap. Remembering the old potato patch in the garden where nothing is planted at present, I decide to bring this gift of food to the earth right outside my bedroom. Excited by this simple solution, I make the twenty-step journey, bucket and shovel in hand, with a quiet intensity befitting the final steps to the top of a Himalayan peak. After digging the disintegrating mess deep into the soil, I sit right on the spot, surrounded by bursts of spinach, tomatoes and zucchini, feeling as if my umbilical cord has been reconnected. I begin to reflect on gardens as places where an intimate daily dialogue with the earth might be re-established. I decide to leave that little spot "unproductive" for a time, with perhaps a few rocks or a bench there, just a place to be, and to celebrate the power of those twenty timeless steps.

Friday, late afternoon. Feeling boxed in and disconnected from too much talking and thinking, I get together with a friend for a walk in the neighborhood. She, too, is word-weary, yet we've been looking forward to this time of sharing with each other. So we agree, as an experiment, to communicate either nonverbally or, when talking, to stay with our present experiences.

We head out on a playful note, conveying through gestures our delight in the clouds, the gnarly old oak trees, and the rollicking children in the day-care center. By the time we're alongside the reservoir, we've settled in quite a bit. From within the embrace of silence, we speak of what is going on around us and inside us: ducks migrating overhead, weariness and longing, background roar of rush hour, spaciousness, relief, waning light of day. All becomes part of our soul poem, part of the song of the place.

Sunday morning. I sense a need for minimal structure and effort in today's excursion, just to follow my feet and be open. After a block or two of wandering freely, I happen upon a golden retriever sniffing out the neighborhood. I start to follow behind him and imagine experiencing the place from his physical level and perceptual framework. Little shrubs and clumps of grass take on greater significance, as do hubcaps, hidden alleyways, and faraway smells. He leads me to an old stone wall, and from there down to a section of creek that I have never noticed before. Dropping onto all fours and crawling and sniffing through the underbrush together, I soak up the aromas of the place and become my contented creature self. Exhausted, I finally roll onto my back and feel the nurturing energy and solid support coming from the warm, wet earth beneath me.

A walk in the park, out to the yard, or around the block with a friend or a dog. Each of these experiences, on the surface, seems like a routine interlude of ordinary urban life. Yet a few subtle shifts of attitude and perception helped foster an experience of myself and where I live as delicately and deeply interwoven. Each walk, lovely in itself, became for me another small step toward reweaving the voices of earth, wind, creatures, and friends into the fabric and soul of my daily life.

As I began to share these adventures with other people, I discovered — and helped inspire — other pilgrims on this path of reinhabitation. Our backgrounds, styles, and home bases were often quite different. Yet as we traded stories and shared journeys, a number of common threads to our healing excursions emerged. I share these with you now, not as recipes, but as catalysts to your own back-home approach to connection and healing.

The challenge in a back-home pilgrimage is in your ability to change gears and penetrate through the driven quality of modern life. Find out what simple transitions help you prepare for your midstream escapade. It might be the choice of a small, symbolic gift to give back to the place, a journal entry about your intentions, a brief shower, or a self-massage. You can contact your inner landscape by taking a few minutes to sense and follow your breathing, and let its energy and rhythm bring you back to your bodily and earthly presence.

Each place can mirror and empower a different part of yourself if you are open to its particular presence. Relax your mind and consult your intuition as you prepare to go out. What place and what pace will suit the grief, the restlessness, or the expansiveness that you are feeling? Do you need to encounter your tree self, your creek self, your seashore self, or your flowers-in-the-cracks-in-the-sidewalk self? Perhaps you need to go with no plan at all and let your feet and heart direct you.

Consciously play with your perceptual system to loosen up the hard boundaries within which we're accustomed to functioning. Imagine your physical and psychic boundaries as they naturally can be—flexible, permeable, preserving of your integrity, yet also places of contact, expansion, and exchange. Let your vision soften and widen so that you can shift from the outsider mode of looking "at" things to being "on the inside," seeing patterns and connections. Let your thoughts connect with and reflect your situation. Cultivate your connected self.

The wisdom of your body and the playfulness of your inner child will probably bring you home much more directly than an overdose of mindful solemnity. Try dropping the upright "on top of things" habit. Stretch, climb, crawl; sniff, roll, float; spiral, slither, swing. Feel your steps as sensuous meetings with the earth, your breath as the ocean of air pulsing through each of us. Feel how each of your senses opens you to a particular way of contact and communication with your world.

Solitary natural places are not hard to find, even in a big metropolis. Staying on the wide, designated trails of neighborhood parks often keeps us in a safe observer role. Traveling narrower paths or animal trails, provided you are sensitive to the impact you're making, can create a time for quietude as well as heightened contact, as you literally brush up against the world around you.

Include your whole body, your car, your walking shoes, jet and siren sounds, in your experience of the journey. Follow the paths made by children or leading to abandoned warehouses with the same devotion you would give to a deer trail or the approach to a shrine. Let your pilgrimage help bridge the devastating separation between the human and the natural world. See your life as the life of your place.

Be aware of places on the journey that are tempting to sidestep. Steep places, dark places, trashed places, your own places of desolation, disconnection, and despair. Make a pilgrimage to the nearest, biggest source of toxic waste and be open to its teaching. Sense when you're ready to stretch your boundaries gently and to encounter these places and parts of yourself.

Reinhabiting your self and your place is a creative discovery that begins right at your doorstep. The love you nurture in your local soulwork is a vital step in building an ecologically and spiritually grounded community. As it grows and embraces the whole matrix of your place, it inevitably helps transform the global nightmare of violation and despair. So as you slither and sniff and step softly on the path, know that you are slowly and subtly finding your place in the regenerative network of roots that hold the earth together.

WATERING THE GARDEN

Jeff Poniewaz

Jeff Poniewaz teaches Literature of Ecological Vision at the University of Wisconsin-Milwaukee. His poems have appeared in numerous publications, such as *Earth First!*, *Greenpeace Chronicles*, and the *Los Angeles Times*. His collection of eco-poems and meditations, *Dolphin Leaping in the Milky Way* (Inland Ocean Books, 1986) is in its third printing and includes "Watering the Garden." He has compiled an anthology of eco-poems titled *On What Planet—Poems in Praise and Defense of the Earth*, which awaits a receptive publisher.

> At first I regarded it a chore.
> Now I savor it, desperately
> needed relaxation, a respite
> from the squirrel-cage of thoughts,
> a sudden listening to all that is there.
> Birdsong once more more awesome
> than the most intricate flights
> of human-wrought fancy available
> on vinyl, more delicious to hear
> than even the most foresty woodwind
> passages in Dvořák, Sibelius,
> greener even than Delius.
> Suddenly the mockingbird alights

once more at the zenith of
the Norfolk Island Pine,
its throat no less melodious
than Keats' Nightingale.
Announcing itself to the universe
more eloquently than the most "trained"
opera singers, more poignantly,
more jubilantly. Wingéd aria
Out of the Cradle Endlessly Rocking
apparition. Do I Wake or Sleep?
The Bird Sang Me. Beyond Word.
Trills and runs beyond notation.
Watering my garden and really breathing.
Time out for timelessness. A "breather."
A brief reprieve from a life
sentence to "urgent concerns."
My breath and my heart reunion'd
with the wilderness
snuck up on me in my own backyard,
my spirits rising indomitably as
the 15-foot purple hollyhocks
springing beside my garden
in southwest San Francisco,
emerald hummingbird
come to hover holyghostly
in the rainbows of my hose-spray.

MYSTERY, HUMILITY AND THE WILD

Steven Harper

Steven Harper, M.A., Psychology, has taught for Colorado Outward
Bound and National Outdoor Leadership School and founded Earthways
Wilderness Journeys. He coordinates Esalen Institute's Wilderness
Programs. For twenty-five years he has led both traditional and experimen-
tal wilderness expeditions on five continents. In addition to wilderness
work he facilitates individual and group change. Steven lives with his sons
Kai and Kes in Big Sur, California.

It was late August. The tundra had already begun to take on fall colors and the nights were finally getting dark enough that the northern lights could put on a show. My two-month expedition across the Northwest Territories of Canada was coming to an end, and I was living with the Inuit community of Chesterfield Inlet on the upper region of Hudson Bay. Before I came north I had seen what I had thought to be impressive northern light displays. I had read a number of books and the latest articles giving the scientific explanations of what and why. None of this prepared me for what I experienced.

At one in the morning, I was up walking the gravel streets of Chesterfield Inlet with a few of my newly made Inuit friends. As we walked out of the small settlement and across the tundra, the display of northern lights became richer in color and more intense in frequency. Even my Inuit friends, who had grown up accustomed to such exhibits of the cosmos, stopped to look up. Curtains of multicolored light rippled across the night sky. Each successive wave grew closer and intensified. At its crescendo, an undulating curtain shot across the expansive sky and came so low that I instinctively hit the ground fully expecting to be struck by the light itself. My Inuit friends were bent with laughter as I lay surprised on the ground looking up at the ongoing dance of light (though I noticed they, too, had been impressed). There on the cold tundra, humbled and laughing at myself, I felt in awe of the mystery of all life, of all existence. Overcome by a feeling of wholesome contentment, embraced by mystery, all became sacred.

The mystery of wilderness is exactly what draws so many of us to it, just as the wild that lies within draws many seekers inward. Through the eons, our human urge to explore has led us toward unknown frontiers to find the source of mystery. Mystery has the simultaneous ability to drive people to destruction with frustrated desire and also to provide a magic sparkle to life. Without mystery, the magic of life drops away. Paradoxically, as we search out answers to our mysteries we must also be willing to accept and embrace mystery as it is. The Dutch philosopher Aart van der Leeuw best stated our dilemma when he said, "The mystery of life is not a problem to be solved but a reality to be experienced." Contentment and wholeness is dependent to some degree on our ability to be with and embrace mystery. It is a part of ourselves and a part of the natural world. Embracing mystery is not a blind acceptance of unanswered questions but, instead, a curious wonderment of that which is inexplicable—the mystery of it all.

In the civilized environment we are surrounded by human-made, human-explainable things. When we enter the natural environment of wilderness we are met with the inexplicable wonders of nature. While the biological and physical sciences have successfully answered many of our questions in regard to the natural world, the fundamental questions still remain unanswered. Even if these basic questions were answered, most of the answers would only bring with them more questions. The wilderness environment puts us back in touch with the magic of life and the enlivening sparkle that goes with it. The wonder of it all brings a wholesome respect and reverence for all life. When felt deeply, all becomes sacred.

I believe the contentment I felt that August day was not about finding answers, but about finding that I could, for a moment, live with all the magic of mystery for exactly what it is, nothing more, nothing less. Most of us have had those rare moments when all our "stories" about life and the universe fall through and we are touched by raw feeling. We allow the fullness of reality to touch us, without shielding the self with questions. While I value questions, I also see that we can easily use them to protect or remove ourselves from direct answers. Life is "a reality to be experienced." One of the geniuses of modern times, Albert Einstein, gave us these wise words:

> The most beautiful experience we can have is the mysterious. It is the fundamental emotion which stands at the cradle of true art and true science. Whoever does not know it can no longer wonder, no longer marvel, is as good as dead, and his eyes are dimmed. It was the experience of mystery—even if mixed with fear—that engendered religion.

Living in wilderness, we are close to the awesome, incomprehensible, uncontrollable forces of nature. The "stripping down" to a more fundamental lifestyle, and the direct contact we have with both nature and mystery, is humbling. The experience of a lightning storm, an avalanche, or the magnificent beauty of a cascading waterfall gives us a natural perspective on our place in the world. Our culture, with its fear-based reaction to mystery and wilderness, can afford a less pretentious stance, a simple acknowledgment of our shortcomings, and a basic respect for the living and nonliving things of nature. Humble pie may be just the diet for our cultural indigestion. René Dubos has this human-wilderness perspective.

> Humanized environments give us confidence because nature has been reduced to the human scale, but the wilderness, in what-

ever form, almost compels us to measure ourselves against the cosmos. It makes us realize how insignificant we are as biological creatures and invites us to escape from the daily life into the realms of eternity and infinity.

Interestingly enough, the very word *humble* is derived from the Greek word *humus*, which means soil or ground. So, in a sense, to be humble is to be close to the soil or earth. *Humble, humus, homage, human,* and *humane* all come from the same root word meaning earth. Quite literally, we can humbly pay homage to the humus from which we humans came. In other words, with modesty, we can regain respect for our soil—our earth. With our hands and feet well "grounded" in the soil of this earth, we can experience a primal union with the earth and reinhabit our true home. To be humbled by the mystery of wild nature is never to be quite the same.

Mystery and, certainly, humility are not virtues that contemporary culture supports. For example, we get F's for not knowing and humility is often mistaken for weakness. Wilderness, on the other hand, supports and cultivates a taste for embracing and even finding strength in mystery and humility. I am reminded of the Zen teacher who encourages his students to cultivate "don't know" mind: an unassuming mind that is surprised and fresh each moment even with the ordinary and everyday, an alive mind that is simultaneously empty and full of creative possibility—perhaps true mystical experience.

Do you want to transform your life? My recommendation is a simple one: Go out in the wilds, take off your shoes, sink your feet well into the ground, and be touched by mystery.

$\mathcal{U}$NCIVILIZED

Laura Carrithers

For the past four years Laura Carrithers has been living and writing on a remote 670-acre piece of land in the Coast Range of northern California. From here she has begun a passionate and tentative return to wildness, both in her art and in her self. She is an assistant editor at Island Press, and has been writing for almost twenty years from such diverse landscapes as Patagonia, Alaska, and all over the United States. She received her B.A. in poetry at Mills College.

What if I came down
out of my watchtower of worry,
left the watchful room empty,
alone with its great fear,
and bent my head
to the soft landing
of earth below.

What if I were to move away
from the supports and ladder
of the tower of watchfulness
and make my way down the steep
sides of the canyon to the wide river
at its base, press my ear to its surface
till there is no chance of hearing
any sound from the outside world again.

What if I then closed my eyes,
stopped taking notice of whatever of my fear
might have followed me down the ladder
and on down to this river,
turned away from the possibility of some
unknown waiting for me in the brush
or behind the patient trees.

What if finally my hands
were not always ready to grip
or push, if the feeling
were all but gone from them
as they grew to hold only
wind and sun, knowing no
resistance or measure,
not even usefulness.

How tragic would it be
if one woman out of millions
were to come out of that nest
the generations built for us,
refuse the food of our time,
and live only for listening.

How quickly would a world be upset
by the small act of one individual
leaving the race with tension
for a life that is sated with stillness.

How sorry would the trees be
or the rivers, if one woman crossed over
from the cell of her noise
to the freedom of her quiet.

BURIED POEMS

Terry Tempest Williams

Terry Tempest Williams is a naturalist-in-residence at the Utah Museum
of Natural History. She is the author of *Pieces of White Shell—A Journey to
Navajoland* (Charles Scribner's Sons, 1984), which received a Southwest
Book Award. Her other books include *Refuge* (Pantheon, 1991), *The
Secret Language of Snow* (Sierra Club, 1984), *Between Cattails* (Charles
Scribner's Sons, 1985), *An Unspoken Hunger* (Pantheon, 1994), *Desert
Quartet* (Pantheon, 1995), and *Coyote's Canyon* (Peregrine Smith, 1989).
She is a recipient of a Lannan Fellowship in creative nonfiction and was
identified by the *Utne Reader* as one of one hundred visionaries "who could
change your life." "Buried Poems" was originally published in her book
Coyote's Canyon.

There is a man in Boulder, Utah, who buries poems in the desert. He is an
archaeologist who knows through his profession that eventually his words
will be excavated, that although they may not be understood now by his
community, at a later date his poetry will be held as an artifact, mulled
over by minds that will follow his.

This man is alone, walled in by the wilderness he loves and neighbors
who don't understand him. They say he spends too much time with the
dead, that his loyalties are to bones, that the land could be better used for
the planting of corn than the digging of corpses. They say he talks too
little and thinks too much for a town like Boulder.

He has lived among the locals for decades, but he is still an outsider. It
is the Anasazi who keep him here. They are his neighbors, the ones who

court his imagination. It is their echoes reverberating through the canyons that hold him.

He listens and he studies. He pores over the artifacts that come into the museum where he works. When no one is around, he pulls out his glasses, slips on his white cotton gloves, and carefully turns the objects over and over as though some wisdom might speak to him from a sandal or basket or cradle board.

Occasionally, a local drops in. He invites them outdoors and encourages them to sit between sage. He takes his hand and sweeps it across the valley and tells them this site was once occupied by over two hundred individuals, continuously from A.D. 1058 to 1200, that this is twice the population living in Boulder today. He tells them the Anasazi were born farmers, and hunters and gatherers—planting beans, squash, and corn as they supplemented their diet with big game and rodents. He tries to convince them that the Anasazi, through their technology of manos, metates, pinched pots, and atlatls, were remarkable people well adapted to an inhospitable environment. And then he stops himself, realizing how carried away he has become. He lets the visitors wander among the ruins.

On another day, some neighbors ask, "Are you finding anything good out there?"

"It's all good," the archaeologist replies, "corn cobs, charcoal, and chipping debris … ."

The neighbors are unimpressed. He gives in.

"But one time, we were excavating in a particular site and uncovered three ollas—corrugated vessels used for carrying water. Next to these pots were two large balls of clay that had been kneaded. You could still see palm marks from the anonymous hands that had made them. Beneath the pots and clay balls was a burial, the delicate placement of female bones."

He pauses as he rubs his hand over the soil. "I honestly believe she was a potter. We have found no reference to anything like it in the literature. It is most unusual."

The locals look at him, puzzled, and shake their heads. It doesn't register. He sees it in their eyes. They ask him for evidence and he says they buried it for another generation to uncover. They look at the dry land and they look at him, and they walk away.

The man leaves the museum for the day, locks the door behind him, and retreats to his spot in the rocks. He pulls out his pencil and spiral notebook from a front pocket of his cowboy shirt and begins writing. Poems come to him like wild horses to water. He writes a few lines, tears the paper, and burns the edges with his lighter. He writes another verse, tears it from his notebook, antiques it with fire, and places it in a pile that he holds down with his boot. By the end of the afternoon, he has a dozen or more poems. On his way home, he buries them.

The man knows the ways of these people. They ranch and they farm. They know the contours of the land, and if a white triangle of paper is sprouting where corn should be, they'll pull it up. Or if the cows are out grazing and happen to kick a sheet of paper into the air, it'll get read by the wranglers. And when women are planting borders of zinnias around their homes and uncover a poem with their trowel, they'll call their neighbors just to pass the words along.

Which is exactly what happened. Within a matter of days, the whole town of Boulder was reading each other poetry.

Some think they are love poems written by an Indian. Others guess they are clues to a buried treasure left by John Wesley Powell or Father Escalante. And still others believe they are personal messages left especially for them by a deceased family member, which is how they became known as "the ghost poems."

The archaeologist listens. He walks about town with his hands in his pockets. People are talking across fences, over melon stands, and inside their automobiles. Some individuals are even offering to buy them from their friends. But the finders of the poems won't sell. The man who buries the poems quietly slips into the convenience store and buys another notebook and lighter and returns to his place in the rocks.

His poems become shorter, more cryptic, until, finally, they are a series of pictographs—the pictographs found in Calf Creek Canyon, Coyote Gulch and Mimi's Grotto.

The town eventually seeks him out, asking if he knows what these picture poems might mean. He refers them to different canyons, invites them to his slide shows, and tells them stories about the Anasazi who once lived where they do now. He explains how these drawings on canyon walls are a reflection of Anasazi culture, of rituals, and all that mattered in their lives. Now, he tells them, we can only speculate. The townsfolk are listening. He sees it in their eyes.

A local hands him a poem and says, "Read this. My boy found it buried near the overhang behind our ranch."

The archaeologist reads the poem out loud.

SOUNDS
by Larry Davis (an archaeologist in Boulder, Utah)

The ruin clings to the cliff
Under the arching sandstone.
It is quiet now.
No longer do you hear the laughter,
The everyday sounds:
Women making pottery—the slap, slap of clay,
People cooking,
Men returning from the hunt,
The builders,
Children playing,
The cries of sorrow when a loved one passes on.
They are gone now—
The Anasazi.
The survivors.
The adaptors.
The only sounds now
Are those of the wind
The raucous sound of the raven, and
The descending sound of the canyon wren.
The guardians.

By now, the town of Boulder has hundreds of these poems in its possession. They hang in the schoolhouse, where the children are taking up the mystery. The community still wonders who is responsible for these writings, questioning just how long they will continue to be found. But poems keep appearing in the strangest places: in milk cans, on tractor seats, church pews, and irrigation ditches. And rumor has it, the canyons are filled with them. It may be that the man who buries poems in the desert has turned the whole damned town into archaeologists. The next thing we'll hear is that the locals want to preserve the wilderness for its poetry.

VIII

Wilderness Ethics: An Emerging Perspective

Nature is too enormous to encapsulate or control. It is wise to remain mindful that wilderness *is* potentially dangerous. I am concerned that the glowing presentation of the benefits of wilderness experience will inspire people to head for the hills, venturing naively and recklessly into challenging situations, unprepared and uneducated.

I am saddened when I hear accounts of people who die rock climbing without ropes, get hypothermia from lack of adequate clothing, are buried in snow avalanches, or become separated from the rest of their party and get lost. The remote terrain of certain areas is something to be approached thoughtfully. Even the most experienced of mountaineers encounter unexpected circumstances, when the weather turns dramatically for the worse or an accident occurs, when lives are threatened and even lost. A little bit of education and intelligent preparation can go a long way in saving lives. Included in this chapter is one contribution that deliberately warns us—and several others that more indirectly remind us—of the power, enormity, and unpredictability of being in the great outdoors.

Bringing the book full circle in its intent to portray a holistic point of view, the contributions in this section reflect the perspective of deep ecology and ecopsychology, where humans are seen as but one part of the complexity of nature, neither more than nor less than other beings. We are recognized as strands of the web of a wide and intricate tapestry of the animated earth and expanding cosmos. Seeing ourselves and our relationship to wilderness from within the web places us in a frame of reference that naturally holds us in modesty, awe, and respect for the diversity, magnitude, and beauty of life. Naturally, in the perpetuation and support of life, we prioritize and serve the well-being and continuation of the whole, which includes our personal reward and survival.

In the not-so-distant past, many native peoples had little concept of "wilderness"; wilderness was their home. Wilderness fed and nourished life. People established ways of surviving in balance and with reverence for their surroundings. Culture, religion, and lifestyles developed intimately around their unique connection to their environment.

In today's world, we tend to be far more removed from nature, both within and outside ourselves. Most of us spend most of our time indoors, sometimes in apartments many floor levels above the ground. We usually do not know where our food comes from or who cultivated it. We have become estranged from the earth, from our bodies, and from the other beings who inhabit the earth. There is great fear and misunderstanding about wilderness. In general, we lack a familiar and close relationship to the very source of life that sustains us.

On a very practical level, one way of restoring balance is to breathe fresh air more often. Wilderness has a way of creeping into and penetrating the fabric of our lives, organically bringing us into a more harmonious relationship with the entirety of life. Wilderness, as a magnificent and wondrous force of healing, has the potential to transform and renew us completely. Wilderness leads us back to our center. Even the knowledge that wild places exist consoles and frees the human spirit.

At another level, I want to ask, What is already free and wild and has no need of recovery? I wish to suggest that the spaciousness we encounter while in nature also permeates the world of our everyday lives. It is my hope that our individual and collective consciousness enlarges and relaxes to the point where we are able to recognize wilderness wherever we are. In this process, we shed our notions of what is and is not wilderness. Then wilderness is freed to be wilderness, as it always has been anyway. We see the uncontrollable, uncontainable, and impossible-to-possess wildness and inherent freedom that rests within the wilderness of who we are. We rejoice in this seeing. The new frontier is right here, right now.

THE DANCE

Jesse Wolf Hardin

Jesse Wolf Hardin (once known as Lone Wolf Circles) is an acclaimed presenter, recording artist, and the author of *Kindred Spirits: Sacred Earth Wisdom* (Swan Raven Press, 2001). Joanna Macy writes, "Wolf sings us Full Circle to the raw, sweet wildness within, and calls us forward to the future primeval." His hundreds of essays have helped in the defining of deep (spiritual) ecology and environmental ethics, appearing in publications such as *Talking Leaves, Earthlight, Green Egg,* and *Earth First!* Wolf currently hosts seekers for quests, workshops, and wilderness retreats at his Gila wildlands sanctuary under the auspices of The Earthen Spirituality Project. "The Dance" first appeared in *Talking Leaves.*

> *We are dancing on the brink of a world which we know so little of;*
> *we are dancing the dance of life, of death; dancing the moon up in*
> *celebration of dimly remembered connections with our ancestors;*
> *dancing to keep the cold and darkness of a nuclear winter from*
> *chilling our bones; dancing on the brink of ecological awareness;*

dancing for the sake of dancing without analyzing and rational-
izing and articulating; without consciously probing for meaning
but allowing meaning in being to emerge into our living space.
    —BILL DEVALL, *Simple in Means, Simple in Ends*
                  (Gibbs Smith)

I finally found a home a few years back, not just a beautiful place to visit, but a place I bonded with completely and immediately. The landscape of my childhood dreams as well as my premonitions of the future. A place I would do anything for. I fell in love with the touch of the river, and knew it as myself, from sensuous trickle to explosive flood. I knew which cave would wear the painted outline of the red wolf mother long before I ventured there. At the same time, as I pledged myself to this particular land, I realized it was not enough to save and resacrament this place as my own. I knew that to be worthy of it, I must enter the struggle to save and resacrament the rest of this contiguous planet.

I threw myself into the fray, writing articles, reading poems, organizing campaigns and demonstrations, engaging in civil disobedience, and instigating the rituals and dances that empower these efforts. I was rushing from one rally to another when my borrowed car developed an ominous knock. It got progressively louder one day as I approached the Eisenhower Tunnel in the Colorado Rockies. I pulled over at the tunnel entrance just as the damnable engine welded itself shut, an inert block of steel awaiting its return to the earth as iron oxides. I pulled out my unread mail even as the snowflakes fell faster and the last of the stored heat bailed out through the window glass. The first letter was from my child, whom I was not allowed to see. The second was from a lover who had decided I was "a little too much." The third was from an old Hispanic neighbor, alerting me that my caretaker had split and my horse had starved to death.

I quickly hitchhiked home, salvaging from the car only what I could carry. I was awash with grief and for the first time questioned the implicit vision. How could the spirit let me down, allowing my home, the source of my power, to fall apart even as I was doing the work instructed of me? I was surprised, on arriving at the old man's house, by the sight of my pony, fattened on Senovio's hay. He had told me it died to get me to come home and take care of things. He gave me a ride as far as the first river crossing and I walked the last two miles in prayer. Inside my unlocked cabin, above my unwashed dishes, unwatered houseplants flourished, covering over a third of the ceiling! Entering the wind-carved cave where I had slept for years, I performed the most relevant ritual I knew. I knew nothing of what ritual my pre-Odinist Viking ancestors would have held, and those I'd learned from Hopi and Sioux seemed somehow inappropriate. I performed the appropriate ritual for a fallible and very appreciative white boy. I played my drum and cried.

Our real human nature exists only in relation to "Nature." We are most ourselves as part of the language of the land, in context—in the texture of the nonabstracted and nonmanipulated landscape. The empowered truths found in all mystical traditions, from Tantra to Wicca, are rooted in the natural. They are the diverse, animate expressions of the Earthen Spirit, the living planet. What we now call deep ecology is the recognition of the intrinsic, sacred value of each and every manifestation of this Nature. Effective social, political, or environmental activism is empowered not by rational deduction, but by the same heartfelt and spiritual connectedness that was deeply lived by the primal ancestors of all races, and by every other living species.

When the men of northern India refused to endanger their woods-based jobs by opposing the clearcutting of the last forests at the foot of the Himalayas, it was the women who stopped it. Recognizing that they were not only losing the fuel they cook with, but the sacred presence of the trees, they set aside their immediate economic concerns and took a stand. When no one would listen to these "impractical, emotional" women, and their petitions went ignored, they literally wrapped themselves around the trees. The women did not merely think, "There goes my beautiful scenery." They did not accept the traditionally held belief that the lower caste, and women in particular, have no power. They knew their power came from the trees themselves, and from the Devas within all living things. By hugging the trees, they said to their saw-wielding relatives, to the regional and national governments, and to thousands of years of patriarchal destruction, "This tree's flesh is my flesh. When you cut into these trees, you are cutting into my guts."

There are two ways of looking at who we are. One is the "narrow" self, defined by the skins of our individual bodies. We only exist, however, as part of the "greater" self. Not greater as in better, but as in complete, inclusive. We were a part of it before "we" were born, and remain a constituent after "we" die. We cannot put on enough clothes to be separate from the rest of it. No matter how high we leap, we are as submerged within the body of the greater self as a fish is contained within its water. It is not a matter of reconnecting with nature, because we are already connected. We can only imagine ourselves as somehow separate, apart, alone. It is this illusion of separateness, this dis-ease, that allowed for the enslavement of land and suppression of other peoples. All so-called "social injustices" result from what is essentially an "environmental" tragedy. Only by asserting that we are separate from, and superior to, other life forms can we rob them of their dignity and, ultimately, deny them the right to exist.

Once we not only recognize but *experience* ourselves as inseparable parts of the organic whole, it's no longer possible to make excuses for our indulgent and destructive lifestyles, to accept the dispiriting domestication or complete extinction of other life forms. When we feel the earth as an integral and continuous part of our selves, we no longer protect the dying rain forests as a botanical source for medicines or as a scenic resource, as something *other* than us. We know them deeply and completely. They are our lungs—to save them is to save ourselves. And as they are the lungs of the planet, we are the conscience. The extirpation of any species, the extinction of any expression of this self, impoverishes our spirit and threatens our very existence. From giant suffering grizzly bears to the endangered mat of mycorrhizal fungi (which transfer nutrients from the soil to the roots of the trees), the loss of any one life form is the loss of a vital strand in the delicate web of existence and endangers the life of the whole. The birds are more than food for our plates or a feast for our eyes: they are our wings. We feel the portentous vibrations from the core of the earth/body through root and worm, and feel the winds of change through our extended fingers, through our swaying leaf-tipped branches. The memory of our past, and of who we really are, is carried through the blue clarity of oceanic swell and the heavy bodies of the last whales. The truths of spirit and being are encoded in our dancing DNA helix. Not meant to be a secret, they are engraved in the core of our being, scratched into the insides of our bones.

There are no "fifty simple ways" to save the earth. There are as many ways as there are people, difficult ways that demand the most from us and make us worthy of this miracle of life. It is no longer enough to tend to our narrow selves. A global cure mandates the personal health of the individual, and also our impeccable participation in the far-flung processes of change. We have first to reclaim the balance of our true nature, but we must not fail to follow this with a direct and assertive response to the mechanizations of destruction and the paradigm of death.

The Amerindians speak in terms of the "seven generations." They ask that we base every act, every decision, on its possible effect on the seventh generation to come. It is a difficult concept for contemporary white folk with little experience of family or tribe. We are a culture of migrants, perpetually on the move, with little allegiance to a particular bioregion, to a particular place. The significance of the seventh generation is lost without this element of place, without the cultural continuity that comes from knowing and loving the same land that our great-grandmothers loved. A people who believe themselves separate from the landscape can desecrate it with impunity, knowing they can move on, and that neither they nor their direct descendants will likely be there to face the results. The cost of resource extraction and material comforts will be borne by someone else's children, themselves refugees from the exploitive practices of others. Our comfort is not evil in and of itself, but, created by a soulless and insupportable technology, it will be paid for later by the seventh generation, both human and nonhuman inheritors of a toxic playground.

We see Americans satisfying themselves by "shopping green," absolving themselves of guilt by recycling the products of a consumerist lifestyle. They drive smaller cars but have forgotten how to walk. A return to balance is not that easy. It is neither effortless nor painless. Environmentalism is not, however, the denial of joy or the recrimination of self. The return to simpler, more natural ways of being in the world enriches the planet as it enriches our experience of it. The downing of old growth forests, the damming of rivers, the incarceration of wildlife, is real self-denial, not our voluntary unplugging from the machine. Away from society's static, we hear more. Outside our protective walls, we see more. Refusing to accept the dictates of the State, we come to know the real meaning of freedom. Responsibility: the ability to respond. Yes, the last old growth forests on this continent are begging us, crying for us, to do whatever it takes to halt their destruction. But the sun, wind, and rain also call to us, asking to play on our naked skin, as the morning's songbird calls on us to sing.

All the world's in tune, rhythmically and ecstatically sharing the delight of existence. The test for right-living is a musical one. Is it in tune? Does it harmonize? Does it resonate? The answer is found not in the processes of logic, but in the vibrato of our very bones. It is set to the one beat, the bass line we first heard pounding in great waves through those amniotic fluids of the womb: the heartbeat of the greater self, Mother Earth. "And, if we're really quiet," writes Bill Devall, "Pan will come out of his place of hiding, and teach us the will-of-the-land."

It's hard to sleepwalk once you've awakened, hard to pretend once you know. For much the same reason, it is hard to sleep in, here in this magic canyon. Freed of the drone of appliances and the constant prattle of the rational mind, every sound stands out: stark and pure, the perfect note punctuating an endless concert. At the first touch of dawn, the reddened visage of the sacred Kachina Cliffs burns through my closed eyelids. I turn back into my dreams, seeking comfort in their busy familiarity. But, as always, one sound cuts through: the plaintive cry of the ravens circling overhead, the piercing peeps of a ground squirrel at my feet, or perhaps it is a hummingbird that awakens me, hovering inches from my face, or a pebble that falls on me from the ceiling of the shallow cave, arresting the distraction of sleep and accelerating the answering rhythms of my heart.

All of this activity says, "Wake up!" It is an invitation to join the song in progress. It says, "Don't be afraid. Sing out! Sing out!"

WILDERNESS ECOPSYCHOLOGY:
The Art of Sacred Survival

Renèe Soule

Renèe Soule, M.A., Wilderness Psychology, continues her work as an ecopsychologist—teaching, writing, and developing the field. She is currently engaged in a rite of passage bridging wilderness and culture: raising healthy twin boys in modern American society. Rather than restoring native habitats and leading wilderness journeys, she now gardens, tends to her community, and walks the neighborhood with her boys. Ten years later, the theme of this essay, sacred survival, continues to be a pulse that gives authenticity and meaning to life, even in the midst of dirty diapers, long nights, and toy trucks. "Wilderness Ecopsychology: The Art of Sacred Survival" is based on her master's thesis.

Whether we acknowledge ecological interrelatedness or not, the human psyche has become a powerful force of nature. It exhibits its own characteristic movements, unpredictable storm patterns, and seasonal influences. To ignore this would be folly. Nor is it prudent to view psychology as exiled from our encompassing biosphere. We are not psychologically immune to its distresses or warning signals. We can no longer dualistically divorce mind from matter, ecology from psychology, nature from culture, or wilderness from human communities.

The difficulties we find in assuming our responsibilities as members of a global ecosystem have given rise to ecopsychology. It seems to be human psychology that gums up the healthy functioning of self-sustaining ecosystems. To weather the storm of awakening to the cost of our alienation from nature and the depth of our responsibility, we need a psychology that directly addresses ecological healing. In essence, ecopsychology is a psychology of ecological transformation. Its role is like that of a midwife, assisting the inevitable movement toward a more balanced and sustainable human-nature relationship.

Ecopsychology assumes that we are not separate from nature any more than our fingers are separate from our toes. What we suffer from is perceived separation, a kind of myopic trance. Unfortunately, our language and our culture's creations rest on this misperception. Most of what we see, taste, touch, hear and sense in human culture reflects back to us the assumption of alienation from and domination over nature. Therefore, perception and language are two main pathways of ecological transformation. They, too, are part of this planet's ecosystem.

Perhaps if we had the wings of an eagle, or the body of a juicy peristaltic worm, or the swift sure-footedness of a jungle panther, then meaning would merge with experience. These papery symbols would be unnecessary. But we do not. We have language and our imaginations. We live in a self-created world of symbols and interpretations. If accurate, they blend gracefully with the rhythms and fluctuations of the larger ecosystems from which they emerge. If inaccurate, this inaccuracy cascades down into the sea of troubles we are currently experiencing as ecological crises and cultural autism in our relationship to nature.

Our perceived separation from the encompassing biosphere is frighteningly inaccurate and out of sync with the natural order of things. Today we are realizing just how dangerous this perception is as we individually and collectively experience the wrenching death throes of a global worldview. Much of what we know and love in nature is going with it.

In this culture, waking up to ecological interrelatedness can be a difficult realization. And waking up is inevitable. Where are the psychological pitfalls? How are the high costs of our alienation an obstacle? How can they become allies in the daily process of transformation? Can we rely upon a more inspiring motivation to change than fear? For we need encouragement now, not crushing statistics. Are there other, more healing ways of coming to terms with ecological interrelatedness than confronting crisis after environmental crisis?

Deafened by the magnitude of our problems, many of us seek gentler pathways of transformation. We go out in the wilds, away from the roaring insanity of our modern culture. We learn what it means to be "in system" in places where this meaning is healing, not horrifying. We discover that wilderness is a relatively safe place to wake up to our interconnectedness.

In wilderness, there are more kindly pathways to transformation. The daily slaps in the face and consistently pushy scare tactics we encounter in culture are not inspirations for deep transformation. Understanding and awakening to our true interconnection with all elements of nature in wild places is perhaps a more viable (but not necessarily easier) mode of ecological transformation. If approached with ecopsychological wisdom and skills, this transformation can continue back in human culture.

Ecopsychology views this urge to "use" wilderness as therapy as utterly healthy and natural. It need not be an escape. Rather, it can directly address the core problems we face as a species: alienation from our encompassing biosphere—an alienation rooted in dualistic modes of thinking—and an inability or immaturity that prevents us from coming to terms with the mess we have made of our habitat in a creative way.

There are four core facets of wilderness experience as a path of ecological transformation. First, wilderness is a living model of a nondualistic community. It is a safe place to regain a lost sense of belongingness. Second, in wilderness we practice the dance of shifting from "survival" to "sacred" modes of interacting with the ease of breathing. We blend these different modes of relationship in a context of wholeness. Third, with intentional awareness, we flirt with potentially dangerous dualisms and learn the art of embracing paradox. And, lastly, we return to our culture with both the insights and skills of an engaged ecopsychology. This last facet is vital, the key to ecological transformation and ecopsychological healing. It is what makes an ecopsychological wilderness experience more than a groovy camping trip or a temporary rush that dead-ends in sketchy transformation, forgetfulness, and depression.

1. Mirroring Our Wholeness

Dualistic mental processes find nothing in wilderness to confirm their validity and nothing to strengthen their tenets of radical separation of different realities. Wilderness does not mirror dualism; it mirrors intricate, cooperative unity. Life and death, individual life forms and their environment, catastrophe and healing, growth and decay all intermingle in a state of dynamic wholeness. There are no clear demarcations between different systems; where one begins and another ends is highly ambiguous. In this setting, a perception of humans as separate from nature softens.

This softening can happen anywhere at any time. But in our culture, we are overcome by the barrage of painful communication that pours in from the natural system in which we live. The noise, the pollution, the ugliness, all tell stories of ecological interrelatedness, but in a way that can be shattering. So we shut down. But in a wild environment of wholeness, it is safe to wake up again. Our senses open fully. In fact, lifting the barriers of awareness is imperative, or we may stumble off some cliff, get caught off-guard in a vicious storm or become hopelessly lost.

We are rewarded for our wakefulness. Rich in living examples of co-operation and community, wilderness invites metaphoric mimicking of its wholeness. Ancient memories flood in—a circle around the fire, night sounds, clear air, simple diet, survival, aloneness, community; being watchful, wary, wondering. A reciprocal flow of communication with the larger encompassing system is opened—dreams intensify, charity deepens, every moment is filled with peace and surprise. We remember what it is to be a human being in nature, a member of an infinitely intelligent, living system.

The joy of adventure and belonging grows with each day in the wilderness. Naked on a hot rock after plunging into a deep, icy, jewel-green pool, we breathe, "I am home." At times there may be stumbling, a kind of dissonance, as dualistic modes of knowing clash with the irrepressible wholeness of nature. But if given half a chance of silent receptivity, the oceanic rhythms of healthy wilderness, with their patient primordial power, will blend with and soften resistance. Panic comes and goes as we encounter hidden layers of resistance. But with mindfulness and clear intention, the deeper dance begins again and again.

2. The Art of Sacred Survival

With every wilderness experience there is a continual dance from the mundane "survival" mode (of soggy belongings on a rainy morning that need to be packed, charred pots that need to be washed, chapped lips, cat-holes in the woods, stiff stinky socks) to the "sacred" (singing, dancing, praying, panoramic views, a special place, panther tracks) and back to survival again (cold feet, protecting food, blisters, shelter). Every moment is an integration of being a human of culture, lugging a fifty-pound backpack up and down hills, with being wild and at home, frolicking in a swift river like a beaver.

This pulsing quality of contrasts constitutes a complete wilderness experience. The contrasts themselves provide the tension for wholeness.

Deeply knowing the feel of this contrasting wholeness can carry over into all areas of life in a way that simultaneously encourages toughness and softness. A wilderness experience can potentially be dichotomized if "survival" fails to blend gracefully with what is "sacred." Or it can be indelibly integrating, when the experience of both blends into one mode of being. Boundaries merge, but the rhythm remains. This is a dance of the wilderness, a dance whose rhythms extend into aspects of our human lives ... sacred-survival-sacred-survival-sacred-survival. Sound familiar?

3. Dualism as Medicine—Embracing Paradox

Wilderness experience dives into our deepest collective wounds: the loss of community and the loss of nature, in the nondualistic sense of integrated wildness, belongingness and an expansion of being. This happens not by verbally lamenting our loss, but by experiencing directly healthy community in wild places. We feel our loss by "finding" it and then by returning to culture and "losing" it. This paradoxical movement can be healing and guide us toward a next phase of ecological transformation.

If one does not understand this ecopsychological mode of healing, then plunging back into a culture of full-blown dualism from a place of wholeness can be paralyzing. This is the main pitfall of wilderness work, a challenge that demands clear awareness, nondual consciousness and a firm intention to integrate what has been learned. Wilderness, so full of contrasts in the context of wholeness, helps us become painfully aware of how living this wholeness is also an actual choice back within our day-to-day lives, a choice we make (usually unconsciously) moment by moment.

To truly begin to heal the core misperception of separation and alienation, we need to embrace paradox rather than accentuate duality. This is a beautiful teaching of wild places, and it takes practice. Though it is exceedingly difficult, it is possible to use the Going Out and the Return to practice building bridges of connection rather than separation. We learn, usually the hard way, that contrasts can either open us up to embrace wholeness, or shrink us back into an even deeper dualistic denial. It is our choice.

By no means does this choice imply compliance with a wounded culture. An easy transition back is not necessarily a sign of ecopsychological health. Quite likely the opposite will be true. Transition is usually painful and we experience the pain of this new phase of human ecology collectively and individually. In this context, pain may be a sign of health, not disease.

Before a transformative ecological experience, most of us are like the frog in a pot of water that is gradually heating up. The frog just sits there, croaking, as the temperature rises. Not perceiving the danger, he boils to death. So the story goes. Returning from a wilderness trip is like jumping back into the pot of water that we hadn't previously noticed was unbearably hot. Wilderness experience wakes us up to danger, signified by pain. Resuming a peacefully croaking stance is not a sign of ecopsychological health.

Wilderness teaches wakefulness. Staying awake means being aware of all aspects of ourselves in relation to the whole. Staying awake means not only feeling the heat, but scoping out our situation and finding the temperature controls! It is not about bailing ship and leaving our fellow frogs to boil. Staying awake is the one medicine we can truly rely upon. When all else fails, listen, open the eyes, open the heart, be ready to help. Awareness is the antidote for perceived separations that leave us alienated, alone and destructive.

Also, for some mysterious reason, embracing paradox with awareness fosters kindness that is free from motivation. The light of awareness can disperse the shadows of dualism that alienate self from other. From this well-lit place we can make clear decisions about how we want to be "in system." In a state of wakefulness — naked and vulnerable — we remember to be kind not for any ulterior motive, but for kindness' sake. This is the path, the goal and the key to ecological transformation.

4. Diversity, Not Duality — The Dance of an Engaged Ecopsychology

Can we learn to live with diversity without splitting differences into alienated dualities? Can we learn to embrace all variations of life — elemental nature, plants, animals, people — so that we can live together as a healthy, creative community? Can we move from a place of open awareness and open-heartedness to embrace even that which we detest, fear, or wish to ignore? Can we do this and still work toward active transformation that is true to our vision of a healthy human-nature relationship?

Yes, yes, yes and yes again. How? By engaging the teachings of wilderness and by engaging ecopsychology. After an understanding is made clear, it must be engaged. First of all, this may mean discovering that wilderness is not a separate haven. It is right here, right now, with every breath, in every action, every object, every relationship. Like "engaged Buddhism," where practice is taken out of the meditation hall, "engaged ecopsychology" merges its theory and therapy with daily life in human communities. No separation.

Engagement is a skill that can be learned and, invariably, must be relearned every day. Tools are needed for the "return" to daily life—not to cushion the jolt back into mushy forgetfulness, but to enact the vision of wholeness learned from wilderness. These tools can be nondualistic practices that cultivate awareness and understanding (e.g., yoga, meditation, studying, creating community, gardening, involvement in body politic, among countless others). Any experience of wholeness and openness suddenly followed by extreme contraction, untempered by theory, practice and awareness, can wreak psychological havoc. Learning the skills of engagement is vital, otherwise learning will be shallow and temporary.

Wilderness awakens us to a soul connection with ourselves, our families, our communities and the world at large, which is both painful and joyful. The hard work is staying awake. That is, not being fooled by surface appearances or bullied by fears, acting on what we know to be true and not being numbed by disappointment, and knowing there are no mistakes, only lessons.

Shifting our ecologically destructive course will not be easy. Instead of razing virgin forests with macho intensity, we will learn to replant them with the tenderness of a lover-child—on our knees, hands in the soil, head bent toward the earth. Making this transition with grace and beauty is possible if we stay awake through it all.

Gradually, the wilderness experience that continues back in human culture teaches us that we are part of a larger system that includes culture. We, our language, our creations, our music, and our thrills do not float above the systems that sustain them. Though in grave crises, yes, every movement of this system's wholeness seeks balance. We learn to see how our every move can be part of that larger movement.

We also learn to make medicine of the bitterness of our times. In this way we can allow the crises we face to become our ally, a tough friend that helps us grow into our full potential as mature human beings. We learn to use the pain of wakefulness to hone our resolve, clarify intentions, and stretch our boundaries of love. Life itself becomes a Wilderness Experience, in the fullest sense of the words.

Though ecopsychology is still in its growing stages, at its core is a strong intention to heal broken, alienated relationships as a path of ecological transformation. Ecopsychology views wilderness as one of our greatest teachers of integrated wholeness. We go "Out There" and "Return" with intentional awareness to feel and engage in the pulse of sacred-survival, culture-nature, life-death, inside-outside, this world-other world, symbol-meaning, freedom-responsibility. This wild dance of sacred-survival can move us anywhere at any time, once we are awake to its rhythm.

Slowly we learn: *"Whatever is here, that is there; what is there, the same is here .... By mind alone is this to be realized, and [then] there is no difference here."* (Katha Upanishad, iv. 10–11)

WILDERNESS RECONSIDERED

Roderick Nash

Roderick Nash has written ten books and over one hundred essays. He is best known for his *Wilderness and the American Mind.* His most recent monograph is *The Rights of Nature: A History of Environmental Ethics.* A national leader in the field of conservation, environmental management, and environmental education, Roderick has been distinguished with numerous awards and honors. He recently retired from a professorship of history and environmental studies at the University of California, Santa Barbara. He is also a founding partner of Off the Beaten Track Productions, a film and software publishing company specializing in the wilderness experience. "Wilderness Reconsidered" originally appeared in the book *Wilderness in America: Personal Perspectives*, edited by Daniel L. Dustin (San Diego State University, Institute for Leisure Behavior, 1988).

You think wilderness is paradise. You look at brochures and equipment catalogs and outdoor magazines — Early Winters, L. L. Bean, REI, Jansport, *Outside, Backpacker, Sierra* — you know the genre. Everyone is young, tanned, smiling and, especially, clean. They are having something called "a wilderness experience" and it looks like fun. Read the text accompanying those pictures, and you get the impression that wilderness is invariably enjoyable, exciting and therapeutic. Sometimes it seems like a grand conspiracy on the part of equipment manufacturers and outfitters eager to wring dollars from city folk who don't know what wilderness really is all about.

I was one of those city folk. For the first eighteen years of my life, the view from my bedroom window was of a brick wall. Stark, gray, unchanging season to season, the wall faced me from across a New York City alley. My family's apartment was on the seventh floor, but the sun seldom penetrated my narrow concrete canyon. I could look in every direction and not see any living thing — not a leaf, not a weed, not a blade of grass. Around the wall, the big city created one of the world's most controlled environments — the antipode of wilderness. New York's gridlock "blocks" were a synthetic environment superimposed over the old island of Manhattan.

Civilization made me appreciate wilderness. It was a case of the Scarcity Theory of Value. Like diamonds, wilderness was rare in New York City. I stared at walls long enough to covet the great open spaces. And, as a city boy, I always imagined they were uniformly wonderful. How great, I thought, to be on Lewis and Clark's expedition walking and boating from St. Louis to the mouth of the Columbia, or with John Wesley Powell pushing down the Colorado. On winter nights in the city I read their journals and devoured *Field and Stream* where the anglers always seemed to catch the maximum limit of fish on the tiniest dry fly. Ah, wilderness! It was some years before I understood that I had been in love with a myth.

The publicizers of wilderness have done such a thorough job that it is difficult to separate hype from actuality. In a sense, they have created a clientele for something that exists largely in overenthusiastic imaginations. John Muir began the tradition. I call him the first "publicizer" of wilderness. He was a "PR" man par excellence, and he had a reason. At the end of the nineteenth century and into the early twentieth century, wilderness needed friends. National parks, like Yosemite, were new and fragile institutions. Muir understood the need to build public support for their protection, so he dipped his active pen in purple ink. Everything in wilderness was suffused with God's grace. Pines bent in praise; waterfalls shouted His glory. Every hike was an act of worship. "Climb the mountains," Muir exhorted, "and get their good tidings." What he didn't say was that it sometimes got rough out there. We can, however, read between the lines. Traveling without a tent or sleeping bag or even a blanket, and consuming only tea and bread, Muir must have suffered through some long nights. When he climbed Mount Shasta, he avoided freezing to death only by groveling in hot, steaming mud. But the temperature of the springs was so hot that Muir literally scalded his body on one side while freezing the other. He must have feared for his life, but you'd never know it from his journals. It was bad public relations to tell the truth about wilderness.

Theodore Roosevelt also consistently avoided realism when it came to wilderness. A New York City boy like myself, he exulted in the Old West and, later, in Africa. Once, camping with Muir in the Sierra, Roosevelt was surprised by an eight-inch snowfall. As legend has it, the president leaped up from his tentless sleeping spot in the morning screaming with delight, "Bully!" Bull roar?

And there was Robert Marshall, another New York kid, who did much for wilderness preservation in the 1930s. In Montana and Alaska, Marshall routinely hiked fifty, sixty and once seventy miles in a single day. His journals record only joy. Once, in Alaska's Brooks Range, Marshall wrecked his boat, lost his gear, and had to walk out 150 miles in rubber hip boots. It rained thirty-two of the trip's thirty-four days. Marshall allegedly loved every minute.

The Sierra Club, which Muir founded in 1892, launched a whole new dimension to wilderness hype. Executive Director David Brower and Ansel Adams, the photographer, collaborated in the 1960s on the first exhibit-format books. These coffee-table volumes idealized and sanitized the wilderness. The flowers were always in bloom, the blue lakes sparkling, the sunsets glowing with bighorn sheep posed in silhouette. Wilderness was consistently perfect. The romantic adulation of wilderness had gone so far as to overcorrect the old hostile image. One myth had been substituted for another.

But in the course of spending thousands of days in wilderness, I have developed a different point of view. I think it's more consistent with what wilderness is all about.

Let me start with Henry David Thoreau, an honest man. Thoreau was the first American to appreciate wilderness, but he never forgot that it was an alien environment for civilized people. He knew he never could, and probably never should, be "at home" there. Once, on a climb of Mount Katahdin in Maine, Thoreau called the country "savage and dreary." Then, characteristically, he philosophized about his feelings: "Vast, titanic inhuman nature has got [man] at disadvantage, caught him along and pilfers him of some of his divine faculty." Thoreau knew that in wilderness, nature "does not smile on him as in the plains." Later, clinging to Katahdin's summit rocks, Thoreau sensed he was in "a place for heathenism and superstitious rites — to be inhabited by men nearer of kin to the rocks and wild animals than we." And finally, almost hysterically, he wondered, "Who are we? What are we? What is this Titan that has possession of me?" Katahdin had shown Thoreau an aspect of wilderness that the later coffee-table literature would not feature. Gratefully he retreated to the semi-pastoral wood lots of Concord, Massachusetts, where civilized man had more control over both the environment and himself. Thoreau still liked wilderness, but he had gone to the mountains, looked the dragon in the eye and returned a wiser man. Besides, he could afford to be honest. In the 1840s, no one was reading him anyway.

Wilderness is a state of mind. We infuse it with our own meaning. But the essence of wilderness is places, creatures and forces that civilization does not control. The word itself derives from the Old English "will" (uncontrolled, hence "wild") being prefixed to "deor" (animal). So "wilderness" literally means the place of wild beasts. As such, it is a potentially dangerous place for people. It is the strange, weird, mysterious, remote, frightening and unknown. Too many maps and guidebooks and signs and managers and, yes, even wilderness lovers erode the essence of wilderness. And so does the promotional let's-have-a-wilderness-experience hype. It takes some effort to dig through the myth and, like Thoreau, find the bedrock of reality.

My own education began early enough—at ten. I recall the time and the place distinctly: July, at Indian Gardens on the Grand Canyon's Bright Angel Trail. A group from the summer camp I attended backpacked from the North Rim. It was relatively easy going down, but climbing a vertical mile out of the big hole at 105 degrees was something else again. I remember the agony on the switchbacks and the realization—for the first time in my life—that I really had to do something I desperately did not want to do. But this was wilderness and you couldn't phone home. There was no option other than placing one dusty foot ahead of the other. It hurt, and it did not resemble the postcards we sent our parents from the rim, but it was an authentic wilderness experience. And, at least after the trip, I thought I liked it because it was so hard.

In subsequent years I returned frequently to the Grand Canyon, running the Colorado River over forty times. Once, in high water at Lava Falls, I flipped my raft and lost part of the flotation material from an old life preserver that should have been replaced. Helpless in the uncontrolled (wild) force of the big river, I was sucked twenty feet down in whirlpools, then, strangely, left in static suspension as if frozen like a prehistoric fly in a cube of amber. Many seconds passed before a new current tossed me violently. It was so inky black in the silty water, I did not know which way to swim to the surface. I thought, surprisingly calmly, that I might die. But the river spat me out, wiser about the wilderness. Clambering, exhausted and hypothermic, onto shoreline rocks a mile below the rapids, I remember asking myself, "Well, turkey, how do you like river running now?" I concluded I still liked it precisely and paradoxically because of what I had just been through. The potential wilderness always holds for disaster makes an encounter with it meaningful. No pain, no gain. It was an axiom early transoceanic sailors and overland explorers knew intimately. If something was easy, it would not have been left undone. And wilderness is not easy. This is a point contemporary wilderness lovers tend to overlook. Perhaps love of wilderness is both impossible and inappropriate. Lava Falls helped me learn that.

There were other moments of insight. Once, I canoed across a lake in Grand Teton National Park in an unseasonable snowstorm. When I reached my car, my fingers were so numb I could not turn the key in the lock. The car was ten miles from help I knew I could not reach. It was very cold and I thought of Jack London's honest-to-wilderness short story "To Build a Fire." But my matches were soaked. The only alternative was to hold the key between my teeth and turn the lock by twisting my neck. I started the engine the same way; chipped teeth were better than death.

Wild beasts can be dangerous, and wilderness is their place. On two occasions I have been obliged to run for my life from big wild animals. The grizzly on the lower Alsek River in Alaska stopped the chase to maul a day-pack I discarded. The buffalo in northern Kenya fell to a spear my companion threw. Both experiences reminded me that wilderness is an environment people do not control. It places them back into natural selection evolution, into the food chain—and not always as the eater!

Finally, there was Peru, the Andes and the Amazon. I went to South America to attempt a first descent of the headwaters of the world's greatest river. "Attempt" is all my expedition did. Early in the trip, in a canyon twice as deep as Arizona's Grand, my partner lost two oars in a big rapid, missed the planned landing and pinned his raft on a midstream rock only yards from the edge of a sixty-foot waterfall. To make matters worse, afternoon snowmelt in the mountains meant more water in the river and the gradual but inevitable inundation of my stranded companions' lonely perch. Again, wilderness left me no alternative but to run a mile upstream, swim the river with a coil of line over my shoulder and work down to the point on shore closest to the trapped boat. The shore was actually a forty-degree shale and talus slope. With the river rising perceptibly, I managed to get my line to the terrified boaters and, using a Tyrolean traverse, pull them through the racing current to safety. After it was over, I walked behind a boulder and threw up, and the night was no better. For the first time in thirty thousand miles of river boating, I heard no music in the moving water. Instead, the river seemed monstrous, a wild heart bent on destroying our group. Terror gripped our makeshift camp. I lay awake wondering how I could have ever wanted to run wild rivers. We eventually got out of the gorge, but it was several years before I heard river music again. And then it was always with an awareness of the dark chords beneath the surface.

What distinguishes wilderness from other environments is a wildness that is intimidating and, for that very reason, appealing to some visitors. Lose the dark, frightening, dangerous qualities, and you lose the essence of wilderness. A generation or two has been prepared to regard wilderness as a sort of paradise, a sanctuary from the stresses of civilization. This is an illusion. Wilderness has its own stresses associated with the absence of civilization. They are essential to its value. Honesty is essential. The necessary philosophy is one that emphasizes that if you can't stand the heat, get out of the wilderness kitchen. The alternative is to have designated wilderness that is not wild and wilderness users for whom myth replaces reality.

KINSHIP WITH NATURE

James Swan

James Swan, Ph.D., is one of the founders of the modern field of environmental psychology and a principal shaper of environmental education. He is the producer of five Spirit of Place symposiums, which have been held in the United States and Japan, involving nearly three hundred speakers from a broad diversity of professions and ethnic backgrounds. He is the author of *Sacred Places, The Power of Place,* and *Nature as Teacher and Healer;* coauthor of *Bound to the Earth, Environmental Education,* and *Building Networks;* and has published over one hundred articles in magazines and journals. He has taught at the Universities of Michigan, Western Washington State, Oregon, and Washington in natural resources and psychology, and conducted a practice in psychotherapy for a decade. He is now an adjunct professor at the Institute for Transpersonal Psychology. "Kinship with Nature" is an edited excerpt of a keynote address that James presented to the Tenri Yamato Culture Congress in Nara, Japan, 1992. It also appeared in the professional journal, *Environmental Carcinogenics and Ecotoxicology Review.*

> *Nature is prime; it is there at birth: society is next; it is only a shaper of Nature, and a function moreover, of what it shapes; whereas Nature is as deep and, finally, inscrutable as being itself.*
> —JOSEPH CAMPBELL, *The Flight of the Wild Gander*

It is no secret that there are some serious ecological problems in the world that threaten the future of the human species as well as many other species and ecosystems. Solving these problems will require the work of governments, scientists, economists, religious leaders, architects, planners, and businesspeople as well as individuals from all walks of life to create a modern culture that can live in harmony with nature and not self-destruct in the name of "progress." The complexity and diversity of the problems seem overwhelming, and yet there is a common starting point from which to begin to understand our ecological dilemma—all environmental problems begin in the human mind. We need the very latest in human and scientific technologies to cure many forms of pollution, recycle our wastes and restore damaged ecosystems like the tropical rain forests of the world, but we ultimately must look at our attitudes, beliefs and ways of thinking if we want to find strategies to create sustainable societies successfully, for our problems arise from the human tendency to create as a reflection of who we are.

I came to this conclusion about how environmental problems begin in the human mind in the mid-1960s as a graduate student in natural resources at the University of Michigan. In hopes of gaining better understanding of how to solve environmental problems, I began to study psychology for my Ph.D. degree. What I discovered shortly was that there are many psychological theories, but we have virtually no psychology of how the mind and nature relate to each other, which is in contrast to the rich maps of mind-nature synthesis provided by Eastern religions such as Taoism, Buddhism and Shintoism, or the tribal shamanic psychologies of indigenous peoples all around the world. The term "environment," in modern scientific psychology, tends to be used to refer to the social environment. Psychologists have little to say about how the physical environment influences mind, health and behavior of humans. The field of "environmental psychology," which is the scientific study of the relationship between people and their surrounding environment, was officially recognized by the American Psychological Association in 1970 with the creation of the Division of Environment and Population Psychology.

The reluctance of modern psychology to consider the relationship between the mind and nature is related to our heavy reliance on Newtonian-Cartesian mechanistic scientific theories to shape our model of how the world works. Such a paradigm is reductionist and says that the truth about things is ultimately known by comprehending their most fundamental units, like atoms and molecules, with chemistry and physics being able to explain all of life. Mechanical models are very good for working with machines, but when they are widely applied to creating lifestyles, urban environments and educational systems they tend to overlook the systematic consequences of our actions. The failure to apply systems theories to understanding our lives and work is one of the greatest sources of many environmental problems.

When we combine the shortcomings of modern scientific theory to harmonize mind with nature with the tendency of modern religions to avoid any close connection with nature in their theory or practice or to declare nature worship as evil or superstitious, we can see how modern science and religion have played a major role in creating environmental problems by blocking any serious attempts to comprehend living in harmony with nature on a conscious and/or unconscious level. We can appreciate nature from a distance, but not as a participant/observer whose every action influences the web of life in a myriad of ways.

In the last decade in the United States the membership in environmental organizations has doubled from four to eight million, and there are an estimated twenty-five million more people involved with environmental groups on a local level. At the same time, one source of research shows that the average person today in the United States spends eighty-four percent of their life indoors, and over ninety percent of these people live in urban areas where nature may not be much of a presence.

Since 1964, when the Wilderness Act was passed in the United States, eighty million of the ninety-one million acres of wilderness in the United States have been added to the Wilderness Preservation system. Despite all these acres of wild mountains, rivers, deserts, forests, and ocean beaches, research shows that the average visitor to a U.S. National Park spends less than six hours there and does not go more than fifty feet from the road.

These statistics suggest that concern about the environment today is very high but, more than ever before, environmental attitudes are not formed from direct personal experience. Living in cities, often far removed from natural resources and their harvesting, people come to forget that the grocery store is not the source of food, lumber does not come from the lumber company store, plastic does not magically appear on the retailer's shelf, and garbage does not disappear once it goes into the refuse collection truck.

Television sets, newspapers and magazines are the environmental educators of today, much more so than what our senses and our dreams told our ancestors about environmental quality. In this information age, many causes are vying for people's attention and many people are suffering from information overload, which can lead to the disease of our times, well-informed futility—being well informed about problems but feeling one has little or no power to solve them. And, because interest in issues is related to the most pressing crises of the time, while people may be well intentioned, their concern for any one issue may not be very deep at all, and may wax and wane according to the current media hype. Developing environmental attitudes primarily from secondhand information is extremely new in human history, and no one is really certain how adequate it may be to keep us closely linked with nature.

Fears are learned and can originate from lack of familiarity; indeed one of the most common roots of fear is the unknown. Living in indoor environments in urban areas, many people develop fears of nature that may have little base in fact. Some research has suggested that as much as half of the household use of pesticides is based on fear rather than a real need to control insects, one example being spraying to kill spiders, which are very good natural pest-control agents. In the same vein, park planners speak of people wanting to cut down natural vegetation in parks because they are afraid of wild places. From the perspective of Jungian psychology one might say that such attitudes are a projection of inner fears of one's own primal self, created by the overreliance upon thinking as the major mental function. Alienation from oneself is a very common condition for many people today. If a person is left alone in a natural place without books or other distractions for three to four hours, they will tend to think more deeply about themselves and their life's purpose than they normally do. Jungian analyst Maria von Franz has written eloquently about the fear of being alone in nature, which she explains as a fear of revealing the inner self, including the "shadow," or darker side of the psyche. Projecting this fear into technology today results in bulldozing forests, covering school playgrounds with asphalt, and excessive spraying of pesticides to control insects, which may not be a serious threat to human health or property.

Human consciousness is multifaceted, and when we deny any major aspect of human nature for any prolonged period of time, anger and hatred will develop, which will result in psychosomatic illness or aggression, or both. Thus today we are troubled by the twin problems of alienation from self and nature as well as aggression against nature (which is a form of fear), and both arise from supporting our current mental paradigm of "normality." The real question of our age is no longer can we do something, but rather should we do it. And answering the "should" question thoroughly requires more probing questioning than a mechanistic approach usually includes.

Research in biofeedback, depth psychology, dream psychology and consciousness studies, as well as ancient wisdom from Buddhism, Taoism, Hinduism and most traditional spiritual psychologies, asserts that the mind of man includes the entire body. James Lovelock's "Gaia Hypothesis," that modern science should consider the entire earth to be alive, a concept that agrees with most traditional psychologies, offers an organic model of life based on systems theory that we need to help order our new map of mind-nature relations.

Lovelock's "Gaia Hypothesis" is especially valuable for ecological thinking, because in the depths of each of our minds there is a symbol for the earth. Carl Jung asserted that all things in the mind are alive, and so to have harmony between mind and nature, we should have a scientific paradigm that considers the earth to be alive, as the earth within us is alive. Without such inner-outer sympathy arising from the similarity of forms, it is impossible to think in harmony with nature, and true intuition is always hampered. Each place on the face of the earth is unique and special and the more we can become aware of this and integrate it into our lives the more we will find peace and beauty in our lives.

If we come to see the earth as alive and a self-regulating organism, then we might conclude that the desire for humans to visit certain special places in nature for contemplation, inspiration and perhaps even healing is one way that the earth cares for us if we in turn show humility for the planet's power and value to us. We care for the earth and it cares for us. In wild places we can lose our personal ego consciousness and perceptual narrowness and unite with a much larger set of natural systems. Special places simply act as multipliers of this experience, giving us more of a chance for making extraordinary states of mind manifest.

The art of being at the right place at the right time is one of mankind's greatest skills. There are times to undertake pilgrimages to places of great beauty and power—Stonehenge, Mount Denali, Machu Picchu, Palenque, Delphi, Mount Fuji, etc.—but there is also the need to find nature's recreational places near your everyday life space. Studies have shown that spending half an hour alone in quiet contemplation at a place of natural beauty on a weekly basis has positive results for mental health. When we can learn how to adjust our minds so that nature can become a teacher and healer, at the great places of power as well as the quiet places near home, there will be more magic and beauty in our lives.

WE CAN'T OWN IT ALL

Diane Sylvain

Diane Sylvain is an artist and writer who works for *High Country News* in Paonia, Colorado, where she also resides. She has been drawn to wilderness since she was a child. This piece was written in response to what Diane describes as an obnoxious letter from a conservative antienvironmentalist, which was sent to the newspaper, and which raised her normally placid blood pressure to geyser intensity. She is currently putting together her first book, a collection of essays. "We Can't Own It All" was first published in the November 4, 1991, issue of *High Country News*.

A river rock sits in the center of my palm as round and smooth as a world. It is smaller than a robin's egg and a color that I have no name for, so dark a green it is almost black. This stone is older than the river that pounded it smooth. It came from the edge of the Colorado River, from the bottom of the Grand Canyon.

I found it seven years ago on a fifteen-day-long backpacking trip. I did not know then that it would be the last time I picked up rocks in the bottom of the Grand, at least after hiking in to get there. I had no idea that this small stone would come to seem to me, on some sad days, like a letter saved from a friend who had since died.

But I am not writing a eulogy to my former, able-bodied self; I am writing in response to an editorial newspaper letter in which the writer said he "would feel better if more of our public lands were 'improved' to the extent that people with limited time, money or physical abilities could enjoy them."

I thought about this for a long time. I don't claim to speak for all environmentalists or for all those with physical impairments. As disabilities go, mine is comparatively minor. I have a back injury; I use a cane; I wear an orthopedic brace on one leg. After six years of exercise and physical therapy, I get around fairly well: I have even begun to hike again, for short distances on easy trails with a companion.

So in many ways—I am fully aware—I am lucky. But I have begun to accept that I will never again hoist a forty-pound pack onto my back, or stride out into the canyon country for two weeks of adventurous travel. And there are days that I find it difficult to get to the post office, or walk around the block. In this respect, I fit the letter writer's description of one who has no "meaningful access" to many places I would love to reach.

Yet I wonder if he and I mean the same thing by those words. His concept seems to include anything from the installation of escalators in the Grand Canyon, to the opening up of wild areas to all-terrain vehicles and oil drilling.

I would be more likely to take his concern for the "infirm" seriously if I knew that conservatives like him who express it were hard at work installing wheelchair ramps, providing medical care and doing what is needed to give the disabled "meaningful access" to the places we already live in.

He misses the point anyway in this whole debate about whether wild areas should be accessible. It seems to me that a wild area is by definition a place that is hard to get to, that is remote, dangerous, and that takes time and health and strength of heart to find. It is a place that by definition is not easily accessible.

There are those of us who cannot climb mountains who still love the sight of them on the horizon. We love the idea of mystery left in the world, of open spaces and wild places, where only the creatures that are born there roam. What we receive from all this is something the writer of this letter doesn't understand.

Six years ago, when I entered the hospital, I took that Colorado River rock with me and kept it on my bedside table. The weight of it in my hand gave me strength. It reminded me that the river it came from still ran through my heart, that even in the white room of the hospital my bones were as real as Grand Canyon rock.

If I ever do strap on a backpack again, to make my slow way down to the canyon bottom, I will give this stone back to the river because I realize now that I don't need to keep it. The thing about this strange world that breaks our hearts and makes it all so precious is that none of us gets to keep anything, anyway. None of us gets to have all that she wants or see everything he dreams of seeing.

But these thoughts will not make sense to someone who regards environmentalists as "over-paid, greedy-little-white kids that refuse to share their toys." Unfortunately, the person who made this statement in the editorial will not understand my point until he learns to love the things he can't own, until he realizes that the natural world was never his "toy" to begin with.

Fierce Landscapes and the Indifference of God

Belden C. Lane

Belden C. Lane is professor of Theological Studies and American Studies at Saint Louis University in Saint Louis, Missouri. An avid backpacker in the Ozarks, he is the author of *Landscapes of the Sacred: Geography and Narrative in*

American Spirituality (Paulist Press, 1988) and of a forthcoming book from which this essay is extracted and edited, *The Solace of Fierce Landscapes: Studies in Desert and Mountain Spirituality.* "Fierce Landscapes and the Indifference of God" originally appeared *The Christian Century* magazine.

Travel agents, especially those arranging religious tours, rarely book passage to the most fascinating places in this world. Most people aren't interested in roaming the sparse desert near Mount Sinai, trekking the mountain passes on the road from Lhasa, or walking the Scottish Highlands on a wintry day as a cold wind sweeps down from the Hebrides. Yet these are places where people have frequently encountered a God of fierce indifference that seized their imaginations. This was the experience of the children of Abraham, of Tibetan devotees of the Dalai Lama, and even of Scots Presbyterians who made their way to New England in the seventeenth century. In each case, their God was no less foreboding and captivating than the landscape through which they moved. Their haunting vision of the holy, growing out of such austere spaces, reminds us of the inevitable correlation that exists between one's spirituality and one's sense of place. "Tell me the landscape in which you live," wrote José Ortega y Gasset, "and I will tell you who you are." There is a special intrigue in the images of God that come to us out of harsh and rugged landscapes, those that remain so utterly indifferent to our pressing human concerns. We are sometimes drawn, both spiritually and geographically, to that which most ignores us.

I am increasingly uncomfortable with current images of God, as often found in books and workshops that mix popular psychology with a theology wholly devoted to self-realization. They seem to reverse the first question in the catechism I studied as a child declaring that "the chief end of God is to glorify men and women, and to enjoy them forever." I really don't want a God who is solicitous of my every need, fawning for my attention, eager for nothing in the world so much as the fulfillment of my self-potential. One of the scourges of our age is that all of our deities are housebroken and eminently companionable: far from demanding anything, they ask only how they can more meaningfully enhance the lives of those they serve.

I often tell my students that if I weren't a Christian, raised in the Reformed tradition, I would probably be a Jew, and if I weren't a Jew, I'd be a Buddhist. These three traditions engage me by the power of their stories, the seriousness with which they address the meaning of suffering, and their strange, even fierce, attitude toward God. The people of these faiths, formed by mountains, desert and tough terrain, celebrate, oddly enough, a sense of God's indifference to the assorted hand-wringing anxieties of human life. In their grand notions of divine sovereignty and the embrace of the void (with its prerequisite emptying of the self), they undercut altogether the incessant self-absorption that preoccupies the American mind. They discover in the vast resources of divine disinterest a freedom and a joy that cut through much of contemporary pop theology.

These three landscapes and three traditions call us back to the *mysterium tremendum* evoked by the image of the Great Mother, Yahweh, Kali, and Calvin's God of sovereign majesty. They can teach us about the renewed importance of an apophatic spirituality, with its recovery of the *via negativa,* its attention to renunciation, and its emphasis on the importance of being drawn beyond ourselves into the incomprehensible greatness of God. The austere, unaccommodating landscapes of desert, mountain and heath remind us of the smallness of self and the majesty of Being. They point again to what theologians once described as the aseity of God, a divine indifference that has as its goal the ultimate attraction of that which it at first repels.

Occasioning this line of thought for me was a phrase that has rumbled for two years in and out of my consciousness like a nagging koan, teasingly promising a meaning that it never quite fulfills. "We are saved in the end by the things that ignore us." I found it in a book by Andrew Harvey, a Britisher from Oxford writing about Buddhist meditation, the landscape of northern India along the borders of Tibet, and his own pilgrimage in search of a self he meant to lose (*A Journey in Ladakh,* Houghton Mifflin, 1983). Near the Land of Snows, at the roof of the world, he traveled with eager anticipation from one monastery to another, passing rows of large stone stupas erected along the high passes, spinning the copper cylinders or "prayer wheels" that symbolically intone the ancient mantra "om mani padme hum." Moved by the magnificence of the mountain landscape and the esoteric mystery of the lamas, he found himself searching for a Great Experience, wanting to be transformed by what he saw, desiring as a tourist some deep, spiritual memento of his trip. Yet this self-obsessed "wanting" was precisely what kept him from obtaining enlightenment.

It was only as the vast grandeur of the land drew him beyond himself that he began to find what he had sought. Walking one day to a remote monastery at Rde-Zong, he was distracted from his self-conscious quest for spiritual attainment by the play of the sun on stones along the path. "I have no choice," he protested, "but to be alive to this landscape and this light." Because of his delay, he never got to the monastery. The beauty of the rocks in the afternoon sun, the weathered apricot trees and the stream along which he walked refused to let him go. He concluded that "to walk by a stream, watching the pebbles darken in the running water, is enough; to sit under the apricots is enough; to sit in a circle of great red rocks, watching them slowly begin to throb and dance as the silence of my mind deepens, is enough."

Compelling his imagination the most was that the awesome beauty of this fierce land was in no way conditioned by his frail presence. It was not there for him. The stream would continue to lunge over the rocks on its way to tile valleys below long after he had gone. The apricot trees would scrape out a spare existence and eventually die entirely apart from any consideration of his having passed that way. Only in that moment of the afternoon sun in Ladakh, as he abandoned thought of hurrying on to the monastery, did he receive back something he had unconsciously offered. Hence he declares, "The things that ignore us save us in the end. Their presence awakens silence in us; they refresh our courage with the purity of their detachment." Having become aware of a reality that exists entirely apart from the world of cares that keep him in turmoil, he was strangely set free. By its very act of ignoring him, the landscape invited him out of his frantic quest for self-fulfillment.

Judaism and Christianity have a similar tendency to view the divine *apatheia* as a rich and subtle way of teasing us out of ourselves and into relationship with God. The Book of Job poignantly addresses the nagging question of God's indifference. Why does God seem to ignore Job altogether? The answer given in chapters 38–41, weak as it may at first appear, is directly connected with the fierceness of landscape. When God finally speaks out of the whirlwind, it is to conduct a tour of the harsh Palestinian countryside. God points to the wine-dark sea, the towering clouds over a desolate land, the storehouses of snow and hail in the distant mountains. And God asks Job what all this has to do with him. Does the wild ox pay him any attention? Does the calving of a mountain goat on a rocky crag depend in any way on his frail knowledge? Does the eagle mount up at his command to make its nest in the tall cedars? Does Leviathan speak to him a single word? The rich mystery of life continues, stubbornly separate from all of Job's anxious longings. His anxieties are absorbed into a dread landscape that goes on apart from him, when it would seem that nothing could have continued in the bleak corridors of his own imagination. This ultimately, of course, isn't an answer. But somehow, for Job, it is enough. It drives him outside himself and his need for vindication and fulfillment. In the silence that is left when the whirlwind subsides, Job finds what he sought most all along. "I had heard of thee by the hearing of the ear," he cries, "but now my eye sees thee." Job is given no answer, but in being drawn out of himself he is met by God.

This is a strange dimension in Jewish spirituality. It is Moses' experience at Sinai (Exod. 19), Elijah's in the cave on Mount Horeb (1 Kings 19), and Second Isaiah's as he offers "comfort" to Jerusalem by pointing to an awesome God entirely removed from the vanity of human fretfulness (Isa. 40). This is the God who "sits above the circle of the earth, with all of its inhabitants like grasshoppers." It would be easy to miss the subtlety of this religious experience by dismissing it as scaremongering patriarchal primitivism. There is more to it than that. What ancient Israel found in this context of untamed landscapes was a Fierce Mother, as well as Gentle Father, who woos her children to a relationship of deeper maturity. One is astonished, in standing nakedly before the divine resplendence, to discover that a grand and new wholeness comes to replace all that has been lost. John Newton, the ex-slave ship captain and hymn-writer, knew this well when he spoke of a "grace that taught my heart to fear and grace my fears relieved." The indifference of God turns out at last to be but another form of God's insistent love.

In the fixed idea of divine sovereignty that forms the heart of Reformed spirituality, one must discern more than a worn-out devotion to a stern God of patriarchal splendor. Ernst Troeltsch argued that such a theology was also rich in implications for the understanding of the self. A focus on the divine majesty brought with it a corresponding tendency to de-emphasize the ego and its inordinate concern for self-aggrandizement. In Calvinist spirituality, "a constant preoccupation with personal moods and feelings is entirely unnecessary." For Calvin, the chief concern was not with a self-centered personal salvation, but with the glory of God.

This offers an important corrective to the simplistic self-help theologies in religious circles today. To be engrossed in the self is, paradoxically, to lose it altogether, as Jesus suggested (Mark 8:35). Reformed theology would insist that the liberation of the true self in Christ comes only by ignoring the false self, as it is overshadowed and driven to utter silence by a God "in light inaccessible, hid from our eyes." When the self has been wholly abandoned, only then is there the possibility of seeing it restored in Christ. Having lost one's life, it comes rushing back as divine gift.

The desert has always been a good teacher. Poets and theologians alike have known this from Antoine de Saint-Exupéry's *Wind, Sand, and Stars* to Carlo Carretto's *Letters from the Desert,* from Edward Abbey's classic *Desert Solitaire* to David Douglas's recent *Notes in the Desert Silence.* The harsh and

arid land of the American Southwest, in particular, has spurred the spiritual imagination of many. Southern Plains Indians have for centuries located their most sacred places in the vicinity of the "four corners," the
desiccated terrain where the states of New Mexico, Arizona, Utah and
Colorado meet. Spanish Catholics in the seventeenth century spoke ironi-
cally of Death Valley as *la palma de la mano de Dios,* the palm of God's hand.
They were accustomed to finding God in the fierce indifference of barren
mesas and cracked earth.

Fierce landscapes can be read in many ways. Always unpredictable,
they are frightening as well as indifferent, a terror to some and a solace to
others. They offer no guarantee of God, even though the three traditions
considered here are accustomed to experiencing the sacred in the threat-
ening emptiness of space. Not everyone discerns the holy lurking as a
dread presence in a dark canyon before a summer storm. Edward Abbey
was one who exulted in the fact that the desert offers absolutely nothing.
Its hold on the imagination is the power of subtraction, the abandonment
of all names and meanings.

Visiting the remote gorge of Nasja Creek in Arizona one summer,
Abbey walked along its amber stream in the deep shadows of canyon walls
towering hundreds of feet above on either side. At one point he made his
way toward the distant sun in a slow and pathless ascent along the east
wall. No human being had been that way for years, he thought, maybe
ever. But as he reached the canyon rim, breaking into the bright light of
the vast desert floor, he saw the remains of an arrow design laid in broken
stone near the edge. It pointed off to the north, toward more of the same
purple vistas and twisted canyons that he had seen for the past week or
more. He searched in that direction for some irregular line on the distant
horizon, an old ruin or sacred site to which the ancient arrow might have
pointed. There was nothing. Nothing but the desert … and its blessed
indifference. Nothing but a desolate silence that filled the earth with its
emptiness. Nothing. With a savage and unaccountable joy, he descended
the gorge once again, knowing why it was that he had to walk and write
about deserts. The sheer nothingness of it refused to let him go (*The Journey Home*, Dutton, 1977).

The power of Abbey's encounter, and others like it, is found in the fact
that what is met cannot be named. It can be painted perhaps, as Georgia
O'Keefe learned, giving a spare beauty to the dry bones of the New Mex-
ican desert she had come to love. But it can't be named. Fierce landscapes
offer none of the comforts of reason. At the extremities of geography, beyond the civilized precincts of all that is safe, we enter the dread terrain of

our own extremities as conscious selves. Yet in that fearful ending we discover also a joyous new beginning,

Stretched out over the edge of a deep precipice, one hand clutching the branch of a blue juniper growing from the rock, we peer down as far as we dare. We see nothing—only the motionless soaring of red-tailed hawks in the canyon far below. We are drawn, though, by an indifference, whose other name is love. We sense an invitation to emptiness. It begins to grow in us, like a vast silence. There is fear, knowing that in hanging there, we will be destroyed. The roots of the juniper begin to loosen from their crevice in the rock. Yet a senseless joy bids us stay. And when we fall, it is a long, slow descent, feathers being unfamiliar to us. We wing our way across the borders of a new consciousness, adjusting uneasily to warm air currents drifting upward. The circling hawks we had studied from above have drawn us by their indifference far more than we might have imagined. With them, we become part of a great void that seems strangely akin to love. The sky opens out into a thin, orange line over the dark horizon and we head with the others toward home. "We are saved in the end by the things that ignore us."

EPILOGUE

It is important to me to have offered you — the reader — a book that is solid and accessible. While I had a general sense of the broad messages and personal tone I was wishing to impart through this collection, coming to the final chapter titles and their contents was, at times, somewhat arduous, daunting, frustrating, and, almost always, quite mysterious. The primary challenge I kept encountering was that so many of the contributions overlap. The chapters themselves have been retitled, rearranged, and restructured again and again.

Wilderness is like that — circular, unpredictable, moving, and changing. Nature weaves around itself in an unending breath of life. Wilderness is too fluid and flowing and fathomless to be neatly conveyed in the minuscule span of a few hundred pages of tree pulp. That which is truly wild spills over the edges — onto our kitchen floors, into our love lives, through the sidewalk cracks, and in the form of dandelions and emotional outbursts.

One way to return to a lifestyle that is more organic and harmonious with the whole of nature is to get outside more often, to get out of the squareness of your comfortable home and routines, to let the unpredictability of wildness touch the soulful longings within. Wilderness is innate to who we are. You do not have to go far to find wildness, only as far as your own beating heart and the joy you find in life.

Although wildness is impossible to contain, we can use language and the written word as a means of reflecting on our connection with nature. In this light, I wish to point the reader's attention to the Suggested Readings section that immediately follows the Epilogue. This list is a collection of books, many written by the contributors to *The Soul Unearthed*, that are related to the theme of wilderness and spiritual transformation. Many of these books are classics. Some are newer, destined to become well known.

Drawing from the expertise of the book's contributors, the Appendix of Wilderness Resources gives the reader help in finding support to connect skillfully and mindfully with wilderness. The Appendix lists wilderness guides, educators, schools, and environmental organizations that have a unique, grounded, and holistic approach to nature.

If you are so inclined, I welcome any feedback, comments, or questions addressed to me, Cass Adams, in care of Sentient Publications. I hope *The Soul Unearthed* will support you in your journey into the vast unknowns of wildness. But more importantly, put down your books, get outside, and go for a walk.

With love for all that is wild and free,
CASS ADAMS

SUGGESTED READINGS

BOOKS

Abbey, Edward. *Desert Solitaire*. New York: Ballantine, 1971.

Abram, David. *The Spell of the Sensuous: Perception and Language in a More-than-Human World*. New York: Pantheon Books, 1996.

Ackerman, Diane. *A Natural History of the Senses*. New York: Random House, 1991.

Anderson, Lorraine, ed. *Sisters of the Earth*. New York: Vintage Books, 1991.

Antler. *Selected Poems*. New York: Soft Skull Press, 2000.

Berg, Peter. *A Green City Program for the San Francisco Bay Area and Beyond*. San Francisco: Planet Drum Foundation, 1989.

———. *Reinhabiting a Separate Country: A Bioregional Anthology of Northern California*. San Francisco: Planet Drum Foundation, 1978.

Berry, Thomas. *The Dream of the Earth*. San Francisco: Sierra Club Books, 1990.

Berry, Wendell. *Collected Poems*. San Francisco: North Point Press, 1984.

Bly, Robert. *American Poetry: Wilderness and Domesticity*. New York: HarperCollins, 1991.

———. *Iron John: A Book about Men*. New York: Random House, 1992.

———. *Meditations on the Insatiable Soul*. New York: HarperCollins, 1994.

———, ed. *News of the Universe: Poems of Twofold Consciousness*. San Francisco: Sierra Club Books, 1980.

———. *The Night Abraham Called to the Stars*. New York: HarperCollins, 2001.

———. *The Soul Is Here for Its Own Joy: Sacred Poems from Many Cultures*. Hopewell, NJ: Ecco Press, 1995.

Brown, Tom. *The Vision*. New York: Berkeley Books, 1991.

Bruchac, Joseph, and Michael Caduto. *Keepers of the Earth: American Stories and Environmental Activities for Children*. Golden, CO: Fulcrum Publishing, 1988.

Cahill, Sedonia. *The Ceremonial Circle: Practice, Ritual and Renewal for Personal and Community Healing*. New York: HarperCollins, 1992.

Carson, Rachel. *The Sense of Wonder*. New York: HarperCollins, 1987.

Chiras, Dan. *Lessons from Nature: Learning to Live Sustainably on the Planet*. Covelo, CA: Island Press, 1992.

Cohen, Michael J. *Field Guide to Connecting with Nature: Creating Moments That Let the Earth Teach*. Eugene, OR: World Peace University, 1990.

———. *Our Classroom Is Wild America*. Freeport, ME: Cobblesmith, 1978.

———. *Reconnecting with Nature*. Friday Harbor, WA: Project NatureConnect, 1995.

Daniel, John. *All Things Touched by Wind*. Anchorage, AR: Salmon Run, 1994.

———. *Common Ground*. Lewiston, ID: Confluence Press, 1988.

———. *The Trail Home*. New York: Pantheon Books, 1994.

Dean, Barbara. *Wellspring: A Story from the Deep Country*. Covelo, CA: Island Press, 1979.

Devall, Bill, and George Sessions. *Deep Ecology: Living as If Nature Mattered*. Layton, UT: Peregrine Smith Books, 1987.

Dillard, Annie. *Pilgrim at Tinker Creek*. New York: HarperCollins, 1988.

Dunn, Sara, and Alan Scholefield, eds. *Poetry for the Earth*. New York: Fawcett Columbine, 1992.

Ehrlich, Gretel. *The Solace of Open Spaces*. New York: VikingPenguin, 1986.

Elliott, Doug. *Wildwoods Wisdom: Mythic Encounters with the Natural World*. New York: Paragon House, and Union Mills, NC: Possum Productions, 1992.

———. *Woodslore*. Union Mills, NC: Possum Productions, 1986.

Foreman, Dave. *Confessions of an Eco-Warrior*. New York: Crown, 1993.

Fossey, Diane. *Gorillas in the Mist*. Boston: Houghton Mifflin, 1983.

Foster, Steven. *The Book of the Vision Quest: Personal Transformation in the Wilderness*. New York: Prentice-Hall, 1989.

———. *The Four Shields: The Initiatory Seasons of Human Nature*. Big Pine, CA: Lost Borders Press, 1999.

———. *The Roaring of the Sacred River: The Wilderness Quest for Vision and Healing*. New York: Prentice-Hall, 1988.

———. *The Sacred Mountain: A Vision Fast Handbook for Adults*. Big Pine, CA: Lost Borders Press, 1984.

———. *The Trail Ahead: A Course Book for Graduating Seniors*. Big Pine, CA: Lost Borders Press, 1983.

Fowler, Jan. *Living the Sacred Round: Transformation through the Medicine Wheel*. Self-published. Available through Jan Fowler, 28110 Locust Grove Lane, Rapidan, VA 22733, (703) 672-0985.

Fox, Matthew. *Creation Spirituality. Liberating Gifts for the Peoples of the Earth*. San Francisco: Sierra Club Books, 1991.

Fox, Warwick. *Towards a Transpersonal Ecology: Developing New Foundations for Environmentalism*. Boston: Shambhala, 1990.

Glendinning, Chellis. *My Name Is Chellis and I'm in Recovery from Western Civilization*. Boston: Shambhala, 1994.

Griffin, Susan. *Woman and Nature: The Roaring Inside Her*. New York: HarperCollins, 1979.

Halifax, Joan. *The Fruitful Darkness: Reconnecting with the Body of the Earth*. New York: HarperSanFrancisco, 1994.

———. *Shamanic Voices: A Survey of Visionary Narratives*. New York: VikingPenguin, 1991.

Hardin, Jesse Wolf. *Kindred Spirits: Sacred Earth Wisdom*. Portland, OR: Swan/Raven Press, 2001.

Heinberg, Richard. *Celebrate the Solstice: Honoring the Earth's Seasonal Rhythms through Festival and Ceremony*. Wheaton, IL: Quest, 1993.

———. *A New Covenant with Nature: Notes on the End of Civilization and the Renewal of Culture*. Wheaton, IL: Quest, 1996.

Hubbell, Sue. *A County Year: Living the Questions*. New York: Random House, 1986.

Hull, Fritz, ed. *Earth and Spirit: The Spiritual Dimension of the Environmental Crisis*. New York: Continuum Publishing Company, 1993.

Jastrab, Joseph, with Ron Schaumburg. *Sacred Manhood, Sacred Earth*. New York: HarperCollins, 1994.

Jeffers, Robinson. *The Selected Poetry of Robinson Jeffers*. New York: Random House, 1965.

Jensen, Derrick, ed. *Listening to the Land: Conversations about Nature, Culture, and Eros.* San Francisco: Sierra Club Books, 1995.

Kaza, Stephanie. *The Attentive Heart: Conversations with Trees.* New York: Fawcett Columbine Books, 1993.

Kerasote, Ted. *Bloodties—Nature, Culture and the Hunt.* New York: Kodansha International, 1994.

———. *Heart of Home—Essays of People and Wildlife.* New York: Random House, 1996.

Kumin, Maxine. *In Deep: Country Essays.* New York: Viking, 1987.

———. *Up Country: Poems of New England.* Boston: Beacon Press, 1972.

LaBastille, Anne. *Mama Poc: An Ecologist's Account of the Extinction of a Species.* New York: Norton, 1990.

———. *The Wilderness World of Anne LaBastille.* Westport, NY: West of the Wind Publications, 1992.

———. *Women and Wilderness.* San Francisco: Sierra Club Books, 1980.

———. *Woodswoman.* New York: E. P Dutton, 1971.

LaChapelle, Dolores. *Deep Powder Snow: Forty Years of Ecstatic Skiing, Avalanches and Earth Wisdom.* Durango, CO: Kivaki Press, 1993.

———. *Sacred Land, Sacred Sex: Rapture of the Deep—Concerning Deep Ecology and Celebrating Life.* Durango, CO: Kivaki Press, 1992.

Leopold, Aldo. *A Sand County Almanac.* New York: Ballantine Books, 1970.

Lone Wolf Circles. *Full Circle: A Song of Ecology & Earthen Spirituality.* St. Paul, MN: Llewellyn Publishing Company, 1991.

Lopez, Barry. *Arctic Dreams.* New York: Bantam, 1989.

———. *Of Wolves and Men.* New York: Macmillan, 1979.

Manes, Christopher. *Green Rage: Radical Environmentalism and the Unmaking of Civilization.* Boston: Little, Brown, 1990.

Matthiessen, Peter. *The Snow Leopard.* New York: VikingPenguin, 1987.

McClintock, James I., ed. *Nature's Kindred Spirits.* Madison, WI: University of Wisconsin Press, 1994.

Merrill, Christopher, ed. *The Forgotten Language: Contemporary Poets and Nature.* Layton, UT: Gibbs Smith, 1991.

Metzger, Deena, Linda Hogan, and Brenda Peterson, eds. *Between Species: The Bond between Women and Animals.* New York: Ballantine, 1996.

Miles, John, and Simon Priest, eds. *Adventure Education.* State College, PA: Venture, 1990.

Minty, Judith. *Lake Song and Other Fears.* Pittsburgh: University of Pittsburgh Press, 1974.

———. *Yellow Dog Journal.* Los Angeles, CA: Center Publications, 1971.

Mowat, Farley. *Never Cry Wolf.* New York: Bantam, 1983.

Murray, John A., ed. *Nature's New Voices.* Golden, CO: Fulcrum Publishing, 1992.

Nabhan, Gary Paul, and Stephen Trimble. *The Geography of Childhood: Why Children Need Wild Places.* Boston: Beacon Press, 1994.

Nash, Roderick. *Wilderness and the American Mind*, 3rd ed. New Haven and London: Yale University Press, 1982.

Nelson, Richard K. *The Island Within.* San Francisco: North Point Press, 1989.

Nollman, Jim. *The Man Who Talks to Whales.* Boulder, CO: Sentient Publications, 2002.

——. *Spiritual Ecology.* New York: Bantam Books, 1990.

Oates, David. *Earth Rising: Ecological Belief in an Age of Science.* Corvallis, OR: Oregon State University Press, 1989.

Oliver, Mary. *American Primitive.* Boston: Little, Brown, 1983.

——. *Selected Poems.* Boston: Beacon Press, 1993.

Olson, Sigurd. *Reflections from the North Country.* New York: Knopf, 1977.

Peacock, Doug. *Grizzly Years: Encounters with Wilderness.* New York: Henry Holt, 1990.

Perenyi, Constance. *Growing Wild: Inviting Wildlife into Your Yard.* Hillsboro, OR: Beyond Words Publishing, 1991.

——. *Wild Wild West.* Seattle, WA: Sasquatch Books, 1993.

Peterson, Brenda. *Living by Water.* Anchorage, AK, and Seattle, WA: Alaska Northwest Books, 1991.

——. *Nature and Other Mothers: Personal Stories of Women and the Body of Faith.* New York: Ballantine, 1995.

Piercy, Marge. *Circles on the Water.* New York: Knopf, 1982.

——. *The Moon Is Always Female.* New York: Knopf, 1980.

Poniewaz, Jeff. *Dolphin Leaping in the Milky Way.* Milwaukee, WI: Inland Ocean Books, 1986.

Raffan, James, and Bert Horwood, eds. *Canexus: The Canoe in Canadian Culture.* Toronto, Canada: Betelgeuse Books, 1988.

Rezendes, Paul. *Tracking and the Art of Seeing.* Columbia, SC: Camden House, 1993.

Roads, Michael J. *Journey into Nature: A Spiritual Adventure.* Tiburon, CA: H. J. Kramer, 1990.

——. *Talking with Nature: Sharing the Energies and Spirit of Trees, Plants, Birds and Earth.* Tiburon, CA: H. J. Kramer, 1985.

Roberts, Elizabeth, and Elias Amidon, eds. *Earth Prayers: From around the World, 365 Prayers, Poems and Invocations for Honoring the Earth.* New York: HarperSanFrancisco, 1993.

——. *Life Prayers: From around the World, 365 Prayers, Poems, and Invocations for Celebrating the Human Journey.* New York: HarperSanFrancisco, 1996.

Rogers, Pattiann. *Fire Keeper: New and Selected Poems.* Minneapolis, MN: Milkweed Editions, 1994.

Roszak, Theodore. *The Voice of the Earth.* New York: Simon and Schuster, 1995.

Roszak, Theodore, Mary B. Comes, and Allen D. Kanner, eds. *Ecopsychology: Restoring the Earth, Healing the Mind.* San Francisco: Sierra Club Books, 1995.

Sauer, Peter ed. *Finding Home.* Boston: Beacon Press, 1992.

Seed, John, Joanna Macy, Pat Fleming, and Arne Naess, eds. *Thinking Like a Mountain — Towards a Council of All Beings.* Santa Cruz, CA: New Society Publishers, 1988.

Shepard, Paul. *Nature and Madness.* San Francisco: Sierra Club Books, 1984.

Snyder. Gary. *No Nature: New and Collected Poems.* New York and San Francisco: Pantheon Books, 1995.

———. *The Old Ways.* San Francisco: City Lights, 1977.

———. *The Practice of the Wild.* San Francisco: North Point Press, 1990.

———. *Turtle Island.* Boston: Shambhala, 1993.

Storm, Hyemeyohsts. *Seven Arrows.* New York: Ballantine, 1983.

Suzuki, David, and Peter Knudtson, eds. *Wisdom of the Elders: Sacred Native Stories of Nature.* New York: Bantam Books, 1992.

Swan, James. *Nature as Teacher and Healer: How to Reawaken Your Connection with Nature.* New York: Villard, 1992; and iUniverse, 2000.

———. *The Power of Place.* Wheaton, IL: Quest, 1991.

———. *Sacred Places.* Santa Fe, NM: Bear and Company, 1990.

Swan, James, and Roberta Swan. *Bound to the Earth.* New York: Avon, 1994.

———. *Dialogues with the Living Earth.* Wheaton, IL: Quest, 1996.

Teale, Edwin W. *The Wilderness World of John Muir.* Boston: Houghton Mifflin, 1975.

Thomas, Lewis. *The Lives of a Cell.* New York: Bantam, 1975.

Thoreau, Henry David. *Walden.* New York: Knopf, 1992.

———. *Walking.* Bedford, MA: Applewood, 1988.

Tobias, Michael, ed. *The Soul of Nature: Visions of a Living Earth.* New York: Continuum, 1994.

Van Matre, Steve. *Earth Education: A New Beginning.* Warrenville, IL: The Institute for Earth Education, 1990.

Van Matre, Steve and Bill Weller, eds. *The Faith Speaks.* Warrenville, IL: The Institute for Earth Education, 1991.

Watts, Alan. *Nature, Man and Woman.* New York: Random House, 1991.

Wheelwright, Jane Hollister, and Lynda Wheelwright Schmidt. *The Long Shore: A Psychological Experience of the Wilderness.* San Francisco: Sierra Club Books, 1991.

Whyte, David. *Fire in the Earth.* Langley, WA: Many Rivers Press, 1992.

———. *The Heart Aroused: Poetry and the Preservation of the Soul in Corporate America.* New York: Currency Doubleday, 1994.

———. *The House of Belonging.* Langley, WA: Many Rivers Press, 1997.

———. *Songs for Coming Home.* Langley, WA: Many Rivers Press, 1989.

———. *Where Many Rivers Meet.* Langley, WA: Many Rivers Press, 1993.

Whitman, Walt. *Leaves of Grass.* New York: Random House, 1995.

Willers, Bill, ed. *Learning to Listen to the Land.* Washington, DC: Island Press, 1991.

Williams, Terry Tempest. *Desert Quartet.* New York: Pantheon, 1995.

———. *Refuge: An Unnatural History of Family and Place.* New York: Pantheon, 1991.

———. *An Unspoken Hunger.* New York: Pantheon, 1994.

Williams, Terry Tempest, and John Telford. *Coyote's Canyon.* Layton, UT: Peregrine Smith, 1989.

Wood, Nancy, and Frank Howell. *Many Winters.* New York: Doubleday, 1974.

Zwinger, Ann. *Run, River, Run: A Naturalist's Journey Down One of the Great Rivers of the West.* Tucson, AZ: University of Arizona Press, 1984.

PERIODICALS AND JOURNALS

Earth First!
P.O. Box 3023
Tucson, AZ 85702
(520) 620-6900
www.earthfirstjournal.org

This magazine is concerned with promoting deep ecology and environmentally direct political action. Routine articles on current environmental debates and issues are printed.

Earth Letter
Earth Ministry
6512 23rd NW
Seattle, WA 98117
(206) 632-2426

Earth Letter is published by Earth Ministry, whose mission is to engage, educate, and inspire individuals and congregations to deepen our relationship with creation through simplified living, environmental stewardship, and justice for the natural world.

Earthlight Magazine
111 Fairmont Avenue
Oakland, CA 94611
(570) 451-4926

Earthlight Magazine is a magazine of spiritual ecology.

Ecoforestry
Ecoforestry Institute Society
P.O. Box 5070, Station B
Victoria, BC
Canada V8R 6N3

This journal embraces the challenge to adapt our methods, sciences, and philosophies toward ecologically responsible forest use.

The International Journal of Wilderness
University of Idaho
Wilderness Research Center/CNR
Moscow, ID 83844-1144
(208) 885-2267

Published three times a year, this magazine seeks to link wilderness professionals, scientists, educators, and citizens with a forum for reporting and discussing wilderness research, inspired ideas, management strategies, and practical issues of wilderness stewardship.

The Interspecies Newsletter
Interspecies Inc.
302 Hidden Meadow Lane
Friday Harbor, WA 98250
This excellent newsletter is concerned with promoting a better understanding of what is communicated between human beings and other animals. It contains articles, book reviews, and information about ongoing projects around the world.

The Journal of Experiential Education
The Association for Experiential Education
2305 Canyon Boulevard
Suite 100
Boulder, CO 80302-5651
(303) 440-8844
(303) 440-9581 (fax)
www.aee.org

This is a quarterly magazine devoted to the promotion of experiential education. Most of the articles, stories, and book reviews are related to using this approach within a wilderness context.

The New Catalyst
P.O. Box 189
Gabriola Island, BC
Canada V0R 1X0
(604) 247-9737

This is a strong journal about bioregionalism and ecophilosophy.

Orion
The Myrin Institute
195 Main Street
Great Barrington, MA 01230
(413) 528-4422
orion@orionsociety.org
www.oriononline.org

Orion aims to characterize conceptually and practically our responsibilities to the earth and all forms of life, and to help us deepen our personal connection with the natural world as a source of enrichment and inner renewal.

PanGaia: Earthwise Spirituality
Blessed Bee, Inc.
P.O. Box 641
Point Arena, CA 95468
(707) 882-2052

This quarterly magazine explores Pagan, Gaian, and eco-activist lifestyles and concerns.

Raise the Stakes
Planet Drum Foundation
P.O. Box 31251
San Francisco, CA 94131
Shasta Bioregion
(415) 285-6556
(415) 285-6563 (fax)
planetdrum@lgc.org
www.planetdrum.org

Back issues of this out-of-print publication promote the notion of bioregionalism and offer a list of readings on the subject.

Talking Leaves
81868 Lost Valley Lane
Dexter, OR 97431
www.lostvalley.org/TL

A quarterly journal that covers model projects and individuals whose actions are making a sustainable difference both locally and globally in considering the intrinsic value of all inhabitants of the natural world.

Taproot
Coalition for Education in the Outdoors
Park Center
SUNY Cortland
P.O. Box 2000
Cortland, NY 13045
(607) 753-4971
taproot@cortland.edu

Taproot is a quarterly publication containing features about environmental and outdoor education, news, reviews, a comprehensive list of resources, professional opportunities, a conference calendar, and more to keep readers abreast of new developments in environmental and outdoor education.

SUGGESTED READINGS

The Trumpeter
Athabasca University
1 University Drive
Athabasca, AB
Canada T9S 3A3

This quarterly is a transdisciplinary journal dedicated to the exploration of a new ecological consciousness and to the practices of ecosophy (ecological wisdom and harmony).

Wild Earth
The Wildlands Project
P.O. Box 455
Richmond, VT 05477
(802) 434-4077
www.wild-earth.org

Wild Earth, the quarterly publication of the Wildlands Project, inspires effective action for wild nature by communicating the latest thinking in conservation science, philosophy, politics, and activism, and serves as a forum for diverse views within the conservation movement.

APPENDIX OF WILDERNESS RESOURCES

WILDERNESS GUIDES AND TEACHERS

Asklepia Foundation
Graywolf/Fred Swinney
P.O. Box 301
Wilderville, OR 97543
(541) 476-0492

Asklepia is a nonprofit educational and service association that provides opportunities to experience natural healing and creative consciousness processes in wilderness settings. It is located in a remote corner of southwestern Oregon.

Brooke Medicine-Eagle
PMB C401
One 2nd Avenue East
Polson, MT 59860
(406) 883-4686
www.medicineeagle.com

Wakantia trainings, created by Brooke Medicine-Eagle, are geared toward the realization of our roles as caretakers of our sacred home, Mother Earth. These trainings are meant to create groups of dedicated people who work together over time toward the next level of being human. These five- to ten-day trainings will be spent singing, dancing, hiking, praying, and vision questing. Both men and women are invited to join. These trainings will be held yearly in beautiful Montana and also in other wonderful places around the country. Brooke also conducts workshops and seminars internationally, and has Native American music/teaching/women's mysteries cassettes and videos available.

The Earthen Spirituality Project
Jesse Wolf Hardin, Director
P.O. Box 516
Reserve, NM 87830
earthway@concentric.net
www.concentric.net/~earthway

The Earthen Spirituality Project serves as an educational networking tool for the furtherance of Earth-centered spirituality, environmental ethics, primal perception, mindfulness/awareness techniques, and unique contemporary practice. Programs include personal counsel, healing quests, wilderness retreats, and resident internships in the enchanted river canyons of New Mexico's wild Gila—with medicine sweats, mindful tracking, primitive camping and conscious wildcrafting. Special empowering programs for women are offered under the guidance of facilitator Loba, and insightful apprentice Scot Deily leads walking quests and alternative building workshops. Wolf's counsel serves as a unique reality check, furthering the participants' reinhabitation of sentient body, inspirited place, and the intensity of present time.

Earthways
Steven Harper
P.O. Box 303
Big Sur, CA 93920

Doug Elliott
3831 Painter's Gap Road
Union Mills, NC 28167
(828) 287-2960
www.dougelliott.com

Doug Elliott is a naturalist, herbalist, storyteller, and musician. For more than two decades, he has traveled from the Canadian North to Central American jungles studying plant and animal life, as well as the wisdom of traditional peoples. He gives storytellings, concerts, and lectures, and leads basketry/fiber arts and woods lore workshops in natural settings. His books *Wildwoods Wisdom* and *Wild Roots* and his cassette *Crawdads, Doodlebugs, and Creasy Greens: Songs, Stories and Lore Celebrating the Natural World* may be obtained through the above address.

Esalen Institute
Big Sur, CA 93920
(408) 667-3000

Steven (the coordinator of Esalen Institute's Staff Education and Wilderness Programs), along with other qualified individuals, offers a wide variety of wilderness workshops and retreats such as: The Way of Wilderness, Contemplation and Nature, Big Sur Wilderness Experiences for Families, and Path of the River: A Grand Canyon Journey throughout the year. The trips range in length from one weekend to two weeks and offer a mix of movement exercises, writing, meditation, and hiking.

Janet Lowe
P.O. Box 47
Moab, UT 84532

Janet is available for creative writing workshops or campfire programs designed to connect people with the landscape through writing. She has taught poetry to people ranging in age from junior high school students to senior citizens.

John Miles
Huxley College of Environmental Studies
Western Washington University
Bellingham, WA 98225
(360) 650-3284

John provides consulting services for those who would like to explore incorporating wilderness education experiences into their curricula at any academic level from elementary through higher education. He also assists groups in identifying how they can "use the wilderness and have it, too" by reducing the unavoidable physical and social impacts on the wilderness.

Sacred Passage & The Way of Nature Fellowship
John Milton
P.O. Drawer CZ
Bisbee, AZ 85603
(877) 818-1881
officemanager@sacredpassage.com
www.sacredpassage.com

Sacred Passage wilderness programs, with John Milton, are available on a regular basis in Colorado, Arizona, Utah, West Virginia, Nepal, Tibet, Bali, New Zealand, and Baja, Mexico. The programs last twelve days, six of which are spent alone in the wilderness, with several days before and after the solo for preparation and integration of this experience. Deep ecology, specific forms of meditation and awareness training, camping, and safety skills are taught as part of the training. Awareness trainings can be up to a year long with solos up to three months long.

Sustainable Living Associates
Elan Shapiro
EcoVillage at Ithaca
124 Rachel Carson Way
Ithaca, NY 14850
(607) 275-0249

Elan Shapiro, an ecopsychology educator and naturalist, teaches unique means of reconnecting human beings to the natural world by linking sustainable living skills and projects with psycho-spiritual practices and multicultural healing modalities. He offers courses, trainings for educators and health professionals, and private sessions.

Way of Mountain Learning Center
Dolores LaChapelle
Box 542
Silverton, CO 81433
(970) 387-5729

Dolores LaChapelle runs the Way of Mountain Learning Center and offers workshops high up in Colorado's San Juan Mountains. Through the Aspen Center for Environmental Studies, she offers a deep ecology workshop, which takes people into infrequently traveled places in the West Elk Mountains, where they chant, drum, and do ritual.

Wilderness Rites
Anne Stine, M.A., MFT
1257 Siskiyou Blvd., #1172
Ashland, OR 97520
(415) 457-3691
astine@wildernessrites.com
www.wildernessrites.com

Wilderness Rites, founded by Anne Stine, offers vision quests and nature-based therapy, integrating psychology and wilderness experience with various forms of earth-based healing practices, three to ten days in length, for groups and individuals. Her programs take place in the deserts of California, Oregon, and Colorado. Anne's programs in ecopsychology have been offered at the California Institute for Integral Studies and in the graduate program in depth psychology at Sonoma State University.

INSTITUTES FOR WILDERNESS EDUCATION OR TRAINING

The Association for Experiential Education
2305 Canyon Boulevard
Suite 100
Boulder, CO 80302-5651
(303) 440-8844

The Association for Experiential Education (AEE) is a not-for-profit, international, professional organization with roots in adventure education, committed to the development, practice, and evaluation of experiential learning in all settings. AEE serves as a clearinghouse connecting people with various alternative outdoor programs, primarily located in the United States. The association publishes more than ten titles including *The Jobs Clearing House, The Journal of Experiential Education*, and numerous directories.

Audubon Expedition Institute (AEI)
P.O. Box 365
Belfast, ME 04915
(888) 287-2234

The Audubon Expedition Institute is an accredited undergraduate and graduate program in which there is no traditional campus. Our campus encompasses the entire United States, as well as other countries such as Nepal, Mexico, and Canada.

Students travel in buses, live and learn in the outdoors, sleeping outside, taking courses, and immersing themselves in the ecological, political, and cultural issues of the region they are studying.

The Boulder Institute for Nature and the Human Spirit
18679 W. 60th Avenue
Golden, CO 80403

Elias Amidon and Elizabeth Roberts codirect the Boulder Institute for Nature and the Human Spirit, through which they conduct wilderness quests in the Utah Canyonlands, as well as a range of "Spirit in Action" programs around the world dedicated to training environmental activists, supporting the land rights of indigenous peoples, and other peacemaking initiatives.

Coalition for Education in the Outdoors
Park Center
SUNY Cortland
P.O. Box 2000
Cortland, NY 13045
(607) 753-4971
www.cortland.edu/ceo/

The Coalition for Education in the Outdoors is a nonprofit network of businesses, educational institutions, conservation and recreation organizations, nature centers, associations, and agencies cooperating in support of educating in, for, and about the outdoors. The coalition's main publications consist of its critically acclaimed *Taproot* magazine and biennial *Outdoor Education Research Symposium Proceedings*.

The Institute for Deep Ecology Education
P.O. Box 1050
Occidental, CA 95466
(707) 874-2347

The Institute for Deep Ecology Education (IDEE) is a nonprofit project of the Tides Foundation. Elias Amidon is the president and Elizabeth Roberts is a board member. The institute sponsors regional and national trainings, consults on deep ecology curriculum and programs, and works to build coalitions among educators, activists, and others involved in this work. Its goal is to bring the deep ecology perspective to the environmental debates of our time.

The Institute for Earth Education
Cedar Cove
Greenville, WV 24945-0115
(604) 832-6404

The Institute for Earth Education is an international nonprofit organization committed to bringing about earth education programs throughout our world with an emphasis on being in harmony with the earth. IEE offers workshops and conferences in addition to publishing the *Talking Leaves* journal, books, and program materials.

North Cascades Institute
Saul Weisberg, Executive Director
810 State Route 20
Sedro Wooley, WA 98284
(360) 856-5700 ext. 209
(360) 856-1934 (fax)
nci@ncascades.org
http://ncascades.org

North Cascades Institute is a nonprofit educational organization dedicated to increasing understanding and appreciation of the natural, historical, and cultural landscapes of the Pacific Northwest. The institute's focus is on experiential environmental education for children and adults. The Institute offers year-round educational programs for schools, as well as field seminars, workshops, teacher trainings, conferences, curriculum development, and publications.

Prescott College
220 Grove Avenue
Prescott, AZ 86301
(928) 778-2090

Prescott College promotes ecological literacy in the context of an experiential, liberal arts curriculum. Based in the mountains of central Arizona, it offers both resident and distance learning opportunities.

Project NatureConnect
Michael J. Cohen, Ed.D.
P.O. Box 4112
Roche Harbor, WA 98250
(360) 378-6313
www.ecopsych.com

Project NatureConnect, run by Michael Cohen, offers hands-on workshops, training programs, and applied ecopsychology methods for connecting with nature. The project helps people develop cognitive and sensory skills for environmental and social literacy.

The School of Lost Borders
Steven Foster and Meredith Little
P.O. Box 55
Big Pine, CA 93513

The School of Lost Borders, run and founded by Steven Foster and Meredith Little, prepares and trains candidates who are or wish to become, in the initiatory sense, ecological psychologists. The training offers a mixture of self-initiated ceremonies, fasting, exposure to nature, solitude, personal myth systems, deep ecology, traceless camping, wilderness first-aid and safety procedures, and, above all, self-study. Seminars include Vision Fast Training, The Psychodynamics of Mirroring, The Rites of Survival, Advanced Four Shield Seminar, and Consultation and Ongoing Training.

Sierra Institute
1101 Pacific Avenue, Suite 200
Santa Cruz, CA 95060
(831) 427-6618
sierrai@ucsc-extension.edu

The Sierra Institute is an interdisciplinary field school providing environmental studies programs in ecology, natural history, nature philosophy, nature writing, natural areas management, and related subjects. Courses grant transferable college credit and are taught entirely on backpacking trips.

Sophia Center at Holy Names College
Jim Conlon
3500 Mountain Boulevard
Oakland, CA 94619
(510) 436-1046 or (800) 794-8813

A transformative educational process blending religion, art, science, and justice into a new cosmology that nurtures ecology, creativity, and the interior journey that evokes a vision and empowers one to realize it.

The Tracking Project
P.O. Box 266
Corrales, NM 87048
(505) 898-6967
thetrackingproject@earthlink.net
www.thetrackingproject.com

The Tracking Project, run by John Stokes, is a nonprofit community education organization that teaches natural and cultural awareness through the *Arts of Life* — traditional tracking/awareness and survival skills, music, storytelling, dance, and martial arts training. Since 1986, the project team of native elders, artists, and educators has worked with nearly one hundred thousand people in the United States and around the world.

University of Global Education
Michael J. Cohen, Ed.D.
Box 1605
Friday Harbor, WA 98250
(206) 378-6313
www.ecopsych.com

University of Global Education is a United Nations nongovernmental institution that provides ecopsychology workshops and e-mail material on related subjects.

Upaya Zen Center
Joan Halifax
1404 Cerro Gordo Road
Santa Fe, NM 87501
(505) 986-8518
Upaya, founded by Joan Halifax, is a contemplative Zen center with an emphasis on mindfulness practice. It offers programs in wilderness solitude practice, mountain-walking retreats, cultural retreats, and other contemplative activities that introduce individuals into the natural world.

Wilderness Institute
School of Forestry
University of Montana
Missoula, MT 59812
(405) 243-6936
wi@forestry.umt.edu
www.forestry.umt.edu/wi

The Wilderness Institute offers the Wilderness and Civilization program, an interdisciplinary wilderness studies program that explores wilderness and the human-nature relationship. Program courses approach wilderness from a variety of disciplines, including recreation management, ecology, literature, Native American studies, economics, and fine arts. Two extended backcountry trips and fieldwork complement on-campus learning with hands-on experiential education. This program offers students an understanding of wilderness values, policies, and issues. Courses also focus on land ethics and personal connection with the natural world. Upon completion of the program students receive a minor in Wilderness Studies.

ENVIRONMENTAL AND POLITICAL ACTION ORGANIZATIONS

Earth and Spirit Council
6200 SW Virginia, Suite 210
Portland, OR 97201
(503) 452-4483
info@earthandspirit.org

The mission of this Portland-based organization is to reawaken our spiritual connection to the earth and engage ourselves and others in earth-conscious living.

Green Earth Foundation
P.O. Box 327
El Verano, CA 95433

The Green Earth Foundation is a not-for-profit educational and research organization dedicated to the healing and harmonizing of relationships between humanity and the earth. Annual membership is $25, student and low-income $15, Canada $30, foreign $35, and includes four issues of the newsletter *The Green Earth Observer*, which contains brief articles and poetry related to Gaia consciousness. Book and periodical reviews, as well as information about ecological and environmental organizations, are also provided.

Interspecies
Jim Nollman
301 Hidden Meadow Lane
Friday Harbor, WA 98250
www.interspecies.com
Interspecies, founded in 1978, researches and promotes a better understanding of what is communicated between human beings and other animals (especially dolphins and whales) through music, art, and ceremony with a strong emphasis on environmental preservation. The work functions primarily to help people reestablish their emotional, spiritual, and cultural ties with the natural world. Interspecies sells Jim Nollman's book, *The Man Who Talks to Whales*, his cassette, *Orca's Greatest Hits*, and a video, *Orcananda*. The organization also produces the quarterly *Interspecies Newsletter*, articles, book reviews, and information about projects around the world.

Planet Drum Foundation
Box 31251
San Francisco, CA 94131
Shasta Bioregion
(415) 285-6556
(415) 285-6563 (fax)
planetdrum@lgc.org
www.planetdrum.org

Planet Drum Foundation provides an effective bioregional, grassroots approach to ecology that emphasizes sustainability, community self-determination, and regional self-reliance. Planet Drum also has developed and continues to promote the concept of a bioregion, a distinct area with coherent and interconnected plant and animal communities, often defined by a watershed. The foundation publishes *A Green City Program for the San Francisco Bay Area and Beyond*, *Reinhabiting a Separate Country: A Bioregional Anthology of Northern California*, and other titles. Memberships cost $25 per year within North America, $30 elsewhere, and include the biannual newsletter, *Planet Drum Pulse*.

Rainforest Information Centre
John Seed
Box 368
Lismore, NSW 2480
Australia
066-213294 (011-61-2-66213294 from the U.S.)
http://forests.org/ric/
johnseed@ozemail.com.au
The Rainforest Information Centre, formed in 1981, has produced *World Rainforest Report* since 1984 and is responsible for a number of rain forest conservation projects from Ecuador to New Guinea and beyond.

Siskiyou Regional Education Project
P.O. Box 220
Cave Junction, OR 97523
(503) 592-4459

Lou Gold helped found this grassroots organization that advocates protection of ancient forests and provides people with information about the complexity, richness, and potential threats to these forests. A newsletter on this subject is routinely published.

PERMISSIONS AND CREDITS

SPIRIT OF PLACE

"Catching the Sunrise" by Antler originally appeared in his book *Last Words*, New York: Ballantine, 1986. Reprinted by permission of the author.

"On the Blue Glacier" by Dolores LaChapelle originally appeared in her book *Sacred Land, Sacred Sex*, Silverton, CO: Finn Hill Press, 1988. (Second edition is published by Kivaki Press: Durango, CO, 1992). Reprinted by permission of the author.

"The Way of the Mountain" by Joan Halifax is an edited excerpt from *The Fruitful Darkness: Reconnecting with the Body of the Earth*, New York: HarperCollins, 1993. Copyright © by Joan Halifax. Reprinted by permission of Harper-Collins Publishers.

"In Praise" by John Daniel was first published in *Zone 3* (1992). It also appears in *All Things Touched by Wind*, Anchorage: Salmon Run, 1994. Copyright © 1993 by John Daniel. Reprinted by permission of the author.

"The Water Way" by Brenda Peterson is an edited and excerpted chapter from *Nature and Other Mothers: Personal Stories of Women and the Body of Earth*, New York: Ballantine, 1995. Copyright © 1995 by Brenda Peterson. Reprinted by permission of the author.

"Kenai Fjords" by Chris Hoffman originally appeared in *Sea Kayaker* magazine, and was also published in the *Men's Council Journal*, Issue 3, November 1989. Reprinted by permission of the author.

"Ten Years Later" by David Whyte was originally published in *The House of Belonging*, Langley, WA: Many Rivers Press, 1997. Copyright © 1997 by David Whyte. Reprinted by permission of Many Rivers Press.

"The Land: A Sense of Home" by Bill Weiler is excerpted and edited from the introduction to *Close to the Wind: A Northwest Naturalist Is Dreaming* (not yet published). Reprinted by permission of the author.

"The Spirit of the Forest" is an original piece by Michael J. Roads. Printed by permission of the author.

"Solitude Late at Night in the Woods" by Robert Bly was originally published in *Silence in the Snowy Fields*, Middletown, CT: Wesleyan University Press, 1962. Reprinted by permission of the author.

QUESTS AND RITUALS OF RENEWAL

"A Sacred Passage" by Lauren Dasmann first appeared in *Chrysalis* magazine, Spring 1991. Reprinted by permission of the author.

"Wilderness Kinship" is an original piece by Anne Stine. Printed by permission of the author.

"The Morning of the Last Day" by Steven Foster is excerpted from the revised edition of *The Roaring of The Sacred River: The Wilderness Quest for Vision and Self-*

Healing, New York: Prentice-Hall, 1988, and reprinted by Lost Borders Press, Big Pine, CA, 1996. Reprinted by permission of the author.

"Song of the Earth" is an original piece by Brooke Medicine-Eagle. Printed by permission of the author.

"Viking Hiking" is an original piece by Christopher Manes. Printed by permission of the author.

"On Climbing the Sierra Matterhorn Again after Thirty-One Years" by Gary Snyder was originally published in *No Nature,* New York: Pantheon Books, 1992. Copyright © 1992 by Gary Snyder. Used by permission of Pantheon Books, a division of Random House, Inc.

"Beyond the Quest: Bringing it Back" by Fred Swinney originally appeared in *The Dream Network Journal,* Vol. 11., No.2, Moab, UT: Roberta Osana Publishers. Reprinted by permission of the author.

"Praying in Death Valley: A Letter to My Father" is an original piece by Elias Amidon. Printed by permission of the author.

MEN, WOMEN, AND WILDNESS

"Finding Our Place on Earth Again: An Interview with John Stokes" by John Stokes and Forrest Craver first appeared in *Wingspan: Journal of the Male Spirit,* Summer 1990. Reprinted by permission of the authors.

"Healing the Wounded Feminine through the Natural World" is based on a doctoral thesis by Anngwyn St. Just and will appear as part of a tape series entitled *Men, Woman and War* from Mike Henry Productions, River House Studio. Printed by permission of the author.

"October, Yellowstone Park" first appeared in *Plowshares,* Fall 1992 and later in *Connecting the Dots,* New York: Norton, 1996. Copyright © 1992 by Maxine Kumin. Reprinted by permission of W. W. Norton & Company, Inc.

"Pipit Lake" is an original piece by Thomas Lowe Fleischner. Printed by permission of the author.

"A Walk with the King" by Gabriel Heilig first appeared in *Wingspan: Journal of the Male Spirit,* Spring 1990 and later in the book *Wingspan: Inside the Men's Movement,* New York: St. Martin's Press, 1992. Reprinted by permission of the author.

"Wilderness in the Blood" is an original piece by Lorraine Anderson. Printed by permission of the author.

"Bonded by Spirit on Broken Hand" by Jed Swift originally appeared in the 1990 Outdoor Leadership Seminar Trainings brochure. Reprinted by permission of the author.

"North McKittrick Canyon" is an original piece by Janet Lowe. Printed by permission of the author.

"Prowling the Ridge" by Judith Minty first appeared in the book *In the Presence of Mothers,* Pittsburgh: University of Pittsburgh Press, 1981. Reprinted by permission of the author.

"Malduce Cabin: A Fantasy" by Paul Willis first appeared in *Cafe Solo* in 1992. Reprinted by permission of the author.

ANIMAL ENCOUNTERS

"In Wilderness" by Joseph Bruchac first appeared in *Near the Mountains*, Fredonia, NY: White Pine Press. Reprinted by permission of the author.

"Two Looks Away: The Art of Seeing and Belonging" is an original piece by Fred Donaldson, Ph.D. Printed by permission of the author.

"Waiting at the Surface" is an original piece by Monica Woelfel. Printed by permission of the author.

"Making Media, Not Making Media" by Jim Nollman is excerpted and edited from the *Interspecies Newsletter*, Winter 1991. Reprinted by permission of the author.

"Swimming with Loons" is an original poem by Howard Nelson. Printed by permission of the author.

"Bloodties" by Ted Kerasote is excerpted and edited from an essay appearing in the book *Bloodties—Nature, Culture and the Hunt*, New York: Kodansha International, 1994. Reprinted by permission of the author.

"The Night of the Living Skunk" by Doug Elliott first appeared in *Wildwoods Wisdom*, New York: Paragon House, Possum Productions, 1992. Reprinted by permission of the author.

"Intersection: A Meeting with a Mountain Lion" by Barbara Dean originally appeared under the title "Lion" in *Northern Lights*, July 1988. Reprinted by permission of the author.

"Mandlovu" is an original poem by Deena Metzger. Printed by permission of the author.

"Killing the Bear" by Judith Minty first appeared in the anthology *Talking Leaves: Contemporary Native American Short Stories*, edited by Craig Lesley. Reprinted by permission of the author.

"Coming Home" by Joseph Jastrab is an edited excerpt from *Sacred Manhood, Sacred Earth*, New York: HarperCollins, Copyright © 1994. Joseph Jastrab with Ron Schaumberg. Reprinted by permission of HarperCollins and the authors.

TEACHING IN THE WILD

"Rain's Song to Cedar: Teaching in Wilderness" is an original piece by Saul Weisberg. Printed by permission of the author.

"The Students of Albert Camp" is an original piece by John Miles. Printed by permission of the author.

"Thoughts on the Idea of Adventure" is an original piece by Bob Henderson. Printed by permission of the author.

"Kids' Camp" is an original piece by Willy Whitefeather. Printed by permission of the author.

"Reflections on an Outdoor Education Experience" by J. Gary Knowles first appeared in the *Journal of Experimental Education*, Vol. 15, No. 1 (May 1992). Reprinted by permission of the author.

"Wilderness Revisited: The Twilight's Last Gleaming" by Michael J. Cohen is adapted from Dr. Cohen's articles in the *Proceedings* of the 1991 national conference of the North American Association for Environmental Education; *Proceedings of the 1991 International Conference of the Association for Experiential Education; The Science Teacher,* of the National Science Teachers Association; *The Journal of Environmental Education; Legacy,* the journal of the National Association for Interpretation; *Adventure Education,* the journal of the National Outdoor Education Association; *Environmental Awareness,* the journal of the International Society of Naturalists; *The International Journal of Humanities and Peace: The Trumpeter,* journal of Ecosophy, *How Nature Works;* and *The Field Guide to Connecting with Nature.* Reprinted by permission of the author.

IN MOURNING, DEFENSE, AND CELEBRATION OF THE EARTH

"The Peace of Wild Things" is from *The Selected Poems of Wendell Berry* by Wendell Berry, New York: Counterpoint Press, 1999. Copyright © 1998 by Wendell Berry. Reprinted by permission of Counterpoint Press, a member of Perseus Books, L.L.C.

"In the Eye of the Hurricane: An Interview with John Seed" by Kaia Svien is edited and excerpted from an original transcript first printed in *Reconciliation,* Winter 1992/1993. Reprinted by permission of the authors.

"One by One" by Constance Perenyi originally appeared in *Living Birds,* the quarterly publication of Cornell University's Laboratory of Ornithology. Reprinted by permission of the author.

"The Pasar Burung" is an original piece by Eric Paul Shaffer. Printed by permission of the author.

"Bald Mountain Vigil" by Lou Gold is excerpted and edited from two earlier articles that originally appeared in *Siskiyou Country,* Vols. 8 & 15. Reprinted by permission of the author.

"The Gift of Silence" by Anne LaBastille originally appeared in *The Wilderness World of Anne LaBastille,* Westport, NY: West of the Wind Publication, Inc., 1992. Copyright © 1992 by Anne LaBastille. Reprinted by permission of the author.

"Ocean Song" is an original piece by Robin Boyd. Printed by permission of the author.

"Bringing Nature and Grace Together Again" is excerpted from a lecture titled "The Greening of Spirituality" given by Matthew Fox at the Voices of the Earth conference in Boulder, Colorado, during the summer of 1994. Printed by permission of the author.

"Alpine Pond, Cedar Breaks" is an original piece taken from a larger, unpublished manuscript by David Lee. Printed by permission of the author.

"The Beauty of the Wild" by John Daniel originally appeared as a longer essay titled "Toward Wild Heartlands," published in *Audubon,* 1995 and later that same year appeared in *Timeline* and *Resurgence* (England). Copyright © 1995 by John Daniel. Reprinted by permission of the author.

"Alone in the Forest" by David Whyte originally appeared in his book *Songs for Coming Home,* Langley, WA: Many Rivers Press, 1989. Copyright © 1989 by David Whyte. Reprinted by permission of Many Rivers Press.

EXTRA-ORDINARY WILDERNESS

"The Practice and Presence of the Wild" by David Oates first appeared in *Earth-light: Spirituality and Ecology*, Winter 1990. Reprinted by permission of the author.

"A Lake in the Mind" is an original poem by Deena Metzger. Printed by permission of the author.

"Deep Ecology and Wonder: Notes of a Sleight-of-Hand Sorcerer" by David Abram first appeared in *Earth First!*, February 1988, under the title "Deep Ecology and Magic: Notes of a Sleight-of-Hand Sorcerer." Reprinted by permission of the author.

"Voices of the Forest" by Serge King is the epilogue from *Kahuna Healing*, Wheaton IL: Theosophical Publishing House, 1983. Reprinted by permission of Theosophical Publishing House.

"The tree in winter is like" by Nancy Wood was originally published in her book *Many Winters*, Garden City, NY: Doubleday, 1974. Reprinted by permission of the author.

"Fusion: The Soul Is Composed of the External World" is an original piece by Roger Dunsmore. Printed by permission of the author.

"Back-Home Pilgrimage" by Elan Shapiro was originally published in *Creation*, Nov/Dec. 1989. Reprinted by permission of the author.

"Watering the Garden" by Jeff Poniewaz is from *Dolphin Leaping in the Milky Way*, Milwaukee, WI: Inland Ocean Books, 1986. Reprinted by permission of the author.

"Mystery, Humility and the Wild" is an original piece by Steven Harper. Printed by permission of the author.

"Uncivilized" is an original poem by Laura Carrithers. Printed by permission of the author.

"Buried Poems" by Terry Tempest Williams is from the book *Coyote's Canyon*, by Terry Tempest-Williams. Salt Lake City: Gibbs Smith, Publisher, 1989. Used with permission.

WILDERNESS ETHICS: AN EMERGING PERSPECTIVE

"The Dance" by Jesse Wolf Hardin originally appeared in *Talking Leaves Journal*. Reprinted by permission of the author.

"Wilderness Ecopsychology: The Art of Sacred Survival" is an original piece by Renée Soule, based on her master's thesis. Reprinted by permission of the author.

"Wilderness Reconsidered" by Roderick Nash originally appeared in *Wilderness in America: Personal Perspectives*, edited by Daniel L. Dustin, San Diego University, Institute for Leisure Behavior, 1988. Reprinted by permission of the author.

"Kinship with Nature" by James Swan is an edited excerpt of a keynote address presented to the Tenri Yamato Culture Congress in Nara, Japan, in 1992. It

ABOUT THE EDITOR

Cass Adams, M.A., Transpersonal Counseling Psychology, was privileged to grow up in a small and spectacular ski-resort town, where he began his deep love of the outdoors. He has been a wilderness guide for both children and adults, and was the cofounder of Men's Wilderness Retreats, through which he led ritual-based wilderness excursions in the mountains and deserts of the southwestern United States. Cass has published essays about wildness and men's issues in *The Men's Council Journal* and *The Green Man*, and nature poems in the collections *Life Prayers* (Harper-SanFrancisco, 1996) and *Chokecherries: A S.O.M.O.S. Anthology* (1999). He edited both editions of *The Soul Unearthed*, from which he has been quoted on two Celestial Seasonings tea boxes (Bengal Spice and Ginkgo Sharp). Three volumes of his poetry have been self-published — *The Naked Heart* (1998), *The First Six Months* (2000), and *Silence* (2000). His photographs appear in many of the above publications, and in the mythopoetic anthology, *Wingspan: Inside the Men's Movement* (St. Martin's Press, 1992). In addition to time spent in the Rocky Mountains, Cass has traveled in the mountainous areas of New Zealand, Alaska, and the Himalayas. He now resides in northern New Mexico with his partner and daughter.

Sentient Publications, LLC publishes books on cultural creativity, experimental education, transformative spirituality, holistic health, new science, and ecology, approached from an integral viewpoint. Our authors are intensely interested in exploring the nature of life from fresh perspectives, addressing life's great questions, and fostering the full expression of the human potential. Sentient Publication's books arise from the spirit of inquiry and the richness of the inherent dialogue between writer and reader.

We are very interested in hearing from our readers. To direct suggestions or comments to us, or to be added to our mailing list, please contact:

SENTIENT PUBLICATIONS, LLC
1113 Spruce Street
Boulder, CO 80302
303-443-2188
contact@sentientpublications.com
www.sentientpublications.com